MALL

By

Pattie Palmer-Baker

Del Sol Press
Washington, D.C.

MALL

DEL SOL PRESS.

MALL.
Copyright © 2019 by Pattie Palmer-Baker
All rights reserved.
Printed in the United States of America.
Del Sol Press, 2020 Pennsylvania Avenue, NW,
Washington, D.C., 20006.

www.delsolpress.org
ISBN-13: 978-0-9998425-5-3

Our books may be purchased in bulk
for promotional, educational, or business use.

Please contact Del Sol Press by e-mail at editor@delsolpress.org.
First Edition: May 2019
10 9 8 7 6 5 4 3 2 1

Pattie Palmer Baker

DEDICATION

To Ron, my beloved husband.

To Linda M and Mimi B for their support and help.

And to Jack R for planting the seed.

MALL

CHAPTER ONE

"I want to be clear, Natalie: are you saying that you're having sex with this man more often than the Code dictates unless pair-bonded?" Nona asked, fidgeting slightly.

Natalie nodded, red curls bobbing. "Sometimes. The sex is good, but that's not why I seek out his company. I can't find the words to ..."

Puzzled, Nona stopped listening. Was Natalie trying to say the sex was not good enough to pair-bond? If that were the case, any Mental Health Practitioner would know how to remedy it. If Natalie's actions weren't against Mall's Code, Nona would interrupt and tell her. Surprisingly, this restriction pressed on her in an unfamiliar manner, a physical pressure in the area just above her stomach, like the sting she sometimes felt when she adminned a dart. But relief would have to wait.

Natalie's voice dropped again to almost a whisper. "You won't tell, will you? That we have sex secretly? Or that we meet to talk in one of our quarters?"

Nona's interest quickened. "No, anything you say in here is protected by client/patient confidentiality. May I ask why you meet in your rooms when that also is expressly forbidden?"

"Are you sure you won't reveal anything I say to you?"

"Yes. Please know, Natalie, that even if I wanted to, Mental Health Practitioners cannot."

"We meet, well, to talk about what he believes is wrong with Mall." She paused to search Nona's face. "Okay, I'll tell you the part that you can never tell: he's a Junker."

The confession stunned Nona into silence. Never before had any of her clients divulged such a shocking fact. Before she could speak, as suddenly as it had been happening so often in the last few weeks, the lights went out. "I do apologize. You probably have also experienced this annoying event too many times. Usually the lights go..." Light flooded the room at that moment. "See, no harm done, and I will add two extra minutes to your session." Nona inched up in her chair to look more closely at Natalie. "I confess that I am taken aback by your admission that you've been meeting with a Junker. Of course, I will not reveal this, but I can't understand why. We all know that Junkers are causing the disturbances occurring throughout Mall. How do you feel about pursuing this strange relationship with someone who belongs to this group?"

"I admit I find it troubling. But not so much that ... Oh I don't know what to do!" She wrung her hands and lowered her head.

Nona was at a loss. Most of her clients wanted to revitalize all kinds of things, from virtual reality rock climbing to interactive story creation and, most often, sexual experiences. Except for Natalie, the complaint was the same for everyone: the experience lacked novelty, and the client wanted to rekindle the thrill. And strange, wasn't it, that the boredom Nona felt when she listened to the repetitive and stale grievances was for her a symptom of the same problem? The only subject she did find interesting was clients' fear of death, but most refused to discuss it in much detail. All she had to go on was body language—those subtle, involuntary physiological effects revealing intense discomfort. If only she could persuade them to go into detail, but that, too, would be against the Code. *Never insist that someone talk about a subject that would make the speaker uncomfortable,* and that even included Mental Health Practitioners.

She certainly did not feel bored with Natalie. Excited and, yes, a little scared. Not only did she know a Junker, she had a relationship with him. What should she do? She wished she could discuss with her colleague and former pair-bond, Royce.

Suddenly, the entry gong sounded, startling her out of her train of thoughts. Natalie gasped, rising from her chair. "God of Reincarnation, am I in trouble?" She fell back into her chair when the door slid open and a black-and-silver uniformed man strode in.

"Pardon me, may I ask why you are here?" Nona asked, stepping back. She seldom encountered a Finance Policeman.

"Your presence is required soon at a Mall Management meeting," he announced in a deep, authoritarian voice.

"Please excuse me. I am confused—why me? Mental Health Practitioners never attend those meetings."

"They do not inform me about the subject of their meetings. Even if I did know, I would not divulge it."

"Yes, of course," she hastened to reassure him. "I have never been to Level 100, so please, can you tell me when and where to go?"

"Not necessary. I will return and accompany you at the appointed time." He spun around and out the door.

Natalie sighed audibly. "Oh, God of Reincarnation, I thought somehow you had alerted the Finance Police about my code violation."

"No, as I said, I would not and cannot. Please continue."

"I wonder what the meeting will be about." Natalie looked over at the door. "I'm afraid for my friend ..."

Nona interrupted. "Please excuse me for cutting in. You said *friend*. Do you have a heart-friend contract with him?"

"No—I would, but he refuses because...I don't think I want to talk about this anymore."

Nona quashed the desire to try to persuade her. "Do you have anything else to discuss? Our meeting is drawing to a close."

"Sort of. At work, Delta stole one of my ideas. I planned on letting Stan know because I earned the extra credit ..."

Again Nona's attention veered away. What *was* this meeting she was summoned to? Was it about the disturbances? Just the other day her office went dark twice, both times during sessions, and one of the blackouts lasted a half hour. The next words out of Natalie's mouth snagged her attention.

"Delta must have heard or seen him enter my quarters. She red-mailed me into keeping silent about her creative theft in trade for her not revealing that Code violation. To make it worse, she overheard him tell me before entering my room the date for the Junker's next meeting. He wanted me to attend."

Nona shifted in her seat. What should she do? How could she help her? "I, as your Mental Health Practitioner, would not want you to take such a risk. If you are experiencing curiosity I can prescribe something that will eliminate that undesirable feeling—have you heard of the new pharm, Freedomfrum?" Before she could stop herself, Nona asked, "Did your friend tell you where the meeting would be?"

"Thank you for the offer of the pharm prescription. I really don't need it. It's not exactly curiosity. I just can't explain it. I do have an idea where they'll meet: somewhere on one of the lower Levels." She raised her head abruptly. "Why do you want to know?"

Why was a good question. Was it because she wanted to be a proper Mallite and report this meeting? No, that wasn't it. She couldn't, anyway. Did she want to meet a Junker? Was that what she really wanted? No one knew who they were or where they met. What was this unusual tenseness she was feeling? Strangely, it was not unpleasant. The chance to talk with a Junker excited her—that was it—a feeling she had not experienced for a very long time.

Before Nona could answer, an alert gong sounded, followed by a loud voice announcing, "Mall Emergency! You are the MHP on call. Guards will contact you in thirty seconds." Nona stood abruptly and said, "Please excuse me, Natalie; it would be best if you left at once. We can schedule another appointment later."

"Oh, God of Reincarnation, a Mall Emergency! I'll leave immediately," Natalie said, voice shaking. She scurried to the opening door and hurried out.

Nona's communicator beeped. "Yes?" she whispered after she pulled her tiny mouthpiece to her mouth. A neutral voice spelled out basic facts:

"Info on emergency: Subject is a female who ran amok in the Jewelry Section in the Ready-Made Division. Fought with the guards. Appearance unusual, dressed in shabby clothes, no cosmetic alteration, heavy—probably 145 pounds at around 5'5". No ID, no Consumer Card. Taken to holding area, but questioning failed due to holdee's emotional state. Sedation dart adminned. You are expected to stabilize her for questioning. Guard will arrive with her in one minute."

CHAPTER TWO

She never should have dragged her husband to the mall, Sara reproached herself as she tried on the fourth dress. She hoped it would get her mind off the doctor's report that she couldn't have a baby. She rubbed her eyes to staunch tears that threatened. It wasn't a new outfit she needed. It was sympathy—someone to talk to, and Carl was not very good in that department.

As she tried on the dress, she knew all Carl would say was, *yeah, that's okay,* or, *if you like it, I like it.* If he noticed that she had lost five pounds, she might feel a little cheered. Not that she dieted. When the doctor diagnosed her with scarring in her fallopian tubes, the cause of her infertility, she ran out before she broke down in front of him. No wonder she had lost her appetite. She had not eaten much for the last two weeks.

She swept the curtain aside only to find Carl chatting with the curvy blond clerk by the register. Anger surged through her. He was always looking at other women—beautiful women, young women, slim women with well-toned bodies. More than just ogling this time, he was flirting. She hurried over to him and pushed him. "You always do this! You don't even see me—just other women! I'm so tired of it!" she whispered through clenched teeth.

Carl shoved her back. "And I'm sick to death of your suspicions and your insecurities. Get over it!"

"You're worse than my father…!" She started crying.

Carl grabbed her by her arms. "What are you talking about? I'm not a drunk! I don't cheat on you! And, you bitch, I'm not the only one. *You* look at other men all time! You need to go back to your shrink!"

"You don't love me; you never have!" she sobbed. Out of the corner of her eyes, she saw a uniformed man walking briskly toward them. *Oh God,* Sara thought, *store security. I've got to get out of here!* She spun around. "Where's the exit?" she cried, panic propelling her legs toward an unmarked door. Someone called her name and caught her arm—Maryanne, a fellow teacher at Johnson Elementary, the last person she wanted to see. *Shit, she'll tell everyone about this,* she thought as she wrenched free and pushed open the door.

She continued to run, barely noticing the dim hallway she had entered, until tired and almost breathless, she slowed. Where was she? Why was the light so bad? A few yards away, she made out what seemed to be a doorway dotted with blinking colored squares of lights. Moving closer, she realized she was having trouble breathing the thickening air. Did she smell smoke? What was happening? Strange, glittering confetti drifted around her. She felt lightheaded, not in an unpleasant way, but more like she felt after a few glasses of champagne. When she reached the end of the hallway, she saw two doors. The one to her left was circular, and the closest one, rectangular. Was she hallucinating or going crazy? She was sure she heard moans and shouts emanating from the one nearest. She moved through taffy-thick air toward the circle. Stopping in front, she ordered herself to turn around, go back. Instead, she pushed the blinking red light in the middle of the circle. A buzzing sound filled the air and the door slid open. And there right in front of her was a man dressed in a shocking pink jumpsuit, hair maple-leaf red. He staggered through. He started to push her aside then stopped and grabbed her arm. "Where am I? Have I escaped Mall?" he cried, eyes wild.

Stunned and still gasping for air, Sara managed to ask the strangely dressed man, "What … what do you mean?"

"Am I still in Mall? Was this the right portal?" His grip tightened.

"You're in Lincoln Mall!"

11

"Lincoln Mall?" His unnaturally green eyes widened. "You mean there's more than one mall?

"Yes, yes, of course! Now let me go!"

He clamped down on her arm. "I found the portal! I'm free! What kind of world is this? Where should I go next? You have to help me!"

"I said, let me go or I will call the police!" She struggled until she wrenched her arm free and stumbled forward through the opening. The door closed behind her. Although the air no longer felt too heavy to breathe, she felt even more lightheaded. And frightened. She held her spinning head. She was in the parking garage! For a moment, relief surged through her. *Wait, something's wrong.* Although the size of the area was right, nothing else was. No cars, no parallel lines, no pillars, just a large, poorly lighted area with gray walls, gray ceiling, and gray cement floor. This was *not* the parking area, but instead an empty gray space, cold and smelling of mildew. Filled with dread, she turned around to push through the door she came in. No indents or lights. She pushed and pushed. The door would not budge. Across the ash-colored expanse, where a red neon exit sign should have been, she saw the same colored lights blinking in a round door's center. *Out, this is a way out!* On shaky legs she half ran, half wobbled over. She stabbed at the indentation. Anywhere—she didn't care; she had to get out! Legs still trembling, she tripped and fell through the opening door. After scrambling to her feet, she rubbed her eyes. Oh God, where was she? She could not see through the shimmering blue mist. Something sweet and flowery filled her nostrils. If only she could blink away the blue fog! In the distance she heard a kind of murmuring. The sound swelled to a buzzing roar and for a terrible moment, she couldn't remember who she was. She stumbled forward and the roar dissolved into a crowd of people's voices. Shapes appeared. *Breathe, breathe,* she ordered herself. Slowly she became aware she was in a shopping area, although not like any she had ever experienced; *not* Lincoln Mall, in fact not a mall she or anyone else would recognize as one. Frozen with disbelief, she stared. Jewelry floated in the air. The garments on the mannequins – or were they real people? – changed form, color and fabric so quickly she could barely make out what they were. Outlandishly costumed shoppers wandered the area.

No, this was not Lincoln Mall. "I have to get out!" she yelled. She turned to push open the door she used to get in, but it seemed to have disappeared. Hysteria built; her legs itched to run. "Where am I? What is this place?" she shrieked. People, even those she thought were mannequins, stopped and stared. A turbaned man draped with jewels called out, "Get the Mall Guards! I think she is going to amok!" Before she could run, two uniformed men loomed in front of her. When one of them tried to grab her wrist, she kicked out and tried to twist away, but heavily muscled arms seized her by the waist in a tight grip. She couldn't move. As the pressure increased, pain shot through her waist to her ribs. Her screams gurgled and choked. The guards wrestled her to the ground, one covering her mouth with his hands to stifle her moans. Lying on the floor, when she felt something float over her and settle lightly on her body. She started to rise only to be slammed back down to the ground. Her thoughts shattered by terror, she could barely make sense of what one of guards said.

"Who's the MHP on call? Nona? Call her and tell her we got an Amoker for her."

Sara opened her eyes on a room she didn't recognize, unable to move. She seemed to float in the air but felt calm as she took in the circularity of the room and the mirrors almost covering the walls. Her curiosity about her whereabouts was muted, soft like the pale green, enormous chair she reclined on. Sitting motionless in the chair opposite her, smiling kindly, was a lovely woman, white-blond hair twisted into a bun on the nape of her neck and with angular cheekbones, full strong lips, and huge, wide gray eyes shaded by pale, long, white eyelashes. Her hands, her face, her body, everything about her was long and slim. Finding her voice, Sara managed to ask, "Have I been drugged? Where am...I? Who...are...?" She wound down, the effort too much.

"I am Nona, and I am a Mental Health Practitioner. I don't know the word *drugged.* Don't you remember grappling with the Mall Guards in the Jewelry Department of the Ready-Made Fashion Division? They netted you and took you to a holding cell where they had to admin a sedation dart. You were then brought to me for treatment—because you amoked."

Sara stared at her, not comprehending. She struggled to brush away the thick fog clinging to her thoughts. Words stumbled out: "But I don't know what...it's...hard to think clearly. Where am I?"

Nona unfolded from the chair, seemed to flow to a built-in cabinet, and removed something Sara couldn't see. "I will admin a mild stimulant to counteract the effects of the sedation pharm. Then you'll be better able to communicate."

Sara felt her push something small and damp against her neck and saw a pinpoint of light in the fog that widened to a sharp clarity. Clutching the arms of the chair, she cried, "Where am I? Who are you? Am I in some office in the mall? I need to get home! My mother! She's waiting for me. My husband ..." Before Sara could bolt out of the chair, Nona, gently, but with surprising strength, pressed her hands down on Sara's shoulders, restraining her. "It is imperative that you allow me to keep you here until you have been restored to your former state of health and well-being. I cannot allow you to leave with the possibility of your amoking again."

Sara's clutched the sides of the chair. "What, what? *Amoking?* What's that? Just let me go!"

Nona continued to gently but firmly restrain Sara. "I must administer a pharm to calm the urge to amok before we can even consider your departure. If you did leave and amoked again, you would be apprehended. Surely you recall that to amok means to lose all control over yourself. Even if you were calmed to an acceptable state, looking the way you do, Mall Guards would detain you; probably take you to a holding center or to another Mental Health Practitioner."

"How I look? What are you talking about?" She pulled frantically at her hair. "Am I bleeding or something?"

"May I ask your name?

"No, just get me out of here!" She struggled against the woman's hands.

Nona pushed down harder. "I am so sorry you are so agitated. I only mention how you look because—you must remember that creating an appearance pleasing to others is of the utmost importance." For a moment, Sara stilled, mouth agape. Nona continued, "But maybe you are still confused from the effects of the pharms we administered." She paused, as if waiting for Sara to agree, but she just looked at Nona, still unable to speak. "Please, do not be offended if I remind you that our Code specifies that it is discourteous not to provide everyone a pleasurable experience when looking at you. And excuse me for my bluntness, but right now you would offend rather than please. But that's easy to remedy."

Sara snapped out of her trance of disbelief. "I must be dreaming; this is so insane." She twisted in her chair, searching for words. "Don't you get it? I want out! Let me go!" Again she tried to free herself from Nona's iron grip, then stilled. "Wait, I get it, this is some sort of elaborate practical joke, maybe even a kind of Candid Camera thing. Any minute someone will pop out and say, *Smile, you're on Candid Camera*, right?" She laughed wildly.

Nona froze, except for a slight flicker, as though she were a television image electrically disrupted. "Oh dear," she said, "I am sorry. I don't think I realized the extent of your disorder. But don't worry; we will find a treatment." She paused, a frown rumpling the smoothness of her forehead, and looked closely at Sara. For a moment, neither said anything. Finally, Nona continued, "This is difficult to believe, but if I remember the class on Ancient Maladies correctly, you may be suffering from amnesia. We can eliminate this problem by using a Mem-wipe …"

Sara moaned. "What, what? Is that some kind of drug? No, no, let me go, for God's sake!" She pushed against Nona's hands.

Nona held her down. "*Drug*? What is this word?"

"You know! How could you not? Those guys shot me with a drug when I was …"

Nona nodded. "Ah yes, pharms—but why do you call them by this other word? I don't mean to offend or frighten you, but something is indeed wrong with your memory."

"No! I know who I am!" She swung her head back and forth. "Please, please listen to me. I remember everything except where I am. I'm still me, but I have no idea, not one, who you are and where I am or how I got here!"

Nona stared at Sara. "I'll be honest; I don't know what happened to you, but I …"

Eyes still on Nona, Sara stopped listening. What was wrong? Had she gone crazy, had some sort of breakdown? Her muscles tensed for flight. Using all her strength, she shoved Nona, who tumbled to the floor. *The door, get to the door.* Once there, her hands scrabbled against the surface. Where's the knob? She'd have to push the lights in the right sequence! She stabbed her fingers at the buttons and once again felt that damp pressure on her neck.

CHAPTER THREE

As Nona steered the semi-conscious woman to the chair and helped her lie down, the entry bell sounded. Before she reached the door, the Finance Policeman marched in. "I'm here to accompany you to the Mall Management meeting."

"What about my client? She's a special case. I should be here when she wakes."

"How long will she be out?"

Nona considered his question for a moment. "I think at least an hour."

"I am not apprised of the projected length of the meeting. You may or may not be back in the span of time. However, you are aware that an MM summons takes precedence over any other activity." Nona knew she had no choice but to follow him. Together they rode the elevator to the 100th floor where Nona followed him into the Mall Management meeting area, a large room with at least twenty rows of purple chairs, all filled with Mallites. She moved toward a group of MHPs sitting toward the end of the second row and third row and sat next to Royce.

"Hello, Royce," she smiled fondly.

He flashed a smile, revealing startlingly white, ruby-studded teeth. "Hi, Nona." He studied her for a moment. "I never get tired of looking at you. I've been thinking about you lately. A lot. I would appreciate it if you would take the time to meet. As soon as convenient for you."

"I don't know. When we last talked, we agreed not to see each other for a while."

"Yes, I know, and for good reason. But I am eager to talk. Do you think you could meet at the Pod's rec room for a cup of coffee, maybe right after this meeting?"

"I can't. I have a new client. Sort of an emergency case…" she trailed off looking around. "And, Royce, you know what happens when we meet. We usually end up having sex. And then, well, you know, I want to keep seeing you on a regular basis."

"I know, I know." He searched her face. "I have a few things to talk over," he said softly.

"I can't meet after this meeting. The new client is Mall mandated. What about tomorrow after my breakfast date with Fabriana? Around 10:30—is that okay with you?"

"Yes. I'm almost sure. When I get a chance I'll access my appointment calendar. If you don't hear from me, let's meet in the MHP coffee lounge."

A petite woman sitting in front of Nona, whipped around. "You two better be careful. People may think you're violating the Code rule about extending pair-knots." She lowered her voice. "Well, you already did break that rule, but you know I will never tell."

Nona quickly changed the subject, reminding herself to use the affectionate terms recommended for heart-friend conservation. "Hello, dear heart-friend, so lovely to see you. Do you know why we have been summoned?"

Fabriana shook her head, swinging her burgundy striped green hair. "Oh, so good to see you too. I'm not sure why we were summoned. I wager they want our expertise," she replied with a self-important   smile.

"Pardon me for disagreeing, Fabriana, but that seems unlikely. They've never asked before. Why now?"

"Pardon me for saying so, but I think it's obvious. Don't you access Rumor Has It? This is about Junkers. MM must want our opinion how to solve this terrible problem—lights going on and off, elevators stopping in between floors, entrance codes not working, those kinds of things—and," she paused, widening her bottle-green eyes, "a neon artist nearly suffocated in her sleeping quarters." She smiled as she shuddered.

"No, I don't usually access that program." She looked closely at Fabriana. "Excuse me if I am wrong, but you look like you think this Junker problem is somewhat exciting."

Fabriana drew herself up. "Of course not! You know I am a loyal Mallite. I abhor the thought of Junkers contaminating our beautiful world."

Nona exchanged glances with Royce and looked around the room filled with chattering Mallites, including a group of three she'd never seen before. She touched Fabriana, who had begun talking animatedly with the MHP sitting next to her. When she turned toward her, Nona thought her smile looked strained, and not for the first time, Nona regretted agreeing to a heart-friend contract with her. But after Fabriana had asked at least five times, it seemed the height of rudeness to turn her down. "I'm sorry for interrupting, but you are ever so much better informed than I am. I recognize all the merchants, the video artists, the creative teams, the chefs, the techs, the different kinds of artists, and some of the bureaucrats, but who are those three just down a couple of rows sitting next to the three Healers—the ones robed in dark colors?"

"They're Spiritual Practitioners," said Fabriana. "Interesting, aren't they?"

For a moment Nona craned her neck and stared at the one in the middle. Taller than most Mallites, he had a well-trimmed beard, wore his jet-black hair long and—this was odd—his face was unaltered. Before she could study him further, a gong sounded and doors slid open to admit four MMs dressed in peacock blue. Each was bald and wore a diamond tiara. One stepped forward. "Welcome, fellow Mallites. I am Claude. Please allow me to introduce Richard, Rubio, and Tyrone. Please excuse any appearance of rudeness, but necessity demands we address this serious situation immediately. You are here to help solve the most pressing problem Mall has faced since its inception—" He paused, making eye contact with all those in the front row. "—namely, the Junkers. Each of you makes the highest profit in your specific area of employment, and if we don't address this state of affairs, this crisis could very well affect the amount of credit transferred to you. That in and of itself should give you incentive to make a commitment to solve this problem. Also, each of you has been an exemplary Mallite known for strict adherence to the Code."

He scrutinized the Mental Health Practitioners. "Before I go on, it is of utmost importance that you divulge nothing of what is discussed." Those at the table began to mutter and shift in their seats. "With the greatest respect, I ask for silence. Many of you have heard about the problems the Junkers have been causing. Let me give just a few examples. They cut the lighting in the neon artists' studio three days ago—for *four* hours. Now these artists are three days behind the deadline for their new installation. This is the most anticipated and the biggest neon show in years. You can imagine the problem this is creating for those who transferred credit—and a lot of it—for the performance. And yes, what Rumor Has It divulged yesterday was correct. They managed to mix too much carbon dioxide into one of the artist's sleeping quarters. Luckily, they restored the balance before she suffocated."

The strange Spiritual Practitioner, even taller than Nona had estimated, stood. "Pardon me for the interruption. Are you able to instruct us how to identify Junkers?" His words, she noted were respectful, but his tone—did she detect a note of arrogance?

Before speaking, Claude picked up a water bottle and drank deeply. "Excuse me if I am too blunt, Paul. That is your name, I believe? I think we all know that it is impossible to determine if anyone we see is a Junker, which is a large part of the problem. If we could ID them, we would apprehend them. But we can't. These

Junkers have the potential to threaten the Mall way of life. Never have performances in Mall been late. Even more momentous is the fact that someone's life been threatened. We must stop them, because if—"

Paul interrupted, "How do you even know that these Junkers are responsible for these disturbing events?"

Why, Nona wondered, *is he being so rude?*

The Mall Manager drew himself up and stared at Paul. "Your eagerness for an answer must be the reason for your rudeness."

"Please excuse my impoliteness." Paul folded his length back into his chair.

Royce cleared his throat and addressed the MM. "Pardon me. I want to make sure, are we permitted to comment or ask questions?"

"Indeed, yes," he replied. "You need to be absolutely clear on your duty because ... because ..." he stopped and coughed, clutching his throat, then crumpled to the ground.

Richard knelt next to him. "Healers, come quickly!"

Two of the three Healers rushed to him and together they carried him out of the room. Someone shouted, "His number is up!" Other audience members stared, mouths agape, or shouted.

When someone yelled, "Get out of here—we're in danger!" Nona felt her throat close and her legs grow too weak to move. Others sprang from their chairs and began to shove their way to the exit; one of them just missed stepping on two chefs who had fallen. Four burly Mall Guards appeared brandishing gold batons. Everyone stopped moving. A loud alarm rang out, silencing the roar. Richard stood motionless in front of the crowd and said in a commanding voice,

"Take your seats immediately or I will have Mall Guards apprehend you."

Quiet now, everyone returned to his or her seats. Richard retrieved a small device from his pocket. After holding it to his ear for several moments, he announced, "The Chief Healer just communicated with me. Claude was poisoned—"

The audience members began to mutter and mumble until Richard set off the alarm again. "I will not ask for silence again." He looked around, eyes resting on the tall Spiritual Practitioner. "Thanks to the Healers' knowledge and expertise, Claude will recover." He paused and bowed his head. "Of course, the Junkers were responsible. I think now you must know the urgency of our situation. All of you are obligated to help end this problem." He looked toward Nona. For an anxious moment, she thought he planned to single her out. Instead, he said, "Royce, I believe you had a question for comment."

"Yes, thank you, Mall Manager, but in light of what just happened, my question seems insignificant."

"No, not at all. We must be clear what our duty is."

"What about our oath never to communicate with anyone the content of one of our sessions?"

"All Mental Health Practitioners are released from their oath. Are there any other questions?"

One of the other Spiritual Practitioners asked. "Do we know why they are doing this? To disrupt an artistic endeavor seems disordered, but to attempt to end someone's life before his number is up must be deranged."

The Mall Manager in the middle stepped forward. "They must be. How can anyone in his or her ordered mind not only want to disrupt the almost perfect life we live in Mall, but also take a life, something that has never occurred in our three hundred-year history? I have heard," he paused and surveyed the audience, "that some of them want out—can you comprehend this? A Mallite with the desire to escape Mall?"

A chill passed through Nona, thinking of the woman in her Pod. Was *she* a Junker?

One of the Cosmetic Artists spoke up. "We all know there's no way out!" Voices swelled and then subsided.

The Mall Manager continued, "I assume you understand what you must do from now on. You are to tell no one about this discussion. And if we discover that you have not followed these orders, the consequences will be severe. You will lose your license to practice for six months. You will be confined to your sleeping quarters for that amount of time. You may even be forced to have a Mem-wipe, depending on how Judgment goes." He surveyed the room and Nona forced herself to meet his gaze as it passed over. A Mem-wipe! If the woman in her quarters was a Junker and she didn't report her, she could lose everything. And if it was discovered that she'd kept Natalie's secret as well…

"This may be the worst crisis Mall has ever faced. Many of you have experienced a Junker-caused disturbance; am I correct?"

Fabriana looked around the room, smiling while fluffing her hair. "The other day the lights in my office dimmed and flickered and then went out for fifteen minutes. Is that what you mean?"

Nona remembered the blackouts in her office. Things might get worse. The knowledge that both her new client and Natalie could be contributing to these disturbances gnawed at her.

"Yes, a minor example. More importantly, some members of the Entertainment Pod woke to feel their throats so scratchy they had to cough. Air quality fell fifty percent optimum for about thirty minutes in that sector. And you all heard Claude describe what happened to the neon artists, especially the one who almost suffocated. To increase your motivation, if you discover and report an actual Junker, your name will be entered in the Tell-All Lottery. You may not know this, but for each weekly drawing we have added new, more tempting prizes, such as a year's credit-free visits to Relaxnrenu Spa." He spoke next in a loud and authoritarian voice.

"You have your instructions. You may go now. The FPs who escorted you here will take you back to your places of employment."

As the participants filed out, Richard made eye contact with Nona and motioned her to come to him. "Nona? Am I right? Could you please stay behind?"

Nona stepped aside and waited until only the two of them remained. "Yes, I am Nona. Did you wish to speak to me?"

"Yes. I hope I have not offended you by singling you out. I thought I noticed—if you will pardon me for pointing out—that you fidgeted several times. I am wondering if you were uncomfortable. Maybe you need to tell me something?"

"Please forgive any appearance of rudeness. I have a client emergency waiting in my office, maybe someone who is disordered. I sedated her and need to return before she wakes up."

"Ah, perhaps a Junker?" The MM rubbed his hands.

"I don't know enough yet. I had just begun questioning her when I was summoned to this meeting."

"If you discover she is a Junker, of course, you will immediately notify Finance Police." The Mall Manager regarded her closely. "I am aware of your reputation for exquisite care, concern, and follow-up with your clients. Your commitment to your patients must not overrule your duty to Mall."

Nona murmured, "Of course." She lowered her eyes to avoid betraying what she already knew.

The MM studied her for a moment more and then said. "Thank you, Nona, for your time. You many go now."

In the center of her stomach, Nona experienced an unpleasant push-pull. Should she report Natalie or the woman in her quarters? Or both? If she didn't, would they find out? No, she couldn't; she'd promised Natalie not to tell and the session occurred before the meeting. Surely, it didn't count. As for the other woman...

Something about her was so different Nona wanted to investigate further. She nodded and left.

CHAPTER FOUR

When Sara woke this time, she felt alert, and immediately remembered what had happened. For a moment panic bubbled through her body. She leapt from her chair ready to attack the woman who wouldn't let her go, but she was nowhere to be seen. "My purse!" she cried out loud, spotting the familiar object. A wave of relief passed through her. She reached in to retrieve her cell phone. With shaky hands, she entered her passcode and found four messages, all from Carl. She could read them later. She had to get in touch with her mother. She dialed her phone number. No ringing, just silence. Maybe she could send a message after she read her texts.

Fingers trembling, she managed to access the texts. The first one: *Where are you? I am at the car.* Second message: *Stop this, Sara. This is stupid. You look at men all the time. Call or text me!* Third message: *You bitch! Is this some kind of punishment?* Fourth message: *Why should I stick around? Nothing will ever be enough.*

"Fuck you," she said out loud. She tapped her mother's name in her contact list, but the phone went dark. She threw it on the counter and paced. Fear swarmed her body, ordering her to get out, get out now! She headed for the door's blinking colored lights. Before she'd passed out, she'd tried to watch Nona push in a sequence of lights. Taking some deep breaths, she pressed different combinations of the colored squares.

Five minutes later, to her elation and surprise, the door slid open. She slipped through, expecting to find herself back in Lincoln Mall or at least back in the parking lot. Instead she emerged in an area that seemed like a different planet. A long, wide corridor flanked on one side by embossed cream-colored office doors stretched into infinity. Moving belts, like the ones at airports but faster and much wider, carried dozens of people, dividing the area into two. She didn't stop to look at the other side of the moving belt. As she stumbled along the corridor, she barely took note of the myriad of people who thronged the area.

She started when behind her a soft voice called out, "Nona. MHP. Top credit earner in the field." Then she realized that each time someone passed a doorway, a voice announced a name. Everything seemed alien, especially the people, but she was too terrified to make out why. Before she could rationally decide what to do, she ran, eyes darting everywhere, looking for an exit while pushing people aside and sometimes colliding with those she didn't see. Dimly, she heard a voice shout, "Guards, where are the Mall Guards?" And then someone snatched her arm, spun her around and pinioned her.

She looked up into the gold eyes of a black-and-silver uniformed officer. Next to him, a familiar face. Nona, yes, that woman who held her captive. She heard her say, "Please, if you wouldn't mind, bring her to my office. I had to interrupt treatment in order to attend the meeting, and I had to leave her there. She had not recovered sufficiently from—I cannot divulge her condition."

"Did you leave your door open?" He asked frowning. "Wait, is this the woman guards brought to the holding cell on the Mental Health Practitioners level? I heard about her."

"Yes," Nona admitted.

"Why haven't you surrendered her to your Finance Police?"

"I haven't finished treating her. She—"

The Finance Police interrupted her, "She had no ID or Con Card. You need to find out who she is. She may be a Junker."

"Perhaps. However, I believe she may be suffering from amnesia. I will admin a Mem-wipe and then communicate with the FPs attached to the Mental Health Pod."

"And as soon as possible."

Sara, who had stopped struggling to listen, eyes stretched wide, jerked her body as she tried in vain to wrench free from the iron-grip of the uniformed man. "Stop, let me go! Let me go!" When she opened her mouth to scream, he put his free hand over her mouth. "None of that, or you will go to the holding cell now, and, if you remember, not a pleasant place compared to the comfort of Nona's office."

Nona moved closer and whispered to Sara, "If you cooperate, I promise I will find a way to help you. Please don't resist any longer. You will regret it; my office is a much better place to be."

Sara sagged almost to the ground. Slowly she straightened and allowed Nona to guide her to her office. A mantra repeated in her head, *Oh God, what should I do, what should I do?*

CHAPTER FIVE

Back in Nona's office, Sara stood rigid, refusing to sit down. "I went along with you and let you take me back here. Now if you really want to help me, you will let me out of here!" She clenched her teeth.

"To what end?" Nona asked. "You won't get far. Mall Guards will pick you up and either bring you to me, to another MHP, to a holding cell, or even to Judgment." When Nona reached out to take her arm, Sara reared back, then sank into one of the chairs.

"I want to go home!" Sara covered her face. "What am I going to do? There must be a way out!"

"Home? What do you mean? Your sleeping quarters? Your Pod's meeting room?"

"I don't know what you're talking about. If I could just get back to the mall and…"

Nona interrupted. "Excuse me, but you *are* in Mall."

"I mean Lincoln Mall. I don't even know what this place is, but it's not a mall. It's, maybe, I don't know, maybe some weird destination place?"

"*Lincoln* Mall? Mall is mall; there is no other mall." Nona shook her head.

Sara covered her mouth and moaned. "I think I've gone crazy."

Nona frowned. "Crazy? What is this word?"

"When you feel like you've lost your mind."

"You are feeling disordered, but why—what happened to you?" A sudden thought occurred to Nona. "Sara, have you had contact with a Junker?"

"What? I never have even heard of a *Junker*. Is that a name for crazy people?" Tears glittered in her eyes.

29

"Oh no, are those tears?" Shocked, Nona's eyes also watered and her throat clogged. The sensation overwhelmed and panicked her. Why was she also so strongly affected? She remembered feeling a similar kind of pain when she and Royce stopped seeing each other. She couldn't think of that right now; she had to help this woman. "You can't go on hurting this way. I can admin a Mem-wipe almost immediately."

"A what?!" Sara cried.

"Surely you haven't forgotten what a Mem-wipe is? It's a process that eliminates parts of your memories, or in some rare cases, all of the memories."

Sara leapt to her feet. "No! I want to go home! I promised my mother I would visit her. I haven't told her yet what the doctor said. I need to talk to her."

For a moment Nona was stunned into silence. Where were these ideas coming from? "Your mother? I don't understand. Why should you, as you say, *need* her? And doctor? Isn't that the ancient term for Healer? Did you go to a Healer?"

"Healer, healer? What are you talking about? No, I didn't go to a healer; I went to a doctor. Then I went shopping with my husband to get my mind off the news that I can't have a baby." Sara's face crumpled. "I can't think about that now. You probably wouldn't even understand."

Something sharp caught in Nona's throat. She was reminded that she, too, had failed to get pregnant, something she shouldn't reveal to this client. If the memory persisted, a dose of Ezydozit would melt the thought into a pink mist. "I do understand that you are suffering unnecessarily. Won't you let me help you?"

Sara dropped back into a chair. "I don't know what to do next. I need to get out of here to search for the way out."

"Please understand that there is no way out. Mall is a closed system. Besides, no one would ever want to leave." She knew that wasn't exactly true. According to the MMs, some of the Junkers wanted out.

"That can't be right. People must want to go outside. Oh, I don't know—maybe you could show me around this mall of yours, you know, so I can better understand?"

Nona raised her eyebrows. If she allowed this, Sara would draw attention, but it might help her to remember if she were among other Mallites. "I suppose we could do that, if you think it would help. If you stay close to me and change out of those clothes."

What she really needs is cosmetic alteration, Nona thought. Did she want to make that possible? How far would she go to help her? Why didn't she just alert the Finance Police that Sara refused the Mem-wipe? They would force her. Yet Nona felt deeply reluctant to silence Sara's stories. Why? Was it because she felt so energized, so engaged when Sara talked? Yes, that and she felt a kind of connection when she'd mentioned her inability to have a baby.

"I want to keep my own clothes."

"If you don't change, you will attract attention." She walked to a section of wall not covered in mirrors and pushed. Sara stretched her neck to see into another room—a very large bathroom, but before Sara could make out any details, Nona was back with a yellow silk jumpsuit she held out to Sara. "This fits me so loosely, you should be able to wear it."

Sara stared at Nona, disbelieving. "I have to do this before you take me out?"

"Yes, as I said."

"Okay."

Nona watched while Sara turned her back, stripped off the bulky top and faded blue trousers and climbed into the jumpsuit. Could she be a Junker? If she were, she was putting on a good act. No, not a Junker. Her insistence that she was from another world must be a deep kind of disorder, although not one Nona had ever

31

encountered or learned about in training. And what caused her degraded appearance? Why was she so heavy? Why did she talk that way about her mother? And did she have a factual memory of trying to get pregnant? That would mean she had been chosen to conceive. Even more worrisome was Nona's reluctance to insist on the Mem-wipe or to just hand her back to the Finance Police. She had always followed the rules, and with every moment that passed, she endangered her reputation and even her life by not turning Sara in.

Again she asked herself why she cared so much. It must have to do with her struggle with ennui. Although what she experienced was a restlessness deeper than boredom. After her involvement with Royce, nothing seemed pleasurable or even interesting, at least not to the extent she was used to. All she could do was admin more and admin the best, no matter how credit-inefficient. Strange how in such a short time this woman had eliminated some of the flat staleness of her everyday life as well as any pharm could. Maybe Royce could help her understand why this woman had become so important.

Another thought: maybe if Sara's memories would come back to her when she saw familiar things, Nona could use it to her credit advantage. People would spend a lot of credit to hear her explain how she'd treated Sara without pharms. And they would be fascinated by Sara's delusions. Not that she needed more credit, but she liked the idea of more acclaim.

From a hidden pocket, Nona pulled out a tiny communication device and the equally tiny earpiece. She listened for a few seconds. "Now I have the new open-sequence. When we go out, please stay close to me and say or do nothing that will make people notice you. You will be able to reacquaint yourself with many parts of Mall. Maybe this will help you remember all you seem to have forgotten." As she entered the new code and led Sara out, Nona thought again about arranging for cosmetic alteration for Sara. To make this possible, Nona would have to credit-transfer a lot, a fact that she didn't seem to mind, which surprised her. As Sara walked out, Nona retrieved her communicator and quickly made an appointment with her Cosmetic Artist in a low voice Sara couldn't hear.

As she followed Sara her stomach clenched. Why was she willing to do this for so disordered a client and one she had only begun to treat? Why take this risk and credit-transfer so much? She wanted Sara to fit in. Maybe, she wondered, Sara was not the only one disordered.

CHAPTER SIX

As they stepped into the corridor, Sara stopped to stare, trying to take note of everything she'd missed when she made her escape attempt. She remembered the offices lining the passageway but not the thick, midnight-blue carpet or the kiosks lining the thoroughfare on the other side of the moving sidewalks, which continued as far as the eye could see, propelling people at a rapid pace. When the belt nearest to them slowed at a gate to let off a man, she shrank back in shock not so much at his towering height, unblemished ebony skin, and chiseled muscles, but at his attire. He wore only a white satin codpiece and white fur turban. Nona turned to look at her. "You look disturbed. Let's move over to an ER."

"A hospital?" Sara asked.

Nona shook her head. "I don't know where these strange words are coming from." She steered Sara to a giant glass tube. Inside were two upholstered straight-backed chairs separated by a plant with heart-shaped magenta leaves. Nona touched several lighted squares on a small twinkling keypad. The glass opened, and a voice said,

"Please describe the nature of the emergency."

"No emergency. The use is recreational rest," Nona said to the invisible voice.

Irritated, Sara asked, "What are doing here? I wanted to walk down this ... thoroughfare."

"You were obviously feeling discomfort, something the Code specifies to be avoided. Please, sit down, Sara."

For a moment Sara watched people through the glass tube. Another man jumped off the slowing sidewalk, opened a gate, and walked without pause through a cluster of people sitting in a circle outside of one of the offices. She grabbed Nona's arm. "Did you see that? Was that an optical illusion or what?"

"You really don't remember this?" Nona gestured beyond the glass. "All the people in front of those offices are holographic advertisements. We're on the promenade of the Mental Health Division."

Sara looked for Nona's office door, but all she could see was a wall covered in cream-colored paper with a repeating embossed design. Only the small squares of twinkling multicolored lights marked the entrances. "Where is your advertisement? And the ones for the offices next to yours?"

"We choose not to advertise."

"Why not?"

"It saves some credit and we don't need to. We are already the top credit earners in our field. We rely on word of mouth."

Sara thought for a moment. "Why was I brought to a—how did you say it?—a top credit earner?"

"We are the ones trained to deal with Mall emergencies, and I happened to be on call."

Sara craned her neck to take in as much as she could. Her eyes darted back and forth as she strained to make sense of it all, to melt away the alien quality. She could get used to the holograms—her world was technologically advanced enough that she could believe in those—but she couldn't get over one thing: all the people were beautiful, gorgeous, handsome, yet each one's attire was striking and original, like the man who was shirtless, revealing a muscular bronze chest, both nipples pierced with what looked like diamonds. His transparent purple harem pants left nothing to the imagination. For a dizzying moment, Sara thought they were all identical. She quickly realized that their matching flawless and ageless appearance triggered this feeling. And, she thought, unease nipping at the pit of her stomach, their eyes—most were not the color eyes should be, but gold, emerald, red, silver—giving them a nonhuman look.

"Sara, are you recovered enough to move on?"

35

"Yes, let's go." As the door slid open, she searched the promenade. No exits, she realized. "Fuck," she murmured. "Can we go to any of the other levels?"

Nona gasped and grabbed Sara's arm. "There's something else you seem to have forgotten. Mall forbids swearing."

"Why? Everyone swears."

"No, we don't. Swearing is the height of rudeness, which is against our Code. You honestly do not remember this?"

"I told you I don't live in this world! Now can we go to some of the other levels?"

"Yes." Again, Nona activated her communicator and earpiece. She spoke too softly for Sara to make out her words.

As they walked, Sara began to notice passersby staring, some elbowing each other as they looked at her. One woman stopped to ask Nona, "Excuse me, please, but the woman with you seems to be a third-rater. I thought their presence on this floor was discouraged unless they were delivering something ordered, and I might add, in a suitable uniform."

Nona answered, "I understand your concern, but please do not be troubled. I am Nona, the MHP, and this woman is a mandated client. Of course, I know you are aware that I cannot reveal anything about her."

Sara felt shocked and confused. A third-rater? That sounded like more than mere disapproval.

Nona looked over her shoulder as the woman walked away. "Do you now understand that you cannot be in Mall looking like this? Or behaving in ways that go against the Code?" If you want me to help you to avoid the holding cell, you must do as I say." Three Mallites walking by slowed their pace and craned their necks for a better view, their mouths pursed in distaste. Several others muttered as they gave Sara and Nona wide berth.

An icy realization shot through Sara. She had to do what Nona said. She had to look and act like they did or she could be arrested and jailed. And maybe end up in Judgment, whatever that was. If she didn't follow Nona's advice, she would never find a way out of this place.

Nona caught her arm and propelled her toward the moving sidewalk. "Hop on after I slow the Throughway." Nona pressed a large blinking red button next to one of the gates and stepped through quickly, motioning Sara to follow. After riding for about five minutes, Nona pressed one of the yellow lights dotting the area below the railing, slowing the sidewalk so they could step off. With Nona in the lead, they headed toward another glass cylinder looming in the center of a fern-filled garden bordered by small white benches.

"Another rest?" Sara wondered aloud.

"This is an elevator," Nona sighed. As they drew closer, Sara saw the tube contained not chairs but a moving platform. Nona touched some of the pulsing lights on a panel and stopped the platform's ascent. "Floor sixty-eight," Nona directed. A narrow door slid up, allowing one person at a time to enter. Just as Sara's hand reached out to encircle the interior railing—normally she didn't hold on in an elevator, but this all-glass one was unnerving—the platform hurtled up, spinning her view into liquid. Her ears popped just before the elevator stopped.

"Floor sixty-eight," the soft voice announced. Sara raced to keep up with Nona after she exited the elevator. They made their way through another garden, a lawn scattered with small maple trees. Once through the green area, Sara struggled to focus—the holographic ads came one after another; so close they almost bled into each other. She couldn't stop herself from gawking at what appeared to be a doctor of some sort stripping a short, plump patient naked and then prodding and poking while pouring out streams of advice. The stubby man disappeared behind purple smoke and then reappeared when the haze cleared, slimmer, and with more muscle definition. The doctor bowed with a flourish. He seemed to be looking straight at Sara when he said, "As you can see, I can do the miraculous."

"A very motivating holo, don't you agree?" asked Nona as she led Sara toward an entrance. "Perhaps you would like to meet someone who does much better work than José in that holo. I am fortunate to be one Rick's preferred clients so he agreed to make time for you."

Sara pulled away from Nona's grasp. Were they going to do something to her? She tensed her legs to run, but Nona clamped down on Sara's shoulder and forced her through the door. A pretty man, black hair smoothed back, flashed lavender eyes fringed with purple lashes as he ushered them into a small room with mirrored ceiling and walls. "Nona," he gushed, "It is so very pleasant to see you. I am still in awe of your new look that we created. You are simply stunning." Turning toward Sara, he said, "This must be the one you communicated about." His hand flew to his chest. "I beg your pardon but I must be blunt to do my work effectively. Who is this woman? How did she get this way? Only a fourth-rater would have this much appearance degradation." He touched Sara's hair and smoothed his fingertips over the lines at her eyes. For a moment Sara froze. He turned to Nona, "Yes, she must be a third- or fourth-rater. I don't know why you are credit-transferring for the procedures, but it is not for me to ask why. I won't need her Consumer Card; however, I will need her ID."

Nona smoothed back her already flawless hair. "That's part of the problem. As I mentioned when I communicated, she has some sort of amnesia and can't remember the number or where the card is."

"Oh dear, Nona, in light of what we learned at that meeting, I can't do anything unless there is an ID. I am so sorry. What if she is a Junker?"

"She is not, I guarantee. And I already promised you extra credit-transfer—two weeks extra over the cost of your fee—if you agreed to see her immediately and if you did not ask too many questions. I do understand your reticence. After that meeting and after all the unfortunate events, I, too, am on the lookout. Really, you do not need to worry." Rick shook his head. Nona continued, "What if I promise to refer all my clients who want cosmetic alteration to you? That could mean up to four or five referrals a month."

Sara barely listened as she struggled against Nona's hold.

Rick caught her other arm. "You make it difficult to turn down," he said to Nona as he held Sara's other arm tightly. "Okay, I'll do it, and I trust you to follow up on the referrals. No need for a voice sign. Looking closely at Sara, he said, "Don't worry, honey, I promise not to report you."

Afraid, Sara tried to jump back, but he tightened his hold on her arm. "Yes, she is in desperate need for cosmetic alteration. You're sure she is not a fourth-rater?" A memory plucked at Sara's consciousness. Her father. Talking to her mother. *Think of a way to get her to exercise, diet, something, for God's sake* while a young Sara crouched around the corner, eavesdropping. *She'll never have boyfriends...take her to a...Listen, she can't go anywhere looking like...* To stop the memory, she dug her fingernails into her palms.

"No, she is not a fourth-rater, Rick. Please forgive me, but I can't go into the reasons for her appearance. I will say that she can't go about as a first- or second-rater in this condition; she must be altered."

Fear flowed through Sara. Struggling with Nona, she broke free of her grasp but Rick's grip was too strong for her to get free.

39

"Honey, there's nothing to be afraid of. Surely you can't be resistant to this process this top-rated MHP is making possible for you. No? Well, we have something to fix that." With his free hand, he reached around her to a drawer in a black cabinet, and although she struggled, once again, she felt that ominous damp pressure at the base of her neck. Instead of blacking out, she sank to the floor, her limbs unable to move.

Rick and one of the assistants helped her to the red velvet sofa in the corner of the room. He walked around Sara, touching and peering. "Eyes are acceptable, the nose a little large, although interesting. The mouth is too thin, and the teeth need whitening. Her face has a nice oval shape with high cheekbones. Overweight, that's unusual. Yes, we will have to work to bring her up to acceptable standards, but it's certainly possible. Time to admit my fabulous dears." He pushed a lighted button on one of mirrored walls. Four assistants surrounded Sara.

"Please, Rick, we need to see her naked," one of the assistants said as she began to remove the yellow jumpsuit. "Hmm, not only is she overweight, but look at her breasts, small and saggy."

Sara tried unsuccessfully to turn her head away from the judging stares.

The assistant responsible for skin said, "Her face is lined around the eyes and the mouth. I'll remove them and add color to the cheeks. How interesting. Her face is reddening. I wonder why? I so seldom see this happen."

Another assistant, a black woman, skin burnished with copper, touched Sara's hair and scanned her body. "Do you remember that class on The History and Nature of Banned Emotions we all had to take before during Training? I think this face coloring is due to a sort of extreme embarrassment. Hmm, look at this. Her pubic hair is auburn but her hair is a streaked mess. I say make her hair similar in hue." The assistants continued to access and decide what techniques to use.

Sara strained to move her body. Shame, sharp and familiar pressed against her stomach. Once again someone listed her physical faults; ones she knew only too well after living with her father and her husband, both of whom never tired of pointing out her weight, her fine hair, her pale skin, and on and on.

After they made their final decisions, Rick said, "Phew, this was an exceptionally frank and negative discussion." The assistants murmured to each other.

"Please forgive me for pointing this out, but she is in such bad shape, how could we be more positive?" the black woman softly objected.

"Yes, you're right. I myself had to be uncomfortably negative in my evaluation. Time to get to work!"

A sting to Sara's neck and she was out.

Sara floated in a chartreuse sky, breathing in roses and gardenias while strong hands kneaded her body into complete relaxation. Her husband? She turned her head to look up, and there he was, smiling and congratulating her on her beautiful, slim body. His voice thrummed with love. *Let him see all of it,* **she thought as she flipped over to show him her firm, flat stomach. But her belly wasn't flat; it was huge! Her hands flew to touch it, and her mouth rounded in terror as she felt it move and ripple. "Oh my God," she cried out, "I must be pregnant, but that can't be—how could it be? I can't get pregnant."**

A beautiful blonde with a tan body, hard and smooth, appeared from nowhere, linked arms with Sara's husband, and they were gone. Sara heaved herself up and off the table. "Wait, don't leave me!" she called as he closed a door behind them. "I'm going to have a baby!" She tugged open the door and found herself on a white beach bordered by a turquoise ocean.

41

Forgetting her intention to find her husband, she stopped to admire the scores of naked people with perfect bodies walking by. Worry squiggled her stomach; something was wrong. Their faces—that was it. They were flat, without features. A scream rose huge in her throat but emerged as a futile squeak. She whirled around to run back into the building, but the ocean surrounded her. Turquoise waves began to swell larger and larger, rushing to engulf her. No escape. This time when she tried to scream, she awoke with a start.

For a moment she could not remember where she was. She stared at the woman standing over her whose eyes stretched wide as she stared back at Sara. Finally, Sara sputtered, "Where am I? I had such a bad dream ..." she wound down, her body too languid to move.

"*Bad* dream?" The masseuse withdrew her hands as if scalded. "I've never heard of that. Something must be wrong. Don't worry; I'll get someone to help."

Sara lay unmoving. *Where am I? What's happening?* she wondered. She knew she was in trouble yet she felt relaxed, even tranquil. Something pricked at that feeling of comfort. A bubble of sadness and longing rose in her throat as she remembered the dream, an expanding pressure that made her moan. *I wish Carl were here.* Or did she? In the dream, he left her, not at all unusual because all too often he rejected her.

What about the faceless people in the dream? Then she remembered while on the promenade with Nona, all the people with their perfect faces. She turned to see Rick entering, eyebrows knotted in concern.

"Are you all right?"

"I ... don't know." She struggled to sit up, holding the sheet to cover her breasts. "What am I doing here naked? Did you do something to me?"

"Yes, a most wonderful thing; you are the most lucky little darling!" he exclaimed. "We made you beautiful!"

"What?" Still weakened by the medication, she fell back on the bed.

"Oh my dear, please stay where you are. You are still affected by Peectem. Is it not a wonderful sedative?"

Her body felt cosseted, but her confused thoughts spun in lazy circles. "Now I remember. You were talking to Nona about my appearance—that you could improve how I look?"

"Yes, we discussed how to alter your appearance, and, my dearest, we did! You are beautiful. All you need to do is lose a little weight, which will be ever so easy because we have injected you Ezyluze, an appetite suppressant. Don't worry, you will hardly be aware of its effects; you will just feel sated more quickly. Now, would you like to take a look?" Rick offered. She allowed him to help her sit up and held a mirror to her face. When she was close enough, shock electrified her whole body. She was no longer Sara, not on the outside.

"What have you done? My face is not my face anymore!"

Rick's mouth and eyes opened wide. "You looked very fourth-rate before. Aren't you pleased?"

Sara stared into the mirror long enough to see that she still looked somewhat like herself. Her nose was the same—a little large, but a feature her dad approved of. *A nose shows character,* he always said. Her skin was flawless, still light—she never could get a good tan—but her cheeks were dusted with almost translucent cinnamon. Her almond-shaped eyes were now shaded with thick brown lashes and her eyelids touched with copper. The same coppery color shone on her new, fuller mouth. The sheet loosened and fell low enough that she could see almost all of her breasts, fuller and firmer like she had always wanted them to be. She was, as Rick said, altered, and in a shockingly gorgeous way. For a moment she wished her dad were still alive and could see her. And Carl, too? Was she still herself? Had she been changed in other ways? And after she returned—she *would* find that exit—would she change back to her ordinary appearance?

Before the next question rose out of the mist fogging her thinking, Rick offered her a glass of pink soda-like drink. Realizing how thirsty she was, she gulped down the strawberry-flavored liquid. The whole room turned pink and then she was out.

CHAPTER SEVEN

Nona watched Sara stir in the chair. Heavily sedated, Sara had slept part of the afternoon and all night, and Nona was able to return to her sleeping quarters for the mandated eight-hour sleep. What should she do with this woman? The Finance Police on the MHP level would contact her for a report on Sara's condition. The fact that they hadn't, Nona suspected, was probably due to their search for Junkers. Should she start the Mem-wipe process? True, the Code prohibited forced use except in rare cases when the client was a danger to Mall or to him- or herself. Not surprisingly, she felt a strong reluctance at the thought of Sara transformed into an exemplary Mallite. Gone would be this troubled woman whom Nona found both fascinating and puzzling.

She looked more closely at Sara; Rick and his assistants had surpassed her expectations. Sara was not only beautiful; she had an unusual look. The nose, that was it—Rick had left it unaltered—too large maybe by Mall standards, but the effect was striking.

Nona watched as Sara fluttered her new long lashes then opened her eyes and took in her surroundings. She could tell by Sara's stillness and her half-closed eyes that she was still affected by the tranquilizing effects of her sedation. Sara asked, "Am I still in the other world?"

"You mean Mall. You were always here. I am not sure why you insist on the existence of another world. I think you may have amnesia, perhaps brought on by overuse of some pharms, although I don't know how that would be possible; or perhaps you mixed some that were incompatible, or even adminned an illegal pharm. Again, I don't know how that could happen."

Sara shook her head, the effects of the Peectem diminishing. "No," she shook her head several times, "I do *not* have amnesia. I can remember everything about my past." She looked around the room. "See my purse over there? If you bring it over, I can show you things from my world."

"That satchel sort of thing? I admit I forgot all about it." Nona retrieved it and Sara dumped it out on her lap. She raked through the items.

"My cell phone—do you know where it is? Oh that's right— yesterday I took it out and tried to call or text my mom." Her eyes searched the room.

"Cell phone? Do you mean that big, bulky sort of communicator? Over there on the counter?"

"It's important; please, can I have it?"

Nona picked up the phone and stared at it. "Where did this come from? Is this something new from the Fad Division?" she asked, puzzled by how it functioned and why it was so large. After studying it for a moment she handed it to Sara.

"Almost everyone has one. It's how we communicate," Sara snapped. She pushed the button to bring up the screen. Nothing came up. "Goddammit! I forgot that the battery is dead. How can I reach my husband or my mother?" She threw the phone on the floor and put her head in her hands.

"I don't know what a *husband* is, and I don't understand why it is so important to communicate with your mother." Sara closed her eyes.

She looked—what was it? Not a look Nona saw very often, and yet hadn't she just recently seen a young woman on the promenade with that expression? She remembered being struck by its rarity. Perhaps that woman was a Junker. Was that the problem—Junkers were dissatisfied with life in Mall? And there was someone else. That Spiritual Practitioner in the Mall Management meeting. Now that she thought about him, it wasn't just his unaltered face and tall stature that made him stand out; he had almost the same expression as Sara did right now. She searched her memory to name the feeling, one probably described in The History and Nature of Banned Emotions. *Sad?* No, it was more than that. A deeper unhappiness—*what was it called?* she wondered; surely one of the feelings Mall Fathers, in Their wisdom, had not only discouraged but forbade. "Sara, perhaps it would be helpful if you told me more about your mother and why you are so sad."

"I don't know if you would understand how I feel; in fact, I don't think you are able to understand one thing about me. You pretend like you care and yet you won't help me find a way out."

"If I didn't care, I would not have credit-transferred a substantial sum to bring your appearance up to Mall standards. I want to understand about your mother, really I do. Perhaps you can, in turn, try to understand my dilemma. I can't help you find a way out because there is no exit to your so-called Mall. Nothing exists outside of this Mall. But I can administer Mem-wipe to stop your sadness."

"Mem-wipe? Where you erase my memories?"

"Exactly. You admit to being sad, a most unpleasant feeling, which can be eliminated with this most beneficial tool." Nona furrowed her brow in an effort to understand this baffling woman. How was she going to help her?

"Yes, I am sad, although I admit the sedative Rick gave me has taken off the edge."

"It is difficult for me to see you unnecessarily upset. If only you would allow me to erase all the erroneous ideas and implant correct memories ..."

Sara abruptly stood. "I will never agree to this memory wipeout. I won't do it. For all I know, you could be planning on tricking or somehow making me!"

To her surprise, Nona raised her voice slightly. "Trick you into undergoing this procedure? I would never! And the Code forbids me to force you except in special cases."

"Am I one of those special cases? Will you force me?"

You probably are one of those cases, Nona thought. Out loud she said, "No, I won't force you. But I am worried. If the Finance Police discover that you believe you are from outside of Mall, they might very well think you are a Junker, or if not that, deranged. You probably would be questioned in a way that would force you to tell all you think and believe."

"I won't say a thing about where I come from, so I'm safe, right? Especially because I look like one of you guys now."

"No, not safe; not without an ID and Con Card. And the Finance Police will be following up on your case, although right now they are probably preoccupied with the … something more important."

Sara's voice broke. "What am I going to do? You have to help me get out of here!"

"If you won't let me help you with Mem-wipe, I can admin another pharm." Not that she really wanted Sara to agree to either solution. At least not yet. Her outbursts, her claims of another world energized Nona so much her whole body thrummed. She had so many questions but was afraid to ask. What if she also became dissatisfied with Mall?

Sara shook her head forcefully. "No more pharms, and please don't sneak up on me and plaster a patch on my neck. Not again." She looked at Nona with pleading eyes.

"Are we at an impasse? You can't go on like this or, as I have said, I think more than once, the consequences will not be to your liking," Nona warned.

"You mean like forcing me to have a Mem-wipe?" Sara rose and paced the room.

"It would be decided at Judgment."

Sara stopped in front of Nona. "I don't like the sound of that. What is it?"

Nona cleared her throat. "Everyone is aware of Judgment—a kind of procedure where you are tried for Code violations and given a sentence."

"I can't believe being without ID and this other thing would be a crime!" Sara flopped into her chair.

"I don't know what the consequence would be for being without an ID or Con Card. If they found out you used banned pharms, you would definitely be in trouble. They might think you were a Junker. Please listen; Judgment is something you would want to avoid. You might even be sentenced to Forced Labor."

"That sounds really bad. What's it like?"

"Horrible. You have to work, I mean physically work, like cleaning filters in the sewer systems, soaking and scrubbing stained fabrics with harmful chemicals, hand sewing certain attire. Six and one half days a week. Very little entertainment. The list of terrible duties goes on and on."

Sara sank back into the chair. "But I'm *not* that Junker thing, and I didn't take a bunch of drugs—I mean pharms."

"They won't take your word for it and, as a matter of fact, neither can I. You must realize that being with me is a better option than going back to the holding cell and then Judgment."

Once again, Sara held her head in her hands. Finally, she whispered, "I don't know, I don't know. I don't seem to have much choice. I guess I'll try to do what you say if you don't force me to use pharms or have that Mem-wipe thing."

"Maybe there's another way," Nona searched her memory, "to help you with this … this sadness about your mother? Maybe you could help me understand if you explained why."

Sara took a deep breath. "Okay, it's like this. My mom needs me. After my father's death, well, we both had trouble adjusting."

Sara looked up, brown eyes clouded with sadness. "She blames herself—that she wasn't a good-enough wife, that she didn't help him enough with his addiction problem."

"Addiction? Impossible."

"Oh yes, very possible; it happens all the time, in my world, and it happened to my father. You want to know what my mom went through? What I went through? You will never understand. I remember my mother sitting in the house crying while my father waited in the car the one time he agreed to go a treatment center. He went along with it to keep my mother and me from leaving him. Not that my mother would have left him. She didn't, not until much later. My mother was too upset to drive him to the center. I had to do it. Neither of us said a word except when he asked me to stop so he could vomit. When I got home, my mother cried and cried. *It's my fault. I even drank with him—not as much, but enough. I should have stopped him. He'll be okay after this, won't he?* Well, he wasn't. Don't ask for any more details, please! I try to visit her often but not enough—she has no one else to talk about what happened. She's so lonely." Tears spilled over.

"You're crying again! We have to find a pharm!" Concerned, Nona leapt up and started for the pharm cabinet.

"No, you promised. Besides what's so bad about crying? Everyone cries."

Sara's agitation and sadness was affecting Nona. Wisps of sadness brushed against her throat. She needed to admin and soon. She rose, retrieved a small dose of Peectem, and pressed it against her neck before she returned to her chair. "I beg your pardon, but as I said, no one cries. Unpleasant feelings cause this phenomenon. Mall Fathers made sure we would not experience them."

"Mall Fathers? What the hell are Mall Fathers? Some kind of kings?"

"Kings? No, no. They were the beneficent, wise and compassionate founders of Mall. They did everything from the design and construction of the structure to the creation of the Code."

Sara stared at Nona for a moment. "And? Somehow they managed to create a place where people don't suffer? That's impossible!"

"People don't suffer here and that's a good thing." Inwardly for a moment, Nona wondered if that were really true. Was there a cost? No. She didn't want to experience the suffering Sara seemed to feel. Out loud she said, "Wait, are you saying that you experience these negative feelings often? How can you?" The lights flickered and she grabbed the arms of her chair. "I think we are about to—" The lights dimmed and the room plummeted into darkness. Nona gasped.

Sara cried out. "What's happening? I can't see a thing!"

"Please don't worry; this has been happening off and on for the last several weeks. I must admit I am always caught off guard, but usually they come right back on."

"How is this possible? Didn't you say this was a near-perfect world?" Sara whispered.

"Yes, I did say that. I don't know why it happens. We just have to wait; the lights will come back on soon." She hesitated. "I confess that we do have a problem, perhaps not very big," she lied. "It's just the Junkers."

"Junkers? Some kind of group?"

"Yes, a group. I don't how many. As a matter of fact, I've never seen one. No, I take that back—I might have seen one and not have been aware. I think they walk around among us. There is no way to identify them."

"But what do they want? Why are they causing problems?"

"I don't know. Some kind of change? I've heard that some— this is so hard to believe—want to somehow escape Mall when we all know that there's no way out."

51

"You mean they know ways out? I want to find them! They could help me."

Nona heard Sara bump into her chair, groping for the exit. "Sara, stop! You'll injure yourself going about in the dark. First of all, it would be an unacceptable risk. If Mall Management finds…" Nona realized she'd almost revealed what the Mall Managers warned them not to do. "If you were apprehended with one, I'm not sure what would happen, exactly, but Judgment for sure."

"I don't care. And you promised me you would help me! You lied when you said there was no way out!"

Nona flinched. Why was this woman affecting her so severely? "No, I did not lie. These Junkers are disordered to believe this nonsense. No one has ever left Mall." They both jumped when the lights flickered on and flooded the room.

Sara blinked several times and then stared for a moment, eyes unfocused. "I remember something. When I was trying to get out of that damned parking lot, I think I saw—yes, I did—I saw a man appear all of a sudden and shout *I just escaped Mall, help me,* or something like that. They *do* know ways out. You have to help me find a Junker or I will run away again and find one on my own."

Nona stood up. "You think you saw someone supposedly come out a portal?"

"I thought he was in some sort of costume, but now I realize all of you dress that way. I can't remember much more. I don't care anyway. Just help me find the way out!"

"Where were you when you saw this man?"

Sara clenched her fists. "I told you. In what seemed to be the parking lot, but without cars."

Nona frowned. "Parking lot? Cars? What are those things?"

"That's not important. I know, you could take me to where I came through! Do you know the place?"

"It sounds like somewhere in the Ready-Made Apparel Division. I have been there many times; believe me, Sara, there is no portal. I would have seen it."

"Are you saying you won't take me there?"

If Sara ran away again, she'd be caught, and Nona would have to deal with—what was the word to describe it? — Weariness? Emptiness? Feelings no Mallite should experience. She should admin. It would have to be Freedomfrum, the strongest and most credit-inefficient pharm. Other pharms were not effective enough. What should she do with Sara? She could certainly pass as a Mallite based on her appearance. But she had to have clothes, employment, sleeping quarters and, most importantly, she had to have an ID and Consumer Card. She would think of something. She had to or they would both be taken to Judgment. Again, she forced herself to look within to be honest. Did she want to meet a Junker too? And maybe find a portal—to do what? Excitement juddered through her. What did she really want? Maybe she could discuss this with Royce. When they'd been pair-bonded, she remembered not just the sex but talking nonstop for the longest time, something that was not expressly forbidden but surely frowned on. Better not to think about that now, she chided herself. "If you or we decide to search for a Junker, you have to pass as a Mallite. Are you willing to do what is necessary?"

"I had the cosmetic stuff done. What else is there? And remember, no Mem-wipe!"

"Let me think." She paused a moment. Maybe she could find employment for Sara and earn a finder's fee. "Sara, these memories you say you have—are they in detail?"

"Yes; do you want me to describe some of the differences?"

"All right, go ahead."

"Well, for starters, there are hundreds and hundreds of malls and a world exists outside of these malls. There are cities and forests

53

and oceans and mountains and …" Nona held up her hand to stop Sara from talking.

"I know about the forests and cities from Ancient History, although rumor has it that the Virtual Reality depictions are not exact facsimiles. All that you mentioned disappeared eons and eons ago. Now, the outside is a vacuum or something like that. Nothing exists outside, nothing. No one knows what happened. Maybe the Mall Fathers did, but I don't think They left a record. I think you believe you saw these cities and things like that because you visited the Ancient Places virtual reality district, and somehow, probably through the use of illegal pharms, your memories of those experiences seem real." In a way, Nona could understand. Once in a while, a Virtual Reality experience almost seemed real, like the time she tried virtual mountain climbing. The air was cold and the sky achingly blue. She'd even experienced fatigue and a little shortness of breath.

Sara reached into her purse and began pulling out the contents. "Okay, then, what is this?" She proffered her license, then the money in her wallet, the pen, and her credit cards. Nona stared at them without taking them. Sara threw everything on the floor. "How do you explain these things? They're different than anything here, aren't they?"

Nona picked up the car keys and jingled them. "Yes, but excuse me for being rude, but the Fad Division circulates all kinds of weird things hoping they will catch on so they can market them for credit."

"Forget it—this is going nowhere. Just tell me what to do so I can get out of this office and find a Junker."

Nona thought more about her idea. With the right touch, maybe Sara's stories could be transformed into some kind of entertainment. Nona would be able to charge a large finder's fee. And once Sara was employed, she would begin to enjoy Mall's pleasures. Surely then her memory would return. "I have the beginning of an idea; I am acquainted with an ET leader who—"

"What is an ET?"

"Entertainment Team. He might be able to use some of your 'memories' for stories. Not only that, there have been some rumors about him. Once in a while, someone may want to change identities. I've heard that Stan knows how this can be done. He should be able to get you an ID and Con Card with little trouble. However, if the Finance Police find out, I have heard the consequences are most dire—maybe a lifetime of Forced Labor. If I can come up with a way for you to meet him and tell him your story, he may be intrigued enough to help you. His Entertainment Team's ranking has fallen to, I think, number three. Your stories might be just what he needs. And if his ratings rise because of your stories, I will earn that finder's fee. We can go to the Pleasure Palace where I am a member, and so is Stan, and talk it over with him."

"Why would I want a job? What's the point? I want to go home."

"Job? You mean employment. You have to. The Code dictates that everyone must be employed. And once you are, you will be in contact with many people." For a moment Nona was silent. What, she wondered would motivate Sara to go along with her? The possibility of escape seemed the best option to tempt her. "You could very well meet a Junker and find one of those portals you believe exist." *Of course,* Nona thought, *no such things exist.* Or did they? Did Nona, in a way, want these escape portals to be real? Anything, almost anything to relieve the excruciating tedium of her everyday life. Maybe not the same reason Sara wanted escape. A wave of—what was that feeling? She searched her memories of Ancient Emotions. Ah, that was it, compassion.

"You're sure you don't know any of these Junkers?" Sara asked.

Nona thought of Natalie. She'd promised not to tell of her association with a Junker. "No, of course not. So you need to meet Stan. He is a Team Leader of the ET I mentioned. His productions— at least the ones I have attended—are quite original. Your stories about dozens of malls might be just what he's looking for to raise his rankings."

Sara shook her head. "Not dozens of malls. Thousands."

Nona's eyebrows shot up. "Impossible. But that's something he might be able to use in a story line. If we go tonight, you'll need new clothes. I suggest that we go to the Ready-Made Apparel Division to find you something appropriate for the Pleasure Palace and a few more things to wear in the days to come. That way you'll be able to see for yourself there is no portal there. Also, if you are worried that nothing will fit you because of your weight problem …" Nona paused when she noticed Sara's unfocused stare. Tears began to leak from her eyes. "Sara, let me admin something, you can't go on having these spells. Your body will fall apart, maybe your mind, too!"

"How ridiculous!" Sara folded her arms in front of her. "We all know crying is good for you when you feel bad. In fact, I think some kind of enzyme or something is released in the tears."

Nona drew in a sharp intake of air. "I beg your pardon? Are you saying you believe that tears are beneficial?"

"Yes, most people know this." Sara answered, rubbing her eyes.

"No, most people do not, as you say, know this. I remember enough from the class on The Theory and Nature of Banned Emotions that tears come from negative feelings. Really bad ones. You must know by now that if one experiences any kind of suffering, he can admin a pharm."

"There must be a lot of addicts walking around."

"No, our pharms are not addictive or in any way harmful, Mall Fathers saw to that." Although, Nona thought, they can lose

56

effectiveness. Hadn't she experienced this herself? A kind of chronic listlessness for which she had to admin more and more? "If you won't admin, what can I do to help?"

"Help me find my way home!"

"First, please agree to meet with Stan. I'm sure he can use these memories and feelings creatively. And we must find you something to wear for the Pleasure Palace."

CHAPTER EIGHT

When the elevator voice announced, "Floor 210, Fashion Sector", the doors opened to a small garden featuring topiaries in the shapes of men and women, each blooming with multicolored flowers in the form of apparel. They emerged from the garden onto a wide, pink-and-green-carpeted corridor flanked by jewelry kiosks, each specializing in gems of a certain color. Sara slowed and gawked.

Nona tugged at her. "No need to look here. All this reproduction jewelry is for third-raters. Once we're inside the Ready-Made Division, you can see the real things." Sara peered ahead but couldn't see anything that looked like a shopping center, just the kiosks on one side and blank, white walls on the other until they reached a waist-high small slot glowing red. Nona stopped and fed in a small silver rectangle. A huge door opened, and once again Sara saw what she'd glimpsed when she entered Mall—cascading jewels, moving mannequins walking among beautiful shoppers. She stood motionless to watch an emerald necklace float over Nona's head onto her neck. From somewhere a voice said,

"Perfect for such an unusual beauty!" Nona laughed and walked away, leaving the necklace hanging in the air. Grasping at logical explanations, Sara finally realized that the jewelry and models were holographs. She began to search for the door she came through.

As Sara began to walk the area's perimeter, Nona caught her arm. "Please stay with me or you might draw attention to yourself."

Sara's gaze continued to circle the room. Suddenly she stopped and threw off Nona's arm, "This is where I entered Mall; so I could leave from here, too. I have to find the door!"

Nona took hold of her arm again. "I beg your pardon, but the only door is the one over there," Nona said, pointing to the right, a few steps from where they stood.

"I can go home!" Sara cried as happiness mixed with fear swirled through her. If she found the right place, would it work? Would she get back to Lincoln Mall? How much time would have passed? Would she look like she did now?

"Please stay where we are," Nona implored. "You can't access the entrance to that office without a Con Card. Calm yourself, and I will open the door for you. I planned to take you there, anyway. It is the entrance to Tailor-Made for the Elite."

Sara allowed herself to be led to the door she almost believed would be her way out, but when Nona used her Con Card to enter, all Sara saw was an office with a wooden desk where a young woman dressed in a smart black suit and a snow-white blouse sat. She looked up from the huge Inset, removed her tiny headphones and greeted them, "Hello, Nona, how lovely to see you. You look so beautiful in that stunningly original way! How can I be of service?"

"Thank you, Lola. I would like to consult with Ingrid, if she is available."

"She is always available for you, Nona," gushed Lola. She reinserted her headphones and spoke into an almost invisible microphone too softly for either of them to hear. In less than a minute a comely brunette appeared dressed in the identical suit as Lola. "My dear Nona, how delightful to serve you today." She looked at Sara, "How pleasant, you have brought a friend."

"Yes. This is Sara, and I trust that you could help her as much as you have helped me."

"I am so gratified to have your trust. Please follow me." She led them into a small room with three pink-and-red-polka-dotted plush chairs. Mirrors covered the four walls. With a small device shaped like a T, she pointed at Sara's breast, waist, hips and the length of her body. At each juncture, the machine announced her measurements, thirty-eight inches, thirty inches and 42 inches. Although elated at the size of her new breasts, heat rose to her cheeks when she heard the size of her waist and hips. How many times had Carl suggested different workout strategies – *run or bike, lift weights, use this or that machine and you'll look great!* Friends told her she wasn't fat, but she sure wasn't thin, nor did she have the kind of body Carl admired. She cringed when another memory shot through her. Her dad, drunk, had dragged out the bathroom scale and ordered her to get on it in front of her best friend—thin, athletic Amelia—when she was twelve. The memory scalded her.

Ingrid looked inquiringly at Sara and then at Nona. "How did this happen, may I ask?"

Nona shook her head. "Please don't press this matter. Just know that I am unable to divulge the cause. Client/practitioner privilege, you understand."

"Of course, say no more." She turned toward Sara. "Please forgive me if I speak too frankly, and know that I do not intend to offend. Your measurements are beyond the norm. I have not designed for anyone this heavy. Not that it's impossible; however I will have to charge more."

Nona nodded. "The outfits are a gift to Sara. Cost is not an issue."

Ingrid stepped in back of her desk and for several minutes spoke quietly to her communication device. In a short time, one holo after another appeared from nowhere and hovered nearby. Ingrid spoke softly and hesitatingly, "I do so hope you are not offended, Sara, that I am showing you outfits that will make you appear more slender."

"Yes, I understand," Sara said, although she didn't feel understanding. She felt angry, scared, and impatient to finish and resume her search. Finally, the three of them agreed on an emerald-green brocade tunic over black satin trousers.

Nona asked Ingrid, "Will you be able to send this outfit to my office within the hour?"

Ingrid glanced sidelong at Nona. "Um, yes, and I did hear you correctly? To your office?"

"Yes, and I thank you in advance for your discretion. And Ingrid, could you pick three or four more outfits she can wear on different kinds of occasions? And also send them, please, to my office at your convenience. After she loses weight and returns to a normal shape and weight, we can, perhaps, return for more garments."

"Of course. And please do not be offended if I remind you that on top of the fee I mentioned for designing for an overweight woman, I will also charge ten percent for my circumspection."

"I am not offended in the least bit. We are all eager to make as much profit as possible."

"I knew you would understand," Ingrid said and then her voice dropped to a whisper. Nona listened intently, back turned to Sara.

Sara realized they were not paying attention to her. She moved quietly to the door and reached behind her to activate the slide option. *Not locked. I have to find the portal! It has be here somewhere!* Quickly, she exited, bolting toward the wall opposite of the Tailor-Made office. Once there, she ran her hand over the gold brocade wallpaper. *It is here?* A few more steps, no more vacant wall, instead shelves heaped with scarfs. She stood motionless, hypnotized by the vivid colors and silken textures, some shot through with gold and silver threads, others sequined or covered by tiny gems. She stood on her tiptoes. *I can't see the wall!* Legs tensed to bolt toward the opposite wall, she almost collided with a tall red-turbaned black woman. "Please pardon me. You seem to be looking for something—perhaps one of these scarves?"

MALL

"No," Sara hissed. Frantic to continue her search, she tried to move around the woman, failing to notice the woman nod to a guard next to the exit.

Before Sara could turn around to escape, the Mall Guard reached her and grasped her loosely by her arm. "ID number, please," he ordered in a muted voice. Panicking, she wrenched free and began to run toward the Tailor-Made office.

Nona hurried toward her. "Sara, stop!" She grabbed Sara's hand. Taking her other hand, Nona made Sara face her. "You do not want to end up in the holding cell, do you? Why don't you listen? Please, please, remain silent while I talk to the Mall Guard."

Sara stood aside hearing their conversation as a buzzing hum. There seemed little she could do but go along with Nona. If Nona could talk the guard out of holding her—and as he nodded, she knew Nona had succeeded—she would go to the damned Pleasure Castle or whatever it was. Sooner or later, she would find a way out.

That evening while waiting for the elevator, Sara listened with one ear while Nona warned her to stay close and do nothing that would make others notice her non-Mall-like behavior. "If you are apprehended again by a Guard or by the Finance Police, I doubt I will be able to persuade them to leave you in my care; do you understand?"

When the melodious elevator voice announced "Floor one hundred and fifty", it whizzed by. Nona punched the large stop button again.

"Why didn't the elevator stop?" Sara asked.

"I'm not sure," answered Nona. They waited, but once again the elevator sped by. By then, a small crowd had gathered.

A familiar voice called, "Nona, how are you?"

Nona turned. Royce stood behind two elaborately dressed women. "Fine, thank you, Royce. How are you?"

"Fine, except that I'm quite late for an appointment and I'm not happy about this malfunctioning elevator. Do you think the…" Just then the elevator stopped and Nona, Sara and three others boarded. Royce elbowed aside two women standing in front of him so he could just fit in.

Sara could hear one of the women say, "For sure I will report him to the Courtesy Enforcers."

In a low voice, Nona asked Royce, "Did you hear that woman? You may be sanctioned."

"Yes, I heard. If I'm on time, it'll be worth it."

Sara was about to ask what this sanction would involve, when the elevator stopped at their floor. They stepped off into a green space, this time tropical with miniature palm trees and red poinsettias blooming along a narrow pathway. As they approached the Romantic Diversions section, the location of Nona's Pleasure Palace, Sara worried that she wouldn't fit in. She had to or she wouldn't get home. But her nervousness dissolved in the vanilla-scented darkness, winking lights, neon holograms blooming flowers and hearts, and miniature fireworks exploding silently above. Crowds of gorgeously dressed people strolled on the promenade, laughing and talking, some breaking away to enter one of the many establishments' facades that resembled expensive hotels or grand mansions. Sara purposefully slowed her steps while Nona kept pace with a woman dressed in red satin, hair dyed the same hue and wearing shoes that shot off red sparks each time her feet touched the ground. Nona's toothpaste-white dress made keeping track of her progress simple. Sara swept her eyes over the area, searching for doors and for people who looked different or odd enough to be Junkers, not that she knew for sure what strange appearance or behavior marked a person as a Junker. When Sara felt someone brush her shoulder, she started and turned to see a man with a trim beard and dark, hooded eyes. A tall man, but not handsome like the rest of the men she had so far seen.

"Please excuse me, I was not looking where I was going." He spoke in a deep, commanding voice. "I hope you won't think me rude if I say you are exceptionally beautiful." Sara flushed with hot pleasure. *No, no,* she warned herself. *I am not here to be swept away by some guy complimenting me, even if it feels so good.* "I hope you plan to enter this Pleasure Palace; I would like very much the opportunity to accompany you and perhaps admin together. And who knows what will happen then?"

Sara felt that old warmth spread throughout her center that rose to heat her face. *Shit,* she thought, *here I am desperate to escape some alien place and this man is turning me on.* Before she could open her mouth to respond, Nona reached her and took her hand.

"Pardon," she said to the mysterious man, "we need to meet someone." As they walked away she lowered her voice. "Sara, this is exactly what I warned you against. I don't know this man, although I know he is a Spiritual Practitioner; but his appearance is odd, not like a true Mallite. Please do not speak with anyone else."

Once at the Palace of Guaranteed Bliss, they climbed white marble stairs, bordered by gold- and silver-lacquered columns, and walked to the entrance, a gilded doorway in a facade that seemed as long as a city block. Just as they reached the door, a holograph of two women, glittering in red and silver sequined body suits, appeared.

"Welcome," the closest holograph said in a low soft voice. "May we ID you?" She pointed to a tiny glowing red circle with a green slit located on the back of the nearest column. Nona placed her finger on the slot and inserted a small silver card.

"One guest," she instructed.

"May your time here be as pleasurable as you desire." The holo faded into the darkness as the golden door opened, and Sara and

Nona entered a large room lit by an enormous chandelier of tier after tier of flashing crystals. A few people sat at tables scattered throughout, but most stood at or near the inlaid wood bar reaching from one end to the far side of the room. Mirrors of all shapes and sizes lined the walls, including one that stretched the entire length of the bar. Almost everyone seemed powerless to stop looking at their reflections; they posed, postured, and even tried to catch themselves by surprise. All were attractive, none of them looked a day over thirty, and all dressed in evening clothes that ranged from beautiful to outrageous. Sara stood still to stare at a woman in diamond-studded white lace with no body suit covering her very visible nakedness.

Nona nudged her gently. "Openly staring at others is considered rude; try to blend in." She looked around and turned back to Sara. "I don't see Stan, but I am sure he is here. Why don't you stay here? It's okay to look around discreetly, but please don't stray from this location while I look for him. Can I trust you to stay where you are and to not talk with anyone unless courtesy demands?" Sara nodded and after Nona walked away, Sara watched some of the more outlandishly dressed Mallites. Which ones could possibly be a Junker? How would she be able to tell? What about that strange man who'd spoken to her before they entered? As if by magic, he appeared by her side.

"I beg your pardon; I wanted to greet you again," he said. "May I introduce myself? My name is Paul." His smile was slightly lopsided and, Sara noticed, his nose was large and his black hair long, and not styled in novel and beautiful ways, just blunt cut at the shoulders.

"Nice to meet you, Paul. My name is Sara." She could think of nothing more to say as her eyes skittered across the room. Nona wasn't watching her. *Good,* she thought.

"Will you permit me to make an observation? You seem uneasy—is that the right word?—like you are uncomfortable. Is this your first time here?"

"No. Well, yes, it is. I'm a guest."

"As am I. What Pleasure Palace are you a member of?"

"I … don't belong to any." She couldn't stop the tremor in her voice.

"Really? That seems unusual; may I ask what is your employment? Please forgive me, I am being intrusive."

"Oh shit." Sara said aloud. "I…" She stopped when she saw the shock on his face. "Uh oh, excuse me for swearing."

"What are you, or should I say, who are you? Where is your Pod?"

Sara looked around. Carefully. No one was standing close enough to hear them. "Maybe I should I ask about you. You don't look like the rest of these people. Your face isn't made to be perfectly handsome. You're wearing plain dark clothes, although the cape is a nice touch."

"I'm an SP. You know, a Spiritual Practitioner. We always dress in dark colors."

"Something like a Mental Health Practitioner?"

"Maybe a little. Sara, again I beg your pardon, but why don't you know all of this?"

She regarded him closely. Could he be one of those Junkers? Maybe he could help her. On the other hand, if she told him too much, he might report her. But she had no one to turn to unless Nona helped her. "I might tell you, but as an SP, don't you have to keep stuff confidential?"

"That's right."

"You're sure?" she asked, desperate to tell someone besides Nona. Was he like a priest who could be trusted?

"Yes, Spiritual Practitioners and Mental Health Practitioners are forbidden to divulge any confidential information."

"Okay then." She cleared her throat. "Here goes. I'm not from here. I'm from a different world."

Paul took her by the wrist and pulled her closer. "Shh. Not so loud." He looked around before speaking again. "Are you saying you've been Outside?"

"I'm not sure what you mean by 'Outside.'"

"You know," he whispered, lips close to her ear, "about Junkers?" Before she could answer, out of the corner of her eye, she saw Nona's dress flash white. "Ah, there you are," she said as she came closer, a man following close behind. "Hello again," she addressed Paul with a brief smile. "I remember seeing you at the meeting."

"Yes," he said as he stepped away from Sara. "I remember seeing you also. I'm Paul."

"Lovely to meet you. You're an SP, is that right? Although I'm confused by your appearance."

"Yes, and I look this way to advertise. It gets me noticed and increases the number of my clients." Looking at Sara, he said, "I have had the pleasure to meet Sara." Turning to the man next to Nona, he said, "I don't think we've met."

"Pardon me. Sara and Paul, I would like you to meet Stan." Paul shook hands with Stan.

Paul said, "I've heard of you and your Entertainment Team, although I haven't had the pleasure of seeing any of your performances, something I mean to do soon. Perhaps all of us can find a table and share a dose of Plesurcrease?"

Nona replied, "Thank you for your kindness; however, the three of us have made previous arrangements."

As Stan and Nona turned away, Sara clutched Paul's arm. "Where and how can we talk further?"

Paul whispered, "I'll be able to find you," and walked away. For a moment, Sara's attention was seized by five Mallites, whose outfits consisted of multicolored feathers, holding hands and nuzzling each other. When she turned back to Paul, he'd disappeared. Several yards in front of her, Nona turned around and motioned her to catch up. When she was abreast of them, Nona whispered,

"Something's off about that man. If you see him again, I advise not talking to him." Speaking in a normal tone, she said, "I've told Stan a little about your problem. I think you both can help each other. I'll leave you alone to talk." She backed away and then turned to speak to a man who had been watching Nona during the entire exchange. Heads close together, they left Sara and Stan alone.

She was on her own. Confused and a little panicky she thought, what will happen?

"Hey," Stan said, leaning in close, "Nona didn't tell me how gorgeous you are." He was the one who was gorgeous, with his turquoise eyes, full lips and gold-blond hair. She flushed with the same pleasure she felt when Paul complimented her. The sexual part of her body was not getting the message that she was in big trouble, that she was not in her world anymore. Averting her eyes, she searched for something to say.

"I guess Nona told you about my, uh, amnesia. I don't even know if I've been here before, but it certainly is a quite a place. A lot of people come here, don't they?"

"You're right about that." He smiled a flash of white. "And, yeah, she told me a little about your problem. Lucky you to get her; she's the best. And, come to think of it, her fee is the highest. And if employing you makes a difference in our rating, I will have to pay her a hefty finder's fee." Silent for a moment, he stared into her eyes, then said, "If you don't mind my asking, how do you credit-transfer if you don't have a Consumer Card and an ID?"

Panic brushed Sara's ribcage. How should she answer this? "I guess I'm sort of a charity case."

Puzzlement momentarily lined his forehead. "*Charity*? I don't know that word. Something new from the Department of Fads?"

"No, it's my word." She stopped, unable to explain her faux pas. Shifting from one foot to another, she looked around at the milling crowd of colorful people. She met his gaze again, taking comfort in the kindness shining from his eyes.

He smiled back at her. "You made up this word, *charity*? I hope you don't mind my asking if you licensed it at the Department of Fads. If not, better do it fast, before someone else claims it, and there goes your percentage. Tell me what you want it to mean, and I'll help spread it around after you license it."

"Would people have use for it? It means to do or give something for free, I mean, without making a profit. You know, out of the goodness of your heart, like Nona is doing for me."

Stan shook his head. "What Nona is doing is unheard of. It's a really eccentric way to cope with boredom. So I can't think how or when you could use it. Better shelve the idea." Stan backed up so two men could pass. Sara stared at the closer one, who was wearing satin harem pants, a scarlet stripe painted diagonally on his bare muscled chest. Stopping suddenly, he reached out and lightly caressed Sara's cheek.

"Do you like what you see?" He asked, grinning, his jet-black teeth studded with diamonds.

Sara averted her eyes. "I was admiring your costume."

"I'm gratified to hear it. Excuse me if I am too presumptuous, but are you paired for the evening?" His glance flickered over to Stan.

"Don't blame you for asking, but she's with me." Moving closer to Sara, Stan put his arm around her.

69

"You're a lucky man. I wish you a pleasurable single-pairing." He waved as he disappeared into the crowd.

Stan grasped her elbow and began to steer her through the crowd. "Nona said we might profit from talking. I'm thinking I could lease one of these private rooms for, let's say, an hour. What do you think?"

Uh-oh, Sara thought, were these private rooms for sex? Would he come on to her?

Stopping at a mirrored door framed in ebony, Stan placed his finger on an emerald indentation and inserted his Con Card in the glowing slot. The door opened to the small, dimly lit room, a table for two in the middle and, off to one side, a small bed with a silvery coverlet. Motioning her to sit at the table, he asked, "Go ahead and choose a recreational, and something to eat too?"

"Recreational?" she asked.

Stan raised gleaming gold eyebrows. "Hmm, you have forgotten a lot—you know, a pleasure-pharm."

"No, no pharms."

"Anything else?"

"Maybe some wine…white?" She glanced quickly at the bed before moving toward the table to sit down.

"Again you are using a word I don't know." Stan smiled as he pulled out his chair and sat down. "Is this, excuse me if I ask too many questions, but this word problem, is it part of the amnesia?"

"I guess so. You don't have wine? Oh, that's right, alcoholic beverages aren't allowed, right?"

He was looking at her with his mouth slightly open. "Excuse me, but are you aware that you sound disordered? Everyone knows alcohol is poisonous. Is that what happened to you? You used alcohol? But where did you get it?"

"No, no." She struggled to find a way to answer without telling him she was probably from a different world, something that would make him think she was crazy. *No, wrong word. What was their word? Oh, right,* disordered. "I was … imagining the effect if used in one of your dramas. Is that the right word for what you create?"

"Sure, among other things. Hmm. Alcohol in an interactive drama—interesting idea, although a little implausible. How did you come up with that idea, if you don't mind me asking?"

"It just came to me when…" She stopped and took in a deep breath. "This is too hard. I need to tell you something—the whole story of what happened. You'll think I'm so disordered you might want to take some kind of action."

"Do you want us to voice-print a non-disclosure agreement?"

"Yes, if it means you won't do anything after I tell you."

Stan reached for his communicator in an unseen pocket near his waist. After soft-spoken instructions, he handed her the device. "Speak your name after the tone." After she finished he also said his name.

After she sat down across from him, elbows on the table, she leaned forward and told him the story of where she'd come from and how she arrived at Mall.

Stan stared at Sara. Finally, he said, "I get it. Nona tried out some new, powerful hallucinatory on you, and I'm part of the test."

Sara sighed. "Stan, please believe me when I tell you," she hunted for the right words, "I did not take, I mean admin any pharms except for the ones Nona adminned. Hardly any and only ones to help me with feelings I've had since showing up in this world. I'm telling you the truth. Could anyone make up what I've told you?"

Stan pushed away from the table to cross his long legs. For a moment he looked over her shoulder into one of the softly lit mirrors on the wall. He turned back to her, frowning. "I'm wondering the same thing. How could anyone believe a place exists outside of Mall?" He paused and shook his head. "Sara, we all know that Mall is everything and everywhere. Nowhere else exists."

"What about the possibility of a parallel reality? Could that explain my experience?"

"Parallel reality? Hell, Sara ..." He rolled his eyes and smiled sheepishly. "Pardon me, but that slipped out before I knew it. You have to admit that your ideas are like some fantastic story we were told as children to get our imaginations going. Wait a minute!" Stan's almost blurred face hardened to clean planes and glittering eyes. "Now I know why Nona introduced us. We could use these fantasies for profit. Now I understand why Nona mentioned a finder's fee. You could be the answer to my team's creative problem." Stan's languid body tensed, vibrating with sharp interest.

"What do you mean?" she asked.

"Our team had a number-one rating until just a couple of months ago." Shifting his weight, Stan looked away. "I'm almost disordered over our loss of rank. In fact, this is my first pleasure-break in about a month of almost nonstop working." He sighed. "I'm only here tonight because the Finance Police issued a warning. You know how that is. Either I take time for amusement or be sanctioned—probably at least a few minutes' public shun and maybe even a credit debit." He looked closely at Sara. "Maybe you're the key to solving our creative problem." He paused for a moment, searching her face. "I don't care if you think this *other world* is real or not. How many original stories do you think you can create?"

Sara gritted her teeth. Was anyone ever going to believe her? She felt like screaming at him. She knew she better not. She probably needed to take this job. If she wanted to move around Mall. If she wanted to get her own place away from Nona's watchful eye. If she wanted to find the way out. "I am not making up anything. And I don't know enough about your world to know if my life experiences are totally original—there seem to be a lot of similarities but a lot of differences too. Sometimes I am totally surprised, even shocked."

Stan's eyes gleamed. "Really? Give me an example. Please."

"Hmm, well, like tonight, the people in this nightclub—I mean Pleasure Palace—meet and then wander into one of these little rooms and have sex like it is just the usual fun thing to do; this does not happen where I come from."

"Ah, you have a different take on sex—maybe something we could make use of in one of our creative sessions. Now, what have you imagined—" he rubbed his hands together "—about sex? Is it titillating and original?"

"It is *not* imagined."

Stan abruptly stood. "This place, this other Mall, is it—?"

Sara snapped, "Not Mall. *World.*

Walking over to scrutinize himself in a wall mirror, he said, "If you want to call it a world, that is okay with me. What I'm interested in is your ability to create wildly different stories. If you can produce, I want to offer you employment as an ET member. What do you think?"

Sara answered his reflection. "I guess so, but I want to warn you that I am agreeing because Nona said to get around in Mall, I have to have a job."

"Job? Don't know the word."

"Employment, I guess you call it. And I need to let you know that I agreed to do everything I could to fit in so I could find a way back to my world."

"You really are disordered. If I hire you, you must agree to be discreet about this fantasy goal of yours."

"Sure, okay, I could do that."

"Good. Then I will offer you employment on my team."

"I should warn you, I'm not trained in this creative field. I'm a teacher."

Stan spun around, frowning. "Teacher? Are you joking? Not funny. Teachers have little intelligence and training. Speaking of which you do not need much training for my team. We don't need to motivate you to get your creative flow moving. You already have all these so-called memories stored in your head."

"What exactly would you do with them?"

Seated again, he answered, "It depends. Some would be made into holographic theater or interactive dramas."

"If I agree, when would I start?" she asked.

"Of course you will agree, how could you not?" he asked. "We're talking about profitable and amusing employment. Let's start tomorrow. Since you'll be working for me, you will automatically become part of the Theatrical Pod. I'll make sure your sleeping quarters are in the best area, close to me. So, what do you think?"

She looked into his eyes and felt her reluctance yanked into and almost subsumed in this widening center that had always yearned for easy acceptance, easy success. She closed her eyes for a moment remembering long hours preparing lesson plans, correcting papers, dealing with indifferent students and angry parents. What would it be like to have an easy, fun job? On the other hand, what if Paul could offer the right portal? Maybe she could take the job and somehow find Paul. If he showed her the portal, well, there was nothing stopping her. *Yes,* she thought; she would say yes, but she wouldn't stop looking for a way out.

"Okay. I'll give it a try," she said.

"Great! I know we're going to profit from this association. Let's celebrate. How about some Plesurcrese? Oh, that's right, you aren't recreating tonight with pharms. Then, how about something to eat? Maybe some bite food?"

Sara laughed. "Bite food?"

"Little morsels of delight. Okay if I choose?" Leaning over, he spoke softly to the in-set, and almost immediately after ordering, they heard a soft gong. Stan touched the twinkling keypad by the door to admit the server, unremarkable looking except for his ink-black mustache contrasting with his silver hair.

"Your bites," he intoned as he set them on the little table with a flourish. Grinning, he looked meaningfully at the bed and then back at them. "Have a pleasant evening," he said, every word layered with meaning.

As the waiter moved toward the door, Stan slid his silver card into the tiny slot in the table. Looking up at Sara, he said, "Go ahead and choose first."

To hide her burning face, Sara lowered her head to study the selection of bites, finally choosing what looked like a miniature pie. She avoided Stan's eyes as she bit through the flaky crust into an unfamiliar but delicious fruit filling. Ordinarily she would have snatched another, but she was afraid she would appear greedy and rude. Besides she didn't really want another. The appetite suppressant Rick had given her made her feel full, almost too full to even finish the one she had. And she loved pie. She loved any pastry—too much. Too bad she hadn't had this drug available in her world.

"Sara? Excuse me for pointing this out. You're wriggling. Is something making you uncomfortable?"

"I guess I'm just sort of embarrassed; when the server implied—well, you know."

Stan cocked his head as he stared at her. "What, *embarrassed?* Sorry, but I don't get it."

"He assumed we were going to just hop into that bed and…" She stopped and shrugged her shoulders.

"That's what these rooms are for. Well, not for us, of course, because we're doing business, and as you know, sex and business do not mix."

She searched for a new subject. "Speaking of business, what would happen to me if I said no to your offer? And had no job? That is, if I stayed unemployed?"

"We have to make profit, right? So we have to be employed. Without credit, how can you have fun?" He bit into a small, plump purple fruit. "And if you aren't employed, where would you sleep?"

"There must be places to rent."

"Excuse me, but you really do need memory work, don't you? Places to rent, as you say, do not exist. Sorry if I am too direct, but you can't work and recreate without—Sara, are you listening? This is all part of the Code. You have to belong to a Pod."

"Why?" Sara said. "Doesn't everyone have a right to live with who she wants and wherever she wants?"

Stan's eyes widened. "No."

"You're saying everyone has to live in a Pod, whatever they are? And what about people who want to live alone, away from others?" Sara picked up one of the silver goblets to sip the lemon-scented water.

Stan stopped eating. "Our Pod is our family. Sure, we all sleep solo, but that's not what you're talking about, is it? You mean eating and recreating alone. No one could stand that. I can't imagine what it would be like." He leaned forward, eyes narrowing. "Ah, this is what I mean, Sara. Your ideas are original to the point of weirdness. We'll have to remember to bring up this idea about living in a Pod-less environment at one of our creating sessions." He leaned back in his chair. "But remember not to not mention something like this outside of the team workroom."

Sara touched his hand. "I understand. Please tell me what will happen if I don't live in a Pod or if I'm not employed."

Stan withdrew his hand from Sara's. "Well, for one thing, right now you're living in Nona's office. If the Finance Police find out, both of you will be sanctioned. And you wouldn't like what comes next, like a long public shun and a big credit debit. And they'll find out; they always do."

"What's a *shun*?"

"You know, when the whole Pod gathers and turns their backs on you and…"

Sara tried to be patient. "Never mind, just tell me why. What have we done wrong? I mean, what's the harm letting someone use someone else's credit? Shouldn't we all have the right to do what we want with our credit?"

"Look, using your credit to please someone is okay. But living off someone else is the rudest thing you could do."

Sara gripped the tabletop. "Why is this so terrible, if both people agree?"

Stan's mouth tightened. "How can you say that? I'm sorry, I don't mean to be rude, but isn't it obvious? If people started supporting other people, it could lead to dependency. What could be worse? Think about it, Sara, and excuse me for being so blunt, but do you want to continue living off Nona?"

"No, of course not, but sometimes people have no choice but to live with another; isn't that true?"

"Like when? It just never happens. Everyone knows it's forbidden."

"What about the sick or the elderly or the unemployed? You don't include them in this…law, do you?"

Stan crinkled his smooth forehead. "*Sick*? I can't quite remember what that is. It sounds familiar, maybe something from Brief Ancient History in school, something about the body breaking down?" His eyes flashed. "Hey, good idea for virtual horror theater, something else for the creating session. Good work, Sara."

Sara shook her head, part of her reveling for a moment in her hair's silky sway. "I am not working, I am not making something up, Stan, and I am *not* creating. Where I came from, people do get sick. Everyone ages, and many are unemployed. There are old people who need help; you can't deny that."

Stan rubbed his forehead. "Why should old people need help? They're no different from anyone else except they've lived longer. And what do you mean *unemployed*? Everybody is employed."

Stunned by the obvious conclusion, Sara whispered, "Do you mean to tell me that there is absolutely *no* unemployment?"

"Not on your life, honey." He looked at her appraisingly. "I don't know sweetheart, some of these ideas, no matter where they come from, might be a little too odd for the general public. But then again, they're so original; we might create some huge hits."

Sara swallowed the last flaky bite of the little tart, wishing she felt like eating more as she eyed what looked like a cheese puff. She loved any kind of cheese, the smoothness on her tongue, the creamy yet sharp flavor. Wiping her hands on the large napkin, she looked around the room and back at Stan, amazingly handsome and so nice, and she sighed. "God, I get so mixed up in this place. When you describe things about this world, it sounds sort of desirable, yet these values are, well, shallow." Looking down, she sighed again. "I don't want this job to interfere with finding a way home." She jerked her head up. "If you try to stop me or report me, I don't know what I'll do but it won't be good!"

Stan tilted his head, regarding her closely. "Oh, honey, you won't find a way out because there is no way. What would be out there anyway? Void—that's what the Mall Fathers said. Why even talk about it, when there is no way to prove anything? Besides if guards, or even ordinary Mallites see you rushing around looking for portals, you will be reported to the Finance Police. They'll suspect that you're a Junker and you'll be taken in." Touching his mouth with his napkin, he stood and offered his hand to her and said, "It is worrisome that you can't find your ID or Con Card. Luckily, I know someone who can issue an Entertainment Team License and possibly forge these items, which will be very credit-inefficient for me, but I wager you will be worth it." He stood and motioned toward the door. "Good night, Sara, I'll see you tomorrow at the Licensing and ID Department in Employment Division at 9:00."

After he inserted his Con Card, the door slid open. In the distance she spied a man a head taller than others. It was Paul.

"Good night." She pulled away from Stan and hurried toward Paul, only to lose him in the milling crowd. She threaded through people to find Nona. Would Paul be able to find her again? Would he want to? *Better not ask Nona about him,* she warned herself. Nona had made it quite clear to stay away from him.

MALL

CHAPTER NINE

After they returned from the Pleasure Palace, Sara curled up in one of the office chairs. Nona offered her an ampoule of Restzy. "No thanks, I almost always sleep quite well without pharmaceutical help."

Surprised, Nona left and returned to her quarters to prepare for her eight-hour sleep period. Could Sara really sleep without a pharm? Surely, Nona thought, that wasn't possible. She reached for the usual sleep prep but stopped before popping it into her mouth. What would happen if she skipped Restzy? She felt a tremor of excitement. Never had she disregarded the sleep-prep rule; she prided herself on how well she followed the Code. But tonight, with a seldom-felt intensity, she wanted to continue to reflect about the events of the last several days. Restzy was too effective; she would be asleep in five minutes. Flushing it down the toilet, she knew if she stayed awake much longer than five minutes, the sensors in her bed would alert the Courtesy Enforcers.

Surprising herself, she thought, *I don't care.* She lay down and closed her eyes. *Was* it possible to fall asleep without adminning? Her body whirred with alertness, while her mind darted from one thought to another. She wanted to know more. Was it possible that Sara was from a different world or a different time? Even if it were so, she could not go around Mall insisting she lived in a place of a thousand malls. And how strange that she didn't want Sara to stop or to conform, at least not around Nona. She wanted her to talk more, to describe her world. Another thought struck her. How unlikely it was that Sara could make up something like all those malls existing. And those things in that satchel: the weird ID she called a license with her picture on it, those odd-looking metal things she called keys—hardly something the Department of Fads would create, too alien. Nona had never before been so absorbed in anyone and what she had to say. She felt excited, like she could hardly wait to see Sara again. Sitting up, Nona noticed that this sleeplessness was having a strange effect on her, like a stimulant somehow forcing her into a stringent honesty.

No, she did not want her to change. Sara had cut a clean edge along the blunted comfort of Nona's existence. Tossing and turning, she was about to jump out of bed when another novel thought struck her. For once in her life, she wished for someone to talk with about what was going on inside of her. She wanted... She couldn't think of the right word to name it. Her mind flew around, trying to touch this vague yearning, for what? Connection? Something like she had with Royce? A longing to see him pierced her. How could she find out more about these rich, colorful, although sometimes aching feelings? Would she go as far as researching Ancient History? How odd yet thrilling to want to know something badly enough that she would consider this step. Almost no one cared about the long-ago past.

Something interrupted her thoughts. A noise? Holding still, with eyes closed, she strained to hear. Something like fabric rustling? She opened her eyes, startled to see Sara looking at her, dressed in one of Nona's iridescent white garments. As she struggled to move, her limbs grew heavier and heavier until she felt paralyzed. The kindness in Sara's gaze filled Nona's eyes with tears. Gently, Sara pulled Nona out of bed, and together they floated across the room out through the wall into a tunnel of darkness illuminated only by Sara's prismatic garment. When they stopped, Sara pushed open a round door to a chamber filled with plants of various sizes and shapes, all talking at once. Their words sounded like bells tinkling. "What are they saying?" Nona asked Sara. "I can't understand."

"Don't you speak their language?" asked Sara with surprise as she began to turn into a tree, blooming pearlescent flowers. She, too, began to talk in an indecipherable tongue.

"I don't understand what is being said. Please, help me!" Nona whirled around to see the plants growing denser and taller, slowly crowding her toward the exit, all the while gibbering at her and touching her with feathery leaves. Shaking them off, she reached for the door but instead clutched at a branch on a black tree, stark and leafless, growing larger and larger until it was huge and menacing. She tried to scream but sharp chunks of ice had replaced her breath. *I'm dying,* she thought; *this is what it's like to die.*

With a jerk she awoke and sat up in her bed, making strangling noises. Her eyes sought the familiar as she gulped huge breaths, trying to slow the staccato beat of her heart. She stumbled to the built-in cupboard, scrabbling at the buttons, willing her hands to stop trembling enough to punch in the correct code. Snatching the Baktoslep patch in her still-shaking hands, she slapped it on her neck.

Her whole body had been affected. *What happened?* Dreams were always pleasant, an extension of the day, never filled with ugly and alien images. Would this happen to anyone who didn't take a sleeping prep? The Mall Fathers knew what They were doing. This was why sleep-adminning was required. She drifted off to sleep.

The next morning, she woke feeling strange. Pinpricks darted over her body. A not unpleasant feeling, was this an effect of Baktoslep, a pharm she had never needed to admin before? Or was it the strange dream she had, one that frightened her to remember? And fear was a decidedly uncomfortable feeling. *Don't think about, it* she cautioned herself.

Last night while walking together back to her office, Sara recounted the highlights of her meeting with Stan. One thing less to worry about, thank the God of Reincarnation; Sara could pass for a

Mallite, especially after she lost some weight. Yet something pricked this relief, the thought that Sara would not need her. How could Nona keep her close? She needed her. She helped to fill the gaping hollow within, partly due to not being with Royce. She had to be so careful how much she met with him. Nona tried but could not name what was happening inside of her. She thought of the frightening dream of last night, wondering if Sara, in her disordered state, dreamed in that manner. A pain pinched her just below her heart. What was that feeling? Not exactly sadness, something to do with hurting because of Sara's suffering about her mother? Her pain ricocheted onto Nona. Why did Sara hurt over her mother? People had little to do with their parents after the age of six. Yes, she cared about her clients but not in the way she did for Sara.

Her communicator beeped. Inserting her earpiece, she heard Royce's voice. "Nona, I beg your pardon if I am interrupting your morning routine. I wanted to check if we are still on for our meeting this morning."

Nona searched her memory. Sara mentioned a meeting with Stan this morning. Was it for 9:00? Nona had no client appointments until noon. She could see him after her time with Fabriana. Reluctance slowed her response. She knew what would happen; she would want more than a casual get-together. And more was not possible. If she avoided him, he would continue to communicate with her to ask for other times and dates. She knew him. Another thought occurred to her. She could discuss Sara with him. "Yes, after my 9:00 with Fabriana. Did we agree on 10:30 at our Pod's rec room?"

"Yes, that works fine, and thank you." He discontinued the communication.

She stared at the tiny communicator thinking about Fabriana, her heart-friend. She seldom felt eager to see her. Not that she wasn't entertaining. She often made Nona laugh. Yet Nona felt keenly that unwelcome flatness, that emptiness when with her. Oh well, she had to keep seeing her until the contract was up.

She rushed to get ready, pulling her hair into the bun so quickly, some of the hair strayed around her neck. Uncharacteristically, she threw on the white jumpsuit even though she wore it yesterday. She wanted to get to Sara as soon as possible.

CHAPTER TEN

Waiting for Nona, Sara sat in the over-sized chair she had slept in. What had she done, agreeing to work for Stan's company? She squirmed with frustration. *I can't do this,* she thought, *I have to get out of here. I did it before and I can do it again!* She was about to get up and randomly punch lights in the entry pad when the door opened to admit Nona.

"Hello, Sara. I hope you slept well?"

"No, but I don't care about that. Like I told you last night, I agreed to employment with Stan." Sara rose and stood in front of Nona. "But I don't want to do the job!"

"His employment is not to your liking?"

"No—I mean, yes. All I would have to do is describe things about my world that are different from here. I don't want to work. I want to go home!" But, her inner voice said, it *is* a dream job. *Am I a little tempted? Stop, stop. You have to get home,* she warned herself.

Nona shook her head. "You can't. We've been over this. Even if there were a way, it would be so difficult to find, it could take years. For now, you must fit in or it's back to the holding cell. I don't mean to sound rude, but I have told you this many times."

Sara squinted at Nona. She sounded—what? Irritated? "I know, I know. Isn't there some other way? Couldn't you help me make a more thorough search?"

Nona sat down across from Sara and folded her hands in her lap. Slowly and distinctly she said, "As I have said before, I can't help you with that. I am so sorry you still want to find this non-existent escape." She looked down, then raised her head and sighed. "I find myself so concerned about you, Sara. I do so much want to help you, but a Mem-wipe is the most effective means. I know, I

85

know. You refuse. However, there are numerous pharms that will ease your pain and anxiety. Again, I want to remind you that if the Finance Police found out you still believed you were from another world and wanted to find a way out, they would force you to go through the procedure. So I really believe the only thing you can do is to live like a Mallite, and that means you have to be employed."

"I guess you're right. I'll do what you say. You do know I won't stop trying to find my way home. Without attracting attention, that is," she added.

Nona smiled. "Especially do not attract attention. What time is your appointment with Stan?"

"9:00. I should shower before I go. Oh, that's right, no shower in your bathroom," Sara replied.

"Right. Let's take a bath."

Sara walked into the bathroom, not for the first time, yet she had not yet tired of looking at this room, almost as large as Nona's office. She marveled at the huge, sunken silver tub centered in a purple-tiled floor. Three of the four walls were tiled in purple and silver, and a mirror framed in amethyst crystal hung above the vanity that ran along the fourth wall. *So beautiful,* she thought.

She said to Nona's back. "A bath together? I would rather not."

Nona was disrobing. "Why ever not?" She leaned down to turn on the water.

"We just don't where I come from. Nakedness is private. It's hard to explain because..." Sara's words tangled and stumbled.

Nona sat on the edge of the tub. "Why would you want to hide your body? It's who you are."

"No, it's only the outside." She waved her hand as if to sweep away her words. "I know you don't understand. It doesn't matter." Sara began to undress. "You're right, in a way—why should I mind here?" She paused for a moment, looking pensive. "Maybe part of the reason for my hesitation is a kind of shame."

"Shame?"

"You know, my body is not what you would call great."

"No need to be concerned, you'll lose weight. By the way, your breasts look wonderful—the cosmetic artists made them perfect."

Sara averted her eyes as she stepped in and submerged up to her neck. "I guess I do look better." If Carl could see her now, he would be sorry he treated her so badly. Out loud she murmured, "This feels so good. And I love how the water looks almost purple." Another thought recurred. When she returned to her world, would she look like she did now? She flushed with pleasure when she remembered how Paul, that tall Spiritual Practitioner, complimented her. Strange how he seemed to think she could help him. He even said he would find her. Would he? He *had* to find her because he might very well be the one who could help her. Soaking in the tub, they both leaned against the sides, their legs floating.

"You have that sad look on your face again. Won't you agree to adminning?"

Sara interrupted, "No, I'll pass."

"But why? I don't understand this reluctance when pharms could help you."

Sara sighed and turned away. "Pharms and alcohol just about wrecked my life."

"But how? Do you mean the accidental overdose or whatever happened that caused the amnesia?"

"No, and I do not have amnesia. I mean what happened with my father."

"Father? Didn't you say that your— the sadness was caused by your mother?"

Sara hung her head. "Yes. I hurt over her suffering. I suffered too! He used pharms and drank and ruined everything and then..."

"Yes, and then?"

"He," Sara bowed her head and said in an almost inaudible voice, "killed himself."

"What do you mean?"

"Suicide, Nona, suicide. Don't tell me you don't know that word!"

She paled and shook her head. "*Suicide*? No, I don't know this word."

Sara's eyes flared with anger. "Don't you get it? How can I be much clearer?" Sara made a strangled noise. Then slowly and deliberately, she said, "He ended his life."

Nona's hand flew to her mouth. Color drained from her face. Neither of them said a word. Finally, Nona whispered, "You mean he ended his life before his number was up?"

Sara clinched her hands into fists. "Yes, if that's the way you want to put it. I don't want to talk about it anymore. I don't want to think about it!" But she couldn't stop. She remembered how he'd struck her mother, how he'd hit one of the police, how they'd handcuffed him and taken him to jail, how she and her mother bailed him out and took him to a motel. The next morning, she and her mother sat at the kitchen table drinking black coffee and the phone rang. Her mother answered it and said, after listening for a few minutes, *I love you too.* Sara would never forget how the morning after that, someone called and her mother ran down the hall crying, *He took pills—he's dead, he's dead!* She began to sob with so much force, she could hardly breathe.

Nona stood up so fast the water formed waves. She waded over. "Sara, I am frightened for you!" Sara yanked her body away from Nona's touch. Her sobs changed to dry heaves. Nona ran to her office and returned with a patch she pressed against Sara's neck. Almost immediately, warmth spread through her body and then a moment of euphoria exploded in her core. After, a sense of peace and well-being made her feel like she was floating. Nona helped Sara out of the bath and handed her a towel, then left to dress.

Looking like a different person, Sara walked into the office, the towel wrapped around her, smiling and with eyes shining. "That patch you put on – wow! At first this warm wave flowed through me and all my pain disappeared. "

"I am pleased that the pharm worked so well, Nona said also smiling and cheerful. "I too adminned—"

Sara cut in, "But what did you give me? I love it. Not that I want to use it again. It feels too good, and I don't want to get addicted."

"I adminned Peectem, the same pharm you had after your upset, although not nearly as much. Please don't worry. As I have told you, many times, I think—please forgive me for pointing that out—our pharms are not harmful to the body, and they are most certainly non-addictive."

"I guess you mean no one goes through withdrawal if they stop a pharm, but don't people get dependent on them? You know, like won't they rely totally on pharms to get them through the bad parts of life?"

"Well, of course, they are to be used if something unpleasant happens, which is rare. Why is that undesirable?" Nona stopped zipping up her white jumpsuit and looked over at Sara. "Didn't you say your appointment with Stan is at 9:00?"

"Oh right, I better hurry. I'm supposed to meet him at the Licensing and ID Department." She chose the off-white silk tunic and black silk pants Ingrid had delivered last evening. "I don't know where to go; will you go with me?"

"Oh, I beg your pardon, I can't. I have an appointment with Fabriana, and another after that, but of course I will give you directions."

"Could you write them down?"

"What?" Her bright eyes lost some of their shine. "Write them? How could I, and even if I could, how could you read them?"

Sara felt her eyes almost bulge out. "Are you saying you can't read or write?"

"No, why would you think I could? Only Bureaucrats and Mall Managers can read or write. The rest of us can only recognize and write numbers." She stopped for a moment. "Sara, are you saying that you have these skills?"

"Yes, everyone does where I come from."

Shock and disbelief crinkled Nona's face. "How could that be true? Only Bureaucrats and Mall Managers need to use those skills."

"Are serious? Almost none of you reads or writes?"

"Like I said, only numbers." Nona's hand flew to her mouth. "Sara," she whispered, "Is it possible that you *are* from another world?" She started when her reminder gong sounded. "I must leave. I will communicate with you later." Nona walked through the open door and hurried toward one of her Pod's cafes.

Sara started to call for her to wait and ask for the directions. But Nona was out the door. She had enough time to primp, she thought, studying her reflection in the full-length mirror. She wanted to look good for Stan. She might as well enjoy his admiration while she remained here. She rushed out.

CHAPTER ELEVEN

Breakfast finished, Fabriana was accessing the in-set to watch miniature holos of upcoming beauty contests. "Nona, look, Barona's Boutique is sponsoring a contest on original fashion looks. Why don't you enter? I love your—what do you call it? Ah, yes, your natural look, because you use so little makeup. Anyway, the prize is wonderful, a free appearance consultation with Marizon. Isn't she the one all the actresses in the Realized Fantasy ET use? Will you? Please? I want to wager on you."

Nona felt indifferent but she pretended enthusiasm. "Of course, it will be amusing," she lied.

"Oh good! I know you will win." She leaned closer. "Nona, I want to bring something up, something that is worrying me about you."

"Oh dear, what is it?" Nona asked.

"It's about the Passing Ceremony."

"Oh no, has your number been called?" Nona asked, trying to sound upset.

"No. It's about your absences. You weren't there last week or the week before. I noticed and so did the some of our Pod members sitting next to me. Harold mentioned you missed several weeks ago."

Nona clenched her jaw. "Of course you're right, but sometimes at the Ceremony, I experience … such unpleasant ennui."

Fabriana frowned. "I beg your pardon? How could that be? I am uplifted every time I attend. And what do you mean, ennui? That's unheard of! Why didn't you admin? No one is ever bored in Mall."

Nona breathed deeply to calm herself. What should she say? "Yes, of course, you're right. I, uh, neglected to admin because I really believed that I, too, would be positively affected. I don't know what happened to me."

Fabriana shook her head. "Please do excuse me, I'm only saying this for your own good. People notice. People talk. Next time you should try adminning…" Fabriana stopped talking while she craned her neck to watch two men in black suits being seated in the corner. "Look at those Spiritual Practitioners who just walked in. Do you recognize any of them? Isn't it odd how they lean so close to each other and whisper?" She turned back to face Nona. "I've heard some unsettling rumors about an SP who may be a Junker."

"Really? It seems so unlikely. They're trained to help people whose number is up not to cause trouble for us," Nona responded.

"Maybe, but who knows? Do you remember that SP at the Mall Management meeting?" Fabriana studied her newly manicured nails, little rainbows arching over pink skies.

"Yes, wasn't his name Paul?"

"That's the one." Fabriana turned around to look at the SPs. "I've heard he is definitely a Junker."

"Really? How can you know that for sure?"

Fabriana smiled thinly. "I have my ways. Anyway, if you see him, don't have anything to do with him."

"I never go to the Spiritual Peace Sector."

"That may be, darling Nona, but I hear he gets around. Which reminds me, why has it been so difficult to set up a meeting with me the last few days? Does it have something to do with that mandated client you've been treating?"

"Uh, yes …" Nona broke off when a stocky Mall Guard strode past them and stood next to the Spiritual Practitioners' table.

"Stand up," he ordered, "I am apprehending you. You are suspected of Junker activity. Please come with me," he ordered.

Both stood up. The one closest to Nona and Fabriana objected, "This is disordered! We're SPs. We have nothing to do with that group!"

He started to make his way past the guard, who snatched his arm. "Where do you think you're going?" he growled. With his other arm, the guard pulled out a pair of safe-bracelets and manacled him. After cuffing the other SP, he marched them out of the cafe.

Sara and Fabriana stared at the SPs and guards as they left. "Why would they arrest two SPs having tea? It doesn't make sense," Nona asked.

"Oh yes it does. Like I was just telling you. SPs are under suspicion."

Nona remembered that Sara had talked with Paul at the Pleasure Palace and maybe at great length. *What did they discuss?* Suddenly agitated, she wanted to leave and stop talking to Fabriana. "Please excuse me, Fabriana. I suspect that I am holding you up. Didn't you mention you had a morning appointment?"

Fabriana shook her head, swinging her newly dyed shocking pink ringlets. "No, I have time, especially for you, dear Nona. Shall we order another cup of tea? Why are we drinking tea, anyway?"

Nona stifled the urge to raise her voice. "I believe the waiter mentioned a coffee shortage." Nona remembered it clearly. When the waiter had explained, Fabriana had faced the other way to admire her reflection in the large mirror on the wall, obviously not listening.

"Oh right. Probably Junker caused. How dare they? To think we have to go without coffee! We live in Mall and should not experience any discomfort. I hope they catch every last one of them. I really wish that one of my clients would confess. You can be sure I would report him before he got out the door."

Nona wondered why she had ever agreed to a heart-friend contract with someone as fatuous as Fabriana. But then, she really had no choice. If she'd continued to find reasons to delay the bond,

Fabriana would have accused her of rudeness—probably in front of their Pod. Besides, other MHPs had begun to wonder why they remained acquaintances when Nona was the highest earner in her field and Fabriana, the second. It followed that they would contract sooner or later. True, when Nona had told her about her illegal second pair-knotting with Royce, Fabriana had been sympathetic and never reported them, even though her name would have been placed in the Tell-All lottery. The prizes, like a three-week free pass to Liberata's spa, were indeed tempting, especially for someone like Fabriana.

"I probably should leave, much as I would rather stay," Nona added quickly.

"I thought you were free until noon."

"I am so sorry if I gave you that impression." Nona was loath to tell Fabriana that she had a meeting planned with Royce. She would jump to conclusions and maybe even gossip about them.

Fabriana mouth twisted into an ugly grimace. "I distinctly remember your saying ..." Nona's communicator beeped and before she could hit the silencer, they both heard Royce's voice.

"Hi Nona, it's 10:35. Did I get the time wrong?"

Fabriana bristled with avid curiosity. "What? Are you seeing Royce again? Isn't that a bit unwise? I hope you're not planning a third pair-knot!"

"No, nothing like that."

"Excuse my curiosity, please, my dear. I only want to protect you from damaging gossip, not to mention the risk of your being caught." She waited with an expectant look on her face. "Aren't you going to tell your heart-friend the purpose of this meeting?"

"Nothing very important. I just want to discuss my new client."

"You mean the emergency case assigned to you?"

"Yes, I had some ideas I wanted to talk over with an MHP."

Fabriana drew herself up, smiling an obviously fake sweet smile. "Pardon me for pointing this out. I am an MHP and your heart-friend. Why didn't you bring this up with me?"

Nona scrambled to think of something plausible to say. "I planned to but you have been so engaging today, I forgot all about it until Royce communicated."

"Well, yes, I realize that I can sometimes be amusing. Tell me now, please. I want to hear all about it."

What could she reveal so that Fabriana would be satisfied and she could get away as soon as possible? "She seems to have some amnesia and a few delusions."

Fabriana's already huge lime-green eyes widened. "That's almost unheard of! What is there to discuss? She needs a Mem-wipe immediately."

"I know, but I want to try something different, something experimental. You know, so at our annual MHP fete, I can explain my new technique and draw in a big crowd."

"Hmm. I understand that, but I can't think of anything that would work except a Mem-wipe."

"Please forgive me, but I must leave. Royce is waiting."

"Oh, all right. Please remember our appointment at Heavenly Scents to sample the new fragrance everyone is talking about. Terribly credit-inefficient or we would smell it everywhere. We can eat at the attached café and you'll be able to tell all."

"Of course! I'll see you then." Trying not to look relieved, Nona stood and made her way to the door. Royce, not Fabriana, was the person to discuss Sara with. Not only could he be trusted, he was an excellent MHP and maybe she could avoid talking about their past.

MALL

CHAPTER TWELVE

Time to go, Sara thought as she pushed a series of lighted buttons, relieved that Nona had disclosed the code to open the door. She had just about enough time to look at her reflection in one of the dozens of mirrors on the walls. Had she chosen the most flattering outfit among the clothes Nona had had—what was the term?— credit-transferred? Yes, that was it. She did look good in the cream-colored tunic, and her face—she was a knockout! Not that she would allow this newfound beauty to distract her from finding her way home, but oh, how she had secretly yearned for men to find her attractive, not just pleasant looking but drop-dead gorgeous. How gratifying that Stan seemed to find her attractive, especially since she was drawn to him. Of course, it didn't mean anything. It happened all the time. Her psychiatrist had pointed out that her messed up relationship with her dad was the cause. *He never gave you the approval all children need. You keep looking for affirmation from other men. If you feel attracted, don't judge yourself, but you have a choice to not act on it. Better leave now,* she urged herself, *so I will have extra time in case I get lost.*

When she scanned the promenade, she was startled to spy Paul, that SP she'd met last night, leaning against the embossed wall between offices. What was he doing here? For a moment she stared, noticing others looking at him, longer than might be considered polite. He definitely stood out, even without the cape he'd worn at the Pleasure Palace. No one who walked on the promenade dressed like this, so plainly and so somberly. Except for the gold chain around his neck, his attire was as black as his unstyled hair. She drew close enough to him to ask, "Why are you here?"

He stepped away from the wall. "I hoped I might find you."

"Me? Why?"

"I think you know. We need to talk a little more about..." He stopped and looked at the passersby who, except for curious looks at his appearance, seemed lost in their own worlds. "What we talked about last night. *Outside.*"

"But where would we talk? Isn't it pretty risky if someone hears?"

"You're right about that." He grasped her wrist and pulled her closer. "There's a meeting of those who have similar, shall I say, goals? Do you think you can get away and come?"

"I don't know—I don't even know where I'll be after I meet with Stan."

"Stan? Oh that guy with that MHP—what was her name?"

"Nona, and yes, that guy."

"Why are you seeing him?" He frowned.

For a minute Sara thought, *he's jealous*, then dismissed the idea. Maybe she just wanted him to be jealous and to see her as a desirable woman. "He's offered me a job—I mean employment—so I can be part of a Pod, whatever that is. I guess I need to fit in until I find a way out..." Before she could finish her sentence, blackness swallowed the light. "Oh shit," Sara whispered, "Lights out again?"

He still held her close to him, her wrist in his hand. "Yes, he whispered back, "and right on time."

Nearby, she could hear bursts of whispered outrage from nearby Mallites, "Not again! Why don't they do something?"

"Is it the Junkers?"

"Do not kiss me!"

"I hate this."

"I wore my new tiara—now no one can see it."

Sara whispered in his ear, "Was this planned?"

"Yes, indeed. At the meeting we'll talk about the dim-downs, the black-outs, unpleasant odors and other kinds of disruptions." As they waited in the darkness, Sara leaned against Paul, and when he put his arm around her waist, she didn't stop him. She even pressed up against his length. He folded his arms around her and kissed her neck.

"No, no, people might see," she whispered.

"How?" he whispered back as he ran his hand over her rear end. "We can't even see each other this close up."

"They will, when the lights come back on!"

"Well, then we'll stop," he reassured her as he kissed her mouth.

"No, wait!" she hissed, pulling away, "I don't even know you!" Although she kept her arms around him.

"What does knowing someone have anything to do with sex?" He drew her body closer to his.

Here I go again, she scolded herself. *What is the matter with me? I am in the worst predicament of my life and...* A memory swept through her whole body—of the principal she worked for. So attracted to him, she'd found all kinds of excuses to pop in his office and ask advice about her lesson plans, about a troublesome student, or even about Joanne who talked behind her back. During her last visit, David had praised her math unit but—she cringed when remembering what came next—*Sara, you need to wear less provocative clothes. Other teachers have complained. I have to admit I sometimes have trouble with it.* When she heard him admit that, she'd reached out to touch him. He'd stepped back quickly, frowning and shaking his head. Humiliated, she ran out of his office in tears and almost bumped into Joanne. She wouldn't have acted on her desire, would she? Sometimes his approval had felt like he was in love with her. And that made her want sex with him. Once she married Carl, she had stayed true to him but she had fantasized about David. She untangled herself from Paul. "Stop, please stop!"

He let her go. "I thought you wanted this. Probably best, though. This disruption is about to end." At that moment, light stripped the darkness away from the promenade. "And I guess it's a good thing that you said yes to employment with that guy and that you'll be part of his Pod; both things you have to do to get around Mall." He retrieved his communicator and inserted the earpiece. "I've got a spiritual advice appointment. I'll speak with you soon to tell you where and how I'll get you to the meeting." Sara watched him walk away. He must be one of those Junkers. He seemed different from her first meeting with him: less formal, not so polite, and more abrupt. Just because she was so attracted to him didn't mean she could she trust him. She had made that mistake too many times in the past. Doubts squiggled in her stomach. She didn't know one thing about him, she admitted to herself, and her future might be in his hands. Even if she chose to trust him, how could she go with him to this meeting without Nona knowing, or, for that matter, Stan? What would working for Stan involve? Would he be able to trace her movements?

She checked her communicator. *Uh oh, almost 9:30.*

After exiting the elevator, Sara stopped to view the miniature holographic maps glittering at eye level, at the same time listening to the repeating directions to different departments in the Employment Division. She had no trouble finding it, where she spotted Stan waiting by the entrance.

"You're a little late. Everything okay?" he asked, not waiting for an answer. He took her by the arm and guided her through the door and down a long corridor, passing cubicle after cubicle so quickly she couldn't take in the details. Finally, they stopped in front of a small office. Not impersonal or drab as she expected, the cubicle was carpeted in orange velvet and wallpapered in yellow striped satin. There was just enough space for a small wall in-set and two chairs that were occupied by two people talking intently. Outside the opening, Stan placed his finger on the keypad and surrendered his Con Card. A bodiless voice announced, "Number three, green."

"We should have about a five-minute wait. Let's sit down for an EB."

"EB?" Sara asked as she followed Stan to sit across from the yellow and orange room in one of the two purple straight-backed chairs. A disembodied voice startled Sara when it asked for their beverages and entertainment choices.

"Entertainment Break," he explained to her and then spoke to the air. "Two coffees. No, wait, I forgot coffee supply is limited—is tea all right with you? How about something to eat?"

"Tea, if I can have it with cream, please. No food—I, uh, don't seem to have an appetite."

"And a tic-tac-toe puzzle for me. Any game for you, Sara?"

"Tic-tac-toe? You're going to play a game?"

"Sure, nothing else to do here."

"No, not for me." Before she settled into her chair, a waiter served the tea. He handed Stan a black box the size of his hand. Sara stared as Stan activated the puzzle and a crisscrossing of neon green lines bloomed in the air, floating just below eye level.

"Start," ordered Stan, and a glowing red X appeared in the middle of the square while an electric-blue O hovered outside the grid.

Sara asked, "Is it okay to talk while you work your puzzle?" Stan guided his O to a spot within the network of lines with one hand while his other hand stirred thick cream into tea so dark and strong it looked like syrup.

"Sure, talk all you want. Please."

Sara sipped her tea. "Do I have to have this Con Card thing?"

"You bet. Just about the most important thing in Mall. We make all our purchases with it, and I mean everything. We have to consume. Without consumption, there would be no pleasure, and without pleasure—I don't even want to think about it."

"You mean pleasure is *that* important?

"Sure, what else is there to live for?"

"There are lots of things." Strange—at that moment Sara couldn't come up with anything. "This person I will be meeting with, is she part of the bureaucracy?"

"Do you mean is she a Bureaucrat? No, BCs work for Mall Management." He cast a sidelong glance at her. Are you sure you don't remember any of this stuff?"

Sara shook her head. "How could I? I come from another world, I told you," she added, impatience creeping into her voice.

"Okay. If you want, I'll go along with you, but only because I wager that audiences will love your stories. This is about making profit. If we're going to work together, you can't go around insisting you're from some other world. Someone's going to hear. Everyone knows all Mallites love gossip and more than that, many would love to report you to the Finance Police partly because they'd find it amusing, but mostly because they would be entered into the Tell-All Lottery. Some of the prizes are quite attractive."

"All right, I'll be careful."

He swept his arm across the room. "These people are employment agents." Sara glanced at the grid floating in the air as a red X blossomed in the upper-left square. Stan entered a green O in the lower-left one.

"Won't I have to go through some kind of bureaucracy for Social Security—I mean, I.D. numbers?

"I'm not following you," Stan replied while studying the grid for his next move.

Sara sipped more of her tea. "I'm talking about paperwork and endless waiting to get the I.D. numbers."

Stan set his cup down. *Paperwork*? What's that? And waiting? Are you joking? How could these people profit if they kept potential clients waiting very long? You would just change to another—Oh, I get it; you must have another meaning for *bureaucracy*. Now, that is interesting. Something we could use?"

How should she explain it? She began to describe the cold personnel and endless paperwork and waiting. Before she finished, Stan was laughing out loud. He sputtered to a stop. "I didn't know you could be funny. I can't wait to use this in a comedy. And I like that added touch that ordinary people can read and write—very amusing."

Sara frowned. "How could someone who issues an I.D. and Con Card make profit?"

Stan looked up and down the corridor. "Jacqueline gets a fee when she supplies a Con Card—I think she provides them to half of our Pod members when they are of age—and she also is an agent for almost all Entertainment Teams and some in the Virtual Reality Section." He lowered his voice. "What worries me is that you don't have an I.D. We all get one when we're born. We're in luck, though, because Jacqueline and I have an agreement that profits both of us. Once in a while, a Mallite might want to change identities so she issues him a new I.D. number and, for the right credit-transfer, a cosmetic artist changes his appearance. And there you have it—a new life."

Confused, Sara asked, "I don't get it. How does he find employment? Aren't you all trained for certain areas?"

"Yeah, but a lot of us have been around long enough to get bored with what we're doing and to pick up enough information to make it in another line of employment."

"What about you?" Sara asked.

"Nah, I love the entertainment field. Besides, I've only been at it for fifty years."

Oh my God, Sara thought, *He must be at least seventy. If I stayed here, would I look as good as he does at that age? How long do people live here?* What if she stopped trying to find a way home?

What about Carl? Would he grieve over losing her? She doubted that. He'd find another woman as soon as he felt a little lonely. Maybe he'd had one all along. She remembered all the times he'd said he was working late, gone bowling with the guys, had drinks with his boss, and how many times he'd said, "Sorry, Sara, I'm wiped out" when she'd wanted sex.

But her mother needed her. And what about her students? "So about this agent, Jacqueline," she said, "she can give me the necessary stuff so I can work for you and get around the Mall? And I won't be caught?"

"Stop game," Stan ordered, and the black box swallowed up the grid along with the Xs and Os. "Hasn't happened before. She's the best. You can use her as an employment agent, too. I transfer extra credit every time she signs up someone who would be profitable for my business." Frowning, he stopped and turned to look at Sara. "Legally, Jacqueline should give you a list of all employment opportunities in this area."

"No, that's okay. I'll stick with you."

"No need to be polite. Would you like to look at the competition?"

Sara searched his face. "Listen, Stan, I don't want to work with anyone else. I don't want to try explaining what happened to me, and then try to convince him or her that this is not some pharm-induced fantasy or a product of a crazy mind. No, thanks."

Also, she thought, Stan was going along with her; another might not. And if she were honest with herself, she had another reason. She felt that familiar undertow of sexual attraction.

"Hey, I like that word, *crazy*. Let me guess, would it mean something like disordered?"

"Good guess. Am I required to interview with other employers?"

"No, but are you sure you wouldn't want to? Everyone wants to make the most profitable connection he can."

"I know, but I want to stay with you because I feel, well, like you're my friend." Again, the warmth of sexual attraction flowed through her. Bending closer, she reached out and caressed his hand. Although he smiled his warm, white-toothed smile, he jerked his hand away. For a moment his rejection burned. *Oh shit,* she thought, *I just made a fool of myself.* She backtracked, trying to save face. "What I'm trying to say is, this is about loyalty too."

Stan turned his whole body toward her. "*Loyalty?*"

"Another word you don't use? It means that I would put our friendship above profit because I value it more."

Stan sat up straighter. "I don't understand; we're not heart-friends. Besides, men and women don't make that friendship bond. If employment with someone else means more profit, any Mallite would switch. In fact…"

"Three, number three, please," the bodiless voice announced, and in midair, a huge three-dimensional number flashed fluorescent green.

"No. I know you, and you seem to be someone I can trust. Let's just leave it at that."

As they walked into Jacqueline's office, Stan said, "Look, I'm glad you trust me, and, of course, I want you to work for me, but I want you to be clear that you might be missing out on a better deal."

They sat down. Sara noticed how well Jacqueline matched the décor. With her orange satin turban and a yellow brocade kaftan she almost disappeared into the wallpaper. Even the cinnamon fragrance she wore complemented the color scheme.

She looked at Stan, then at Sara. "Early this morning, I listened carefully to your requests. Let me see if understand. Not only do you want employment licensing for this woman, you want a new I.D. number for her. Please excuse me, but I have forgotten her name."

Stan answered, "First of all, Jacky, thank you for agreeing to an appointment today. I know you are very in demand. As always, you are a pleasure to work with." Touching Sara's shoulder, he added, "This is Sara."

"Yes, that's right. Sara, please give me your old I.D. so I can place it in the shred bin. Then we can proceed."

Sara looked at Stan who cleared a nonexistent clog in his throat. "That's part of the problem; she lost her I.D. and can't recall the numbers."

Jacqueline frowned. "That's easy enough to remedy. Contact a Bureaucrat with her name and ask for a new I.D. Or I could access my records to determine if I was the issuer, which, of course would take more time because, unlike the BCs, I am the only one who would be listening to all that info. I really do need those numbers."

"Beg your pardon, Jacky, but no can do. Why not just give her a new I.D. number like you do with the other special clients I refer to you?"

Jacqueline shook her head. "These are not, shall we say, ordinary times? I was at that Mall Manager meeting too, remember? I sat just in front of you." She looked sharply at Sara. "I probably shouldn't have mentioned that; you would need to voice-promise that you will never mention my reference to that meeting."

"Never mind; I'll take care of that," Stan reassured, "I wouldn't want her to refer to it, or I could be in trouble, too."

Jacqueline put her hands on the table as if to rise. "You realize that this is highly suspicious. For all I know, she is a Junker."

Stan put his hands on hers. "Wait, please. I think I can make this worth your while. I will credit-transfer you an extra three weeks above the cost of your fee if you agree."

Watching Jacqueline's eyes dart back and forth as she drummed her fingers on the table, Sara made a mental bet that this woman would agree. True, she'd been almost hysterical when Nona and that cosmetic artist talked, but she remembered that Nona, too, had offered more credit to Rick and he'd accepted. She was learning fast that these people were indeed profit motivated.

"Five weeks," Jacqueline stated.

"Four weeks," Stan countered.

"All right, it's a deal. However, if she is a Junker and is caught and I am implicated, I will do everything I can to bring you down, Stan."

Sara trembled inwardly. This woman was not to be messed with. What if I do something so contrary to their ways that I arouse suspicion? Would someone think she was a Junker? It was a chance she had to take in order to blend in and find the way home.

CHAPTER THIRTEEN

At the snack bar, Nona nibbled a cookie dotted with sparkles. When Royce walked in, she smiled at how attractive he looked with his auburn hair slicked back and his lithe body clothed in a skintight copper-hued jumpsuit. No wonder she'd been so attracted to him and agreed to secretly extend their pair-bond.

Royce took the chair opposite her. "Thank you for coming, Nona. Please excuse me if I skip pleasantries to save time."

Nona nodded. "Of course, Royce. I, too, have something urgent to discuss."

Royce raised his eyebrows. "Really? I'm so pleased that you've decided to talk over whatever it is with me. Why don't you begin?"

"I don't think you know that I have a mandated client."

Royce shook his head. "No, I hadn't heard. What was the nature of the emergency?" Nona told him Sara's story from the beginning. After she finished, Royce looked around the room and then at her. "I hope no one heard anything you said because you would be in big trouble. Let me see if I understand you correctly. You have neglected to admin a Mem-wipe because of how you feel about her?"

Nona sighed. "Yes, that among other things. Like the chance to earn some extra credit by drawing in a big crowd at the annual MHP Extravaganza and ..." she stopped. She knew better. Credit was not the primary motivation.

"Do you think this has happened because we agreed to stop adminning Nepenthe to see if our perceptions would be clearer?"

"Maybe. I don't know. I didn't notice anything except my thinking did seem clearer, sharper. I'm not sure that stopping made any difference. I still felt hollow. But then Sara came along. If I were still adminning Nepenthe maybe she wouldn't affect me as strongly.

To be honest with you, Royce, I don't want to stop feeling the way I do about Sara." She touched his hand briefly. "Why did we ever start that pharm?"

"Excuse my bluntness, but you know the answer to that. After we failed to conceive, and MM removed us from the list of parents-to-be, we both sunk deep into a—what was it like? I sort of forget."

"I have a hard time remembering also. It was like we could hardly move, like our limbs were weighted. I had to take appetite enhancers. So incredible. And my interest in sex disappeared, even with you."

"Right; I remember experiencing almost the same thing, and after quitting that pharm something very strange and surprising happened. I found myself missing you in an almost piercing way."

"Royce, don't you see? We both encountered the same thing! Heightened feelings. I don't want to go back to what life was like before. I like what I'm feeling—excited, sort of like bubbles are flooding my blood."

"Pardon me for pointing this out, Nona, but you just raised your voice." He turned to look at the couple closest them who seemed oblivious to everyone and everything around them as they fondled and kissed each other.

"I'm so sorry." She looked at the couple. "I doubt they heard anything. I don't think they even know anyone else is here. Royce..." She fell silent.

"What is it?"

She leaned in close and whispered, "Do you ever think the Code should never have forbidden certain things?"

"Yes." He whispered after checking that the couple still seemed oblivious to anyone or anything in the room. "I have. A lot. Like staying in the same employment for your entire adult life if you an MHP."

"What—I mean, pardon me? I thought you enjoyed helping people."

"Sometimes, but you have to admit, it gets a little repetitive, doesn't it? Sexual problems most of the time or some kind of issue with pleasure. I tell them to take this or do that, and so what? Sometimes it seems like anyone could do it. I find myself thinking about other occupations. I know there are other things I could do."

"Like what?" Nona asked, puzzled.

"Well, I am very drawn to the creative field. Like neon art. If I had the time and space, I know I could teach myself how to do it."

"Really?" She was surprised to find out something new about him. "But there's no way you could change employment."

"I could get a new I.D. number. I've heard there are ways." He leaned forward and folded his hands on the table. "I'm going to tell you something that may alarm you."

Dread pinched her stomach. "Is it dangerous? I don't want anything to happen to you."

"I feel the same way about you. And yes, it does involve danger. One of my clients told me where a Junker meeting will be. I'm tempted to go. I want to know what these Junkers are after. I wager they're dissatisfied with some of the things that you and I are talking about."

"They have scheduled meetings? Now I'm concerned about you and Sara. I suspect she and this SP, Paul, had a long discussion. He's rumored to be a Junker, maybe even the leader. She believes Junkers could get her out of Mall."

"Well that isn't going to happen, so maybe you're worried for nothing."

Nona nodded. "No, leaving Mall isn't possible, but she could be talked into attending a meeting. If she's even seen with a known Junker, she'll have to go to Judgment."

"Maybe she *is* a Junker. An undercover one."

"No, I'm sure she's …" She stopped when sudden darkness engulfed them, followed by a sickening stench. Something toxic was blowing in through the air vents. Nona gasped and clutched his hand.

The woman nearby shrieked, "Let me out of here!" followed by the sound of a chair toppling. The man retched and moaned.

"Nona, are you okay?" Royce's voice trembled.

"No. Something's wrong with the air. I'm dizzy; my stomach feels odd. Can we get out of here?"

"Where's the …" Lights returned as suddenly as they went out. Just as quickly, fresh air pumped through the vents. For a moment Royce and Nona gulped in the clean air and watched the couple get to their feet and scramble to the exit. Royce broke the silence, not bothering to lower his voice. "Another disturbance. I really need to know what they want."

"Do you think anyone knows?"

Still holding her hand, he replied. "Maybe they want what we want. More—how shall I say it?—excitement. More freedom to explore, to have relationships like ours."

Nona thought for a moment. "I see what you mean."

Royce rose from his chair looking at his communicator. "If I don't leave now, I'll be late for my next appointment." He leaned down and said in a low voice, "It's with the client who gave me a pretty good idea where and when some of the Junkers will be meeting next. I'm strongly tempted to go." He walked off and called over his shoulder, "I'll communicate with you soon."

For the third time, the sleep chime warned Nona to lie down and rest the mandated eight hours, but she remained standing, staring at the prep in her open palm. In five minutes, the sensors would record her failure to be in bed. No matter that it would be her second sleep infraction. She just didn't care. Strange, her lack of concern, when before just the possibility of a negative entry in her dossier would be enough to jar her into corrective action. Thinking about it now filled her with apathy. Deciding to lie down, she wondered: should she or shouldn't she admin? If she didn't, she might be vulnerable to another one of those frightening dreams. But she wanted to think more about Sara. Did the world she claimed to come from truly exist? More and more, Nona was inclined to believe her. She turned over to her left side, then to her right. One thing was clear. She didn't want to administer Mem-wipe to Sara. When else had she experienced such excitement? She sat up, careful to stay on the bed to avoid sensors recording her absence, which would count as one of the three times allowed out of bed.

Yes, she did indeed crave more of the exhilaration her interactions with Sara brought. It was more than that. She wanted her company. She liked looking at her. She liked the animated way she talked. And she felt—what? Responsible. Yes, that was it, for her safety, for her well-being, a feeling that went far beyond what she felt for her other clients. Her function was to guarantee they experience as much pleasure as possible, something she could do blindfolded. This sense of responsibility for Sara, was this the cause of the kind of dull ache at the pit of her stomach? A sort of desire? What did she want? To have sex with Sara? No, that wasn't it. She liked men. She was not a same-sexer. If it wasn't a sexual pull she felt, what was this longing? For some other kind of joining? Not heart-bonding. That was too diluted, really just a convenience, a pledge to be available as company at social events, for dinners out, for gossip.

She wanted a connection, a smudging of the boundaries between them. Something like she and Royce had before their failure to conceive a baby, before adminning the recommended Nepenthe. Sleeping prep still in hand, Nona lay back down, her heart in her throat. Were these thoughts disordered? Better take a pharmaceutical to calm her to the point of indifference. No. Not yet. What she felt was so unusual, certainly uncommon for Mallites. Was this because Sara was so unlike any Mallite she knew? To be this different, she *must* be from somewhere else. She needed to talk more about this with Royce. There hadn't been enough time in their meeting today to go into detail. It certainly wasn't something she could talk about with Fabriana. Fabriana might report her, and Sara too, because Nona had not yet convinced Sara to undergo Mem-wipe. If Fabriana told the Pod, Nona's expertise would be judged. Would they take away the award she had recently been given? She hoped not. She'd won that fairly by making the highest profit in the Pod for three months in a row.

The bed sheet twisted around her body as she tossed and turned. If the Pod found out about Sara, someone else would be appointed to take over her case. She felt her stomach plummet. She pressed the palm of her hand against her temples to slow her racing thoughts. No use. She adminned the Restzy.

CHAPTER FOURTEEN

Sara half lay and half sat on the small single bed, studying her surroundings. The furnishings were functional: a bed, a nightstand, an easy chair, and an Inset in the middle of a wall papered in off-white linen. Such austerity seemed hardly appropriate for such pleasure-loving people, but Stan explained that because the Code dictated eight or more hours of sleep, sleeping quarters must be devoid of stimulation, including guests. Sara had balked at that. "Why shouldn't people be allowed to do what they want in the privacy of their own rooms?" she demanded.

"Because," according to Stan, "sleep is crucial to keep our body in shape so we will look and feel as good as we can."

After showing Sara her quarters, Stan mentioned his was three doors down. So if she asked Stan to visit her, could he? What if she visited him? She could creep down the corridor, knock on his door, and what? Fuck him silly? Shit, this place with sex all around was influencing her. To distract herself, she jumped from her bed to look at her bathroom. How many times could she get up? Three? Nona told her that bathrooms were important for *maintaining optimal appearance.* "Beauty," she had said, "is one of all Mallites' most important goals."

No one could really believe that, Sara had thought. How long had she worked with her therapist Dr. B on the idea that her 'inner self' was beautiful and the real her? Five years! Marrying Carl hadn't helped. Now more than ever she realized that she hadn't grown past the desire for beauty and for men's approval. Stan and Paul had stirred up that part of her.

A memory seeped through: a time when she'd overheard her mom and dad talking just before Sara graduated from college. Her father said, *Let's hope she marries that guy she's been dating.*

What's his name? Gary? He's got a job, doesn't he? Yes, her mother answered, *he's a nurse, but he's too quiet. He hardly says a word.*

So what? Nurses make good money, her father had said. Sara remembered the familiar sound of the cupboard opening and the clink of a glass. He was drinking again. *Better than some nobody who makes a pittance. If she were prettier or smarter or even more charming, maybe she could find someone better."* Why hadn't she married Gary? He'd been kind and gentle. Oh, she knew: he wasn't exciting enough. What a fool she was. Instead she'd slept with too many men, drank too much. No wonder, now that she was separated from Carl and from her mother—two people who sometimes dampened that gnawing need for approval and affection—that she was falling back into that sexual addiction.

Carl hadn't really eased her loneliness and self-esteem. He no longer found her desirable. So, not surprising that she felt such joy when she looked at her reflection. Would she look like she did now when she got back home? How would her mother and Carl react? Would he fall back in love with her? Would she even want him to? Her mother was the only person she could be sure missed and loved her. She stood motionless in the doorway, eyes closed, panting. *Think about something else!* she told herself. She opened her eyes to look at her bathroom, more beautiful and luxurious than anything she had experienced in her world. The chandelier rotated slowly, spilling light on the magenta-tiled floor and the large, circular, teal tub. An entire wall consisted of mirrors to which her eyes flew, like butterflies in search of just the right flower. She could find absolutely nothing about her face to criticize. Her beauty loosened a huge knot of self-disgust. She'd never stopped wanting people to stop and stare at her. Now, gone was that razor-sharp longing for beauty. For a moment, peace radiated through her whole body.

Back in the bedroom, she reached for the mandated sleeping prep and rolled it in the palm of her hand, surprised that it wasn't a dart or a patch. So they don't poke themselves or slap on a patch every time they want an upper or a downer. Stan warned her to admin this pharm or she might be sanctioned. *How would they know if I don't?* Sara had asked. He explained Mall dispensers placed one pill and one ampoule a day in every Mall's sleeping quarter, and if during their random searches they found two unused in the trash, they would report this to Mall Guards. Not only that, somewhere in the bed, sensors recorded the amount of time lying down and how much time you spent asleep. The first time she would be given a warning; the second time she would be sanctioned. She swallowed it, wondering if it would knock her out. It would have to be strong, because after all of the alien things she'd experienced, she was wired. And worried about escaping. And troubled about taking a drug.

She lay down on a bed that contoured perfectly to her body's shape. Just as she thought, she wasn't sleepy. Maybe if she breathed deeply. After several breaths, she noticed a musty smell. She began to cough and then gag. She sat up and grasped her throat. What was happening? Something was wrong with the air! And then she was out.

Someone called her name. She struggled awake. It was so dark she couldn't even make out a shape. She heard a familiar voice say, "Sara, it's me, Paul. I'm going to dart you with an antidote. You were knocked out from breathing too much carbon dioxide." Too sluggish to stop him, he turned her body over and she felt a sting in her neck.

"What ... can you turn on the lights?" she asked in a hoarse voice.

"No, we blacked out the lights in this section and pumped a little too much carbon dioxide into the circulating air." Sara gasped and tried to get up. Paul held her in place. "Don't worry, we've corrected the problem. This time, no one will be harmed, but they will be uncomfortable." The lights glimmered and then illuminated the darkness. Sara rubbed her eyes. "How did you get in? What are you doing here?"

"Almost all the entry codes are just slight variations of a color sequence. Anyone could do it with a little thought and practice, if he or she is good at detecting patterns." Paul pulled on Sara's hand. "Come on. We have to hurry if we want to make the meeting I told you about."

"I don't know." She pulled back.

"Do you want to get out of Mall or not?" Paul tugged at her hand again.

Sara sighed. "No. Yes. I'm frightened," she admitted, although she allowed him to pull her up and away from the bed.

"No one will see you. Most people are either in their Pods, at a Pleasure Palace or at a Virtual Reality scene." He waited while she threw on some clothes and then guided her toward the door where he pressed the correct sequence of lights.

"It scares me that you know the right combination. Can just anyone come in?"

"If they wanted to. No one knows how easy it is. Besides who would go to the trouble? Almost everyone follows the rules like mindless babies." Outside, Sara looked up and down the empty corridor of Entertainment Pod. She glanced quickly at Stan's door. Was he okay? Paul led her out the door to the Entertainment Division promenade where the lights still flickered. Even the elevator voice wasn't working and stuttered its question, "Wh-wh-what fl-floor?" When the door bumped as it opened, Sara refused to step through.

"I don't trust it to work. What about the outage?" At that moment, the lights swelled and the melodious voice repeated its question.

Paul said, "Nothing to worry about. We timed this little disturbance to the very second." To the elevator he said, "Floor K." As they plummeted down, Sara held on. What *was* on the lower floors? She'd never asked.

"Floor K, Mall Maintenance level," the voice announced while the door opened, this time smoothly as usual. They stepped out into a dimly lit corridor lined with numbered metal doors. She followed Stan to door number eight. He punched in the code and they entered a room stacked with unopened boxes, each with an image of their contents, too difficult to make out in the gray light. Paul pulled her behind the highest pile and knocked quietly on what seemed to be a smooth wall. A door slid open to reveal a man dressed in an off-white jumpsuit. "Who's she?" he asked, blocking them.

Paul elbowed him aside. "She's with me." They entered a room painted gray; no wall hangings, no carpeting. About twenty-five people sat around a large rectangular table draped with a flowered tablecloth so much like one of her mother's she stumbled. Paul caught her and gently pushed her toward one of the empty chairs. Only three dressed the way Sara was used to seeing, like the man closest to the door wearing a red velvet vest over an orange silk shirt. All the rest wore jumpsuits—some off-white, others brown, and a few wore navy blue. After seating Sara, Paul sat down in the vacant chair at the head of the table.

Everyone stared at her. Was it because she was the only woman there? The red-vested man blurted out, "Who in the hell is she?" Sara, already nervous, grew more uncomfortable.

Paul answered, "She is," he stopped looking around the table, "someone from Outside." For a moment, silence, then muttering, and finally loud, incoherent voices. Paul shouted, "Quiet!" The clamor died down and he continued, "Do you want to find out more or not?"

"Where did she come from?"

"Why do you believe she's from Outside? Maybe she's disordered."

"We need proof!"

"Sara," Paul turned to her, "tell these people what happened."

At first she had trouble starting, then stopping, even stammering until she decided to go ahead and trust these people. The events rolled out smoothly until she was finished. All except Paul stared at her, shocked into silence until one of the uniformed men asked, "What's a parking lot?"

Sara tried to explain. "A parking lot is where cars are parked while people shop. Cars are vehicles for getting places."

"So if you do live in a mall Outside, what's different about living there?"

"Like I tried to tell you, there are thousands of malls. We don't live in them, but in houses. I lived in one on a tree-lined street where lots of flowers grew. It had three bedrooms and a kitchen and two bathrooms and a yard..."

The Mallite dressed in black garnet-encrusted satin interrupted, "Excuse me, but so what? We can go to almost any upper level and see trees, flowers, grass, even sand with seashells, everything perfectly replicated from Ancient Times."

"Not the same, I bet. There are huge forests filled with hundreds of kinds of trees and..."

One of the uniformed men exclaimed, "That's not enough. Who cares about trees and grass? Not me. I'm not gonna give up this life and risk being picked up by the Finance Police 'cause I want to see a lot of green stuff."

"What do you want, then?" Sara asked, exasperated.

"I know what I want," asserted the Mallite dressed in black satin. "To live in the same room with Andre." He put his hand on the shoulder of the red-vested man. Loud voices erupted again.

119

One man shouted above all the other voices, "What for? Don't you guys get enough fucking in your clubs?"

After Paul shushed them, Andre responded in a quiet voice, "It's because of how we feel about each other. It's a very deep...liking?"

Shocked silence flooded the room. Sara finally said, "It sounds like you love each other."

"I'm not here to listen to that kind of crap!" The man who had let them in rose, knocking over his chair in his rush to reach Andre. He grabbed the chair and tipped it over. Andre landed on his back. A few hurried to help him up while two others tackled the man who had pushed him.

Paul shouted, "Stop, stop! Are you deranged?" He strode to the scuffling men, pulled them apart, and slammed them into chairs. "Everyone shut the fuck up! Have you forgotten what you're here for?" Sara shrank in her chair. Hadn't Nona or Paul told her that violence never happened here?

"Yeah, but what Andre said about living with someone, and that woman, she used the word, *love*. What the hell is she talking about? Sure we love a kid, if we get picked to have one, but to talk about two adults..."

"Look," Paul argued, "we've all got our reasons for wanting out. Who's to judge? And if the reason Andre and Peter want to leave doesn't sit well with you, the door's right there." He pointed to a man dressed in a copper jumpsuit. "You look like you want to say something. Maybe you could start by telling us your name."

"Thank you, Paul. My name is Royce. I don't believe that very many of us really want Out. We want changes, and I mean big changes, like the ability to choose our employment and change it when we tire of it. Why should Mall Managers choose not only what we'll do when we're just kids but also force us to do the same thing for all of our lives?"

Another man agreed. "Yeah. Maybe I don't wanna clean corridors when most are down for their eight hours. Maybe I coulda been a neon artist. I say, keep messing things up, then make demands, and they'll come around to our way of thinking."

"How are we going to mess things up? More of the same?" one of the Technos asked.

"How about cutting off the water supply? And cut off the lights more often?"

"More black-outs, sure, but let's ramp it up." Paul answered. "Turn the heat up until they sweat; more odor leaks to make them sick, and I say let's pump carbon monoxide instead of carbon dioxide into some of their quarters."

Silent for a moment, the whole crowd buzzed. One voice called out, "I don't know about taking someone's life before his number is up."

One of the navy blue jumpsuits called out, "So what? That'll shake things up, good." The group erupted again.

"Quiet!" Paul shouted above the clamor. "We need to keep disrupting the hell out of their restricted, empty lives, but I'm not willing to wait to see if it works. Who's with me for another escape attempt?" Only Andre, Peter and one other uniformed man raised their hands; the rest shifted in their chairs or murmured to one another.

Sara wasn't surprised. She'd want to stay if she were one of them. The risks were huge. Anyway, she was beginning to think that this life had a lot going for it. She raised her voice to be heard. "Why do the rest of you want to stay?"

One of them replied, "I know stuff here. I don't like a lot of things here, but I admit it: I'm scared to go to a place I've never been before. Would I even fit it in? And how do I know it's a better place?"

"That's the problem. How would we get by? Where would we live? Maybe we'd end up at Judgment," a brown-suited Techno agreed.

"From what I've heard, Judgment is a scary thing to go through," Sara admitted. "Although you're right, you might not fit in where I come from, and I don't know what you would do once there. I do know that if I hadn't had help here, I would have ended up at Judgment. If you ended up in my world and acted strangely…"

"Like what?"

"I don't know, maybe you would wander around lost; maybe you would be overwhelmed and ask weird questions; maybe you would jaywalk…"

"What's *jaywalk*?"

"What kind of questions?"

"What would happen if we were picked up by guards?"

"Police, not guards," she answered. "Maybe you would go to jail. I'm not sure."

"Ah, you're making all this stuff up. You're disordered. And you're wasting our time!"

"No, I'm not. It's better in some ways. We have more freedom there. We can have children when we want." The bruising memory that no matter that she was free to have a baby if she wanted to—she couldn't. Unexpected tears spilled down her cheeks.

Andre raised his voice, "God of Reincarnation, she's crying. Only children cry. What's wrong with her?"

One of the green-uniformed men knocked over his chair as he ran up to Sara. Before she could pull away, he touched her wet cheek. "I've never seen anyone do this. You *must* be disordered."

"Or she really is from Outside?"

When uproar broke out again. Paul slapped the table to get their attention. "That's what I've been trying to tell you. Let's get back to what we're here for. If you don't want Out, you better come up with a list of demands for the next meeting. In the meantime, you need to do your part to keep the pressure on. Go ahead with pumping carbon monoxide into a few of the first-raters' quarters and keep up the other disturbances like black-outs, heat-ups and anything else you can think of. And release the nauseating odor into all of the Pods' dining rooms. I'll help all I can, and then, I'm out of here. Mac here thinks there's a portal we can use for getting out on the MM level. We both are working on the code sequence and how to get there without drawing attention. Now let's get back to our Pods and get in our eight hours or the FPs will be on our asses." He took Sara's arm to guide her out. Quietly he said to her, "It'll be just a couple of days and you and I will walk through a portal to Outside."

Sara looked up at him. Could she trust him? Did she even want to trust him? Almost dizzy with confusion, she stumbled. Paul took her arm to steady her. "You all right?"

"I guess so." To herself she thought, *not really*. She was scared. Scared of getting caught and then what would happen? Also scared to leave, she admitted. She was having the kind of adventure she never dreamed of. Yet she longed for home—or did she? Then another thought flashed through. What if she escaped to a different, parallel world or even a time in the future? For a moment terror clamped down. Was it safer to stay here? Another idea snuck into the cracks. *It's more fun here.*

CHAPTER FIFTEEN

Sitting on a green cushioned bench in a miniature rainforest, Sara cupped her hand around a few drops of the moisture falling from the canopy. Next to her Nona sat holding a cup of tea. "Are you enjoying the rainforest arboretum?"

"Yes, a much better place to meet than your office." Sara took a small sip of her own tea. "But do I really need to keep meeting with you? Like I said on the phone, I mean the communicator, now that I have an I.D. and Con Card, cosmetic alteration, and employment, I can pass for a Mallite."

Nona floundered. The last thing she wanted was to stop seeing Sara. How could she keep her in her life? "Yes," she answered, "until I report back to the Finance Police that you are ready for questioning. We need to make sure that the answers you give them are credible. So probably we should discuss this today and maybe have one more client-MHP meeting." She looked up at the miniature rubber tree and then sipped her tea. "I was hoping, after you are settled in and cleared by the FPs, maybe you would like to meet on an informal basis, to check in, maybe talk over how you are managing?"

"I don't know. It depends on how busy I'll be working for the Entertainment Team. Probably we can meet occasionally. Maybe after we eat, before sleeping?"

Something seemed to be blocking Nona's throat, a kind of lump? Keeping in touch was not a priority for Sara. Nona swallowed. "Possibly, although you must be careful to sleep the mandated eight hours."

"Oh right. You know, I don't need that much sleep. It seems like a waste of time. And why do we have to admin each night? I always sleep just fine without a sleeping prep."

"What do you mean? Do you mean that in your Mall you don't take sleeping preps?"

Sara said sharply. "World, not Mall. Remember I told you that there are thousands of malls? And no, most of us do not take sleeping pills. Well, some do, but most of us just lie down and go to sleep. I usually sleep like a baby."

"Baby? Babies are given sedatives. They need them for optimum sleep."

Sara faced Nona. "I can't believe this! You people give babies pharms? It's not right! How could adminning sleeping preps to babies be good for their health? No wonder I can't give up the idea of returning home. What a barbaric idea."

Nona could not understand why Sara continued to believe that pharms were harmful. "Please listen, Sara—all pharms have been carefully researched and tested over hundreds of years. Look at each and every one of us; surely you can see that we are all are brimming with good health. Why can't you accept this?"

Sara folded her arms. "I have never seen any babies so... Wait, I've never seen any kids at all. Where are they?"

"In the Children's Pod, of course."

Sara stared at Nona. "You mean they don't live with their parents?"

"No, but the parents visit the little ones every day to hold them and bond with them."

"Why, why would they be separated from their parents?" Sara's voice was rough with disapproval.

Nona frowned. "How could they stay with their bio-parents? Everyone lives in his or her own separate Pods."

"But what about nurturing and caring; isn't that the role of parents?"

Nona took a deep breath, remembering her excitement when she and Royce were selected to have a child and then, the darkness

125

that followed when she could not conceive, despite various methods. Such an occurrence was so rare the technicians subjected her to weeks of testing and pharms before removing her and Royce from the list.

"But why can't they stay with their parents? Are they too busy seeking pleasure or earning credit?" She heard the sarcasm in her voice but couldn't help it.

Nona winced. "Yes, those things take up a lot of our time. After all, they are mandated. Children would suffer if all they had were their parents to guide them."

"What do they do in these Pods?"

"They are trained to be productive Mallites, and learn the necessary skills they will need for their future occupations." And, Nona thought, they can never change occupations. Why did the Mall Fathers make that decision?

Sara whispered, "You grew up this way? Did they brainwash you?"

"Brainwash?"

"I'm not sure how to explain. You know, use ways to train your brain to believe something without question."

Nona shook her head. "I remember that time with pleasure. We learned almost all that was essential for a good and profitable life." Inwardly, she wondered if she would have chosen her occupation if she had the freedom to.

"I bet you never had any fun," Sara said.

"Learning *was* fun, with lots of games and wonderful prizes and," she added, this memory warming her, "it made me so happy when I won. And you can imagine how proud I was that, when the time came, I tested in the high range for credit-earning potential."

"And when did you get to choose what kind of work to be trained for?"

"MMs believed we wouldn't always choose the best occupation that would match up with our abilities and talents."

"What about what *you* wanted to do?" Sara said.

"How could a mere child know what she wanted? I went through dozens of tests before it was decided that I fit into the MHP category, although maybe when older I might have chosen something different; but after all the time and credit spend on my training, that was not an option."

"What would have happened if you had tested in the dumb range?"

"Dumb?" Nona asked.

"You know, the low range."

"Some low-raters are allowed to have a child, just enough so we will have enough people for those kinds of employments. The Mall Managers make up the quotas."

In the silence Nona could hear the moisture drip on the ferns in a steady beat like her heart, not fast but definite, almost loud. Sara's next question cut through the stillness. "What if a woman wanted to have a child? I always did. Badly."

"They taught us that if people had children without licensing or genetic matching, undesirable, unemployable people would overrun the system. Just think of the chaos, the overpopulation. I ..." Unexpectedly, Nona stopped talking and stared off in the distance. "You may not think it possible, but I do understand how you feel." The words tumbled out of Nona. "Royce and I were selected to have a baby."

Sara clasped Nona's hand. "You did have a baby! Why didn't you tell me?"

"No." Nona plucked at her white linen trousers, "They missed something when they tested that was discovered later. How or why they did, I don't know; no one ever explained. I am not able to get pregnant."

Sara pressed her hand to her chest. "You too? But here in Mall, you don't get depressed, right?"

"Depressed? We so seldom use that term, although I know what it means. Yes, both of us were unutterably sad. We had to take a pharm, Nepenthe." Both remained silent until a realization dizzied Nona. She grabbed Sara's hand. "Now it is coming together for me. If your memories are factual, and you are from another world, you grew up with your bio-parents. From what you've told me so far, you suffered immeasurably!"

"I tried to tell you so many times that my world is real. It's about time you begin to believe it." Sara jerked her hand from Nona's.

Nona hesitated. She never knew when her words would ignite Sara's combustible feelings. "I can't imagine living full time with parents. It was terrible for *you*; isn't that proof how this relationship doesn't work for either the parents or the child when they live together for an indefinite period of time?"

"It had its ups and downs." Sara turned away.

Nona sighed and shook her head. "Please forgive me if I caused more of these memories to resurface. Would you like me to admin some Peectem?"

Sara looked down. "I don't know, maybe later. You must know by now that I'm afraid, because of my father's addiction."

"Yes, so you said. Please pardon me for repeating this, but our pharms are not addicting."

"I can't get past the idea that people here take all kinds of chemicals. So do we in my world." She hesitated and then said, "Including alcohol. It can ruin lives."

Nona was having difficulty keeping up. She closed her eyes and said, "How could something as toxic as alcohol be permitted?"

"Small amounts are fine, but too much can be quite toxic, and not just to the body." Sara's eyes unfocused. "The early times with my father, before the alcohol began to take its toll, were the best times in my life." She leaned her forehead against the palm of her hand, a gesture so unfamiliar, so full of pain, a cramp contracted Nona's heart. "Why didn't he see how much his drinking hurt us? I remember sitting with my mother in a small coffee shop where she recounted the years of his drinking and how it had gotten worse since I moved out. She stammered out how he had punched a hole in the kitchen wall. It was the last straw, my mother said. She'd found the strength to stand up to him and insist that he needed to go to treatment, AA, and to counseling, but he wouldn't stick to any of it. I should have been there to help her! He told her, *No more counseling, I'm not a pussy and that other 'woo woo' stuff. So what if I have a few drinks now and then?"*

"Let me help you, Sara." Nona reached out to touch her but changed her mind.

Sara's eyes glittered with unshed tears. "I don't know."

"Come to my office and allow me to admin a light dose of Peectem. Remember how beneficial its effects were?"

Sara twisted away and then back. "Okay. But just a very small dose."

Nona suppressed an urge to hold Sara's hand as the elevator sped up to the MHP level. How could Sara want to go back where such suffering was commonplace? True, Nona was tempted to meet and talk to a Junker, but to step into Sara's world? The thought made her heart pick up speed. And what if Outside was not her world but someplace even worse and even more alien? Oh, she thought, please don't let one of the Junkers talk Royce into an escape attempt!

CHAPTER SIXTEEN

Her father was floating in front of her while he spit out wounding words. *Get that dress off of Sara. She looks like a fat sausage tied in the middle! You're still getting B's and C's? I told you ...*

Then she was in the attic of her childhood home, rummaging through clothes too small to fit. Again he appeared in front of her, mouth distorted in a grimace.

You think you buried me, but here I am, not dead!

She woke to the sound of the communicator beeping. Disoriented, eyes wet with tears, she puzzled over the dream. With her psychiatrist's help, hadn't she dealt with her father's rejection? In her world, she seldom dreamed about him. She remembered Dr. B's words; *I think you know why you're drawn to men who are unable to give you the intimacy you crave.*

Yes, she did know. She chose men like her father so she could get the love and approval he'd never given her. But she'd worked through all that and stopped acting on her attraction to that kind of man, hadn't she? *No, be honest,* she thought. She had married Carl who only *seemed* different.

Not a good sign to have this nightmare about her father, nor was her awakened attraction to men who noticed and paid attention to her like Paul and Stan.

Although she'd awakened sad, she did feel well rested. Whatever that Number 11 was, it had worked better than she expected and without any sleeping pill after-effects. Maybe the small dose of Peectem Nona had adminned had helped.

Rising from the bed, she stood naked in front of the wall-size mirror. Yes, Carl would approve of this new polished beauty. She could tell she had lost a little weight. She thought of how he put her down with what he thought of as constructive suggestions to help her achieve her goal of improving her appearance: *I bet you would be a knockout if you colored your hair red and let it grow really long, and have you tried that new machine at the gym? Great for toning arms.*

Sometimes he'd insisted he loved her for herself, but what did that mean? How would she even know? He never said anything about enjoying her company nor did he try to find things for them to do together. She was the one who tried to accommodate him, like going to sporting events that bored her. There had been only one thing he hadn't been able to talk her out of—the desire to have a baby. *I'd be a bad dad. You're enough for me*, he insisted over and over. She doubted that. What about those late nights out with "the guys"? Maybe he wasn't a good choice for a father, but that hadn't stopped her from skipping the pill for almost a year. And no pregnancy. She was unable to conceive. Just one more thing wrong with her.

She closed her eyes to call up her husband's image. Only parts of him emerged—his hands, his mouth—instantly fading into a blankness that enlarged with every effort she made to remember. What was happening to her? The clarity of her past world was losing its defining edge. What should she do? Surrender to this place or try to survive while she searched for a way back home, clinging to what was left of her old self? Because there was no doubt that this place was starting to erode parts of her. Would living with these people change her? Perhaps more of her was changed than her face, or perhaps she'd been altered the moment she squeezed through some temporal warp into this world.

The communicator beeped in a different tone. It was Stan reminding her to meet him and his Entertainment Team.

"Will you tell them that I crossed over from a different world?" Sara asked as she and Stan walked toward the team's workplace, knowing the answer before he spoke.

"Not on your life, honey. No one would believe that, including me. No one would want to work with someone that disordered, except for me, if you can pull off making your delusions sound like stories you created," Stan answered while they waded through a red cashmere-soft carpet several inches deep toward a doorway where the center flashed red and purple neon stars and moons. A low-pitched voice announced, *Realized Fantasy Workspace.* "To them, you will be a slightly eccentric creative consultant for second- and third-raters who fooled around with some illegal pharms and ended up with amnesia."

Sara winced at his words. "You'll tell them that?"

"Pardon me, tell them what?"

"You know—about my supposedly taking illegal substances? Won't they judge me? Some people might hate the idea of illegal pharm use."

"*Hate*? Not a word we use. Almost like a curse of some kind. You have to remember that swearing is illegal. No time to talk anymore. We need to get to work. You wait here. I'll be about ten minutes while I brief the team. Then I'll come get you."

While he was gone, Sara paced, thinking about Paul and the Junker meeting. She could be arrested if the Finance Police found out. What did she want to do? Stay here? Have sex with Stan and Paul? Or did she want to find the way out and go home? She felt buffeted by the conflict. Would communicating with Paul help?

The door slid open and Stan appeared to lead her into a room of muted grays dominated by a gleaming stainless steel table, almost as long as the room, surrounded by about ten people, each sitting in front of a blinking Inset.

"Good morning, all. I want to introduce the new team member, Sara." As Stan went around the table announcing each member's name, Sara's face froze into a smiling mask. How could she remember all the names? Some nodded and they all smiled. The man on the end waved and said,

"Welcome, Sara!"

What would they expect of her? Would she say something that would make her seem crazy? She didn't care! Oh yes, she did. Crazy people had to go to MHPs for Mem-wipes. Or they might think she was a Junker. Nervous as on her first day of teaching, she sank into the chair Stan indicated and busied herself with her headset, averting her eyes from the team's fixed stare.

Stan looked at each team member. "I know some of you have already accessed today's profit info for creative teams. Third place, team, is not acceptable. For six months we were the top profit-makers—a great run, guys, and proof that we have it in us to get to the top again." He turned his head to look at Sara. "I believe Sara is the answer to our creative problem. I suggest we get right to work."

"Excuse me, Stan, isn't that rather rude?" asked one of the team members. "We usually take a little time to chat with a newcomer."

Stan glanced around the table. "Look, we're in a bad spot. You know how Mallites are. If we stay in third place for much longer, none of the top-raters will attend our events. We will be forced to reduce our admission costs so only second- and third-raters can afford us. How many of you are willing to get by on less credit?" He glanced around the table at the solemn faces turned toward him. "Okay, let's start." His eyes found Sara's. "How about trying out some of your ideas on the team, Sara?"

"Stan and I…" For a moment anxiety clogged her throat. "Well, we were talking about swearing..."

"Swearing? How could a subject like that amuse an audience?" A woman with diamond-studded black hair asked.

133

"Uh, I'm thinking of a different world where … I forgot what happens when you swear."

When the team all started to talk once, Stan sounded a gong. "Like I told you, Sara had amnesia and occasionally still has a few episodes. I'll refresh your memory. Non-uniformed Courtesy Enforcers wander throughout Mall. There's no way to identify them because they're dressed like all of us. So what's your idea?"

Sara thought hard. "Big Brother watches over you?"

His eyes lit up with interest. "You can imagine a place where a bio-relative would monitor your behavior?"

"No, no." She didn't know whether to laugh or be annoyed. "It's just an expression for a place where everyone is being watched through electronic devices."

"Why would those devices be necessary when we have Courtesy Enforcers everywhere? They issue Shun or Derision Citations when a rule is broken."

"What kind of citation?"

"Shun is when you stand in front of your Pod and they turn their backs on you for a designated period of time. For derision, you stand there, and they face you, laughing and pointing at you."

Sara laughed. "That's silly."

"Not if it's you it's happening to. Right, guys?"

"Right!" they all cried.

"A while back I was caught for being rude and," Stan continued, "I tell you, ten minutes of shun was not amusing." He shuddered.

Sara tried to imagine people she had known and cared about turning their back on her, maybe booing or laughing. Maybe it wasn't as silly as she thought. She had to come up with another idea. *What? What?* She began to stammer, "What about telling stories about people living in an alternate world, where things are the same but not really—only superficially—and…"

A petite, delicate blond, wearing nearly transparent pajamas randomly studded with pearls, cut in. "Excuse me for cutting in, but, Stan, what rules are we using? Rules of Evaluation or Brainstorming? I think the latter would work better."

"Thanks for the suggestion, Shirley. How about a quick vote? All those in favor of Rules of Brainstorming? Good, it's unanimous." Looking at Sara, Stan explained, "When Rules of Brainstorming are in effect, we're allowed to criticize, and we're not penalized for interrupting. Any questions?"

Sara swallowed several times before she could answer. "No. It's okay with me."

Shirley inclined her head toward Sara, speaking slowly and emphatically to make her point. "It goes without saying that I don't wish to be rude or unpleasant, but we've tried dozens of different world stories, and they have not proven to be profitable. The problem is that the people only appear different. And the events, well, usually, they end up being the same old thing in a different setting. Now, I don't wish to be discouraging, but you're going to have to come up with something really unusual or original, or I, for one, will veto your ideas."

"I think I do have an original idea about a relationship." Should she describe her relationship with her husband? Did they know anything about commitment to a man who made her stomach twist in anger and hurt, about staying together so they could work it out? Or was that just another word for resignation? In her real life outside of this world, she had seemed fated to be in a difficult marriage that forced her into the nooks and crannies of herself, her life, and her world. How tiresome that sounded now. But here no one seemed married. Think, she thought, think! Would a play about her marriage be original enough to interest them? Why hadn't she asked more about how their relationships worked?

135

Across from her, the short, thick-necked man, muscles bulging everywhere, interrupted her reverie. "Relationships? Good! Hot sex always pulls them in. Do you envision something radically different, something really titillating?"

Next to him Natalie, the redhead snickered, "Oh, Tom, that's all you ever think about, create about, and do!" Leaning over, she whispered something to him and he laughed.

Shrugging, he retorted, "As if you don't. You're more into sex than I am, any day."

Natalie licked her shiny red lips, eyes gleaming. "Who isn't into sex?"

Forgetting her discomfort, Sara jumped right in. "Of course there can be more to a relationship if…" She slowed to a stop, noting confusion in all the faces turned toward her. Careful, she thought. "I mean, in this world I made up. Sometimes men and women would not only have sex, they would love each other too."

"Love?" exclaimed the man on the end. "That sounds interesting, but…"

Tom cut in. "What do you mean, *love?* People only love children. I wouldn't know because I've never been selected to be a father. Anyway, I don't get it. How can you even conceive of two people of the opposite sex loving each other? It seems too weird to me, almost perverted."

"What do you think, Shirley?" asked Stan.

"It could be so radically different that…I need to hear more before I make up my mind."

"Yes, I agree, and I think some of you have forgotten to switch to record mode on your Insets," Stan reminded them.

Heads down, whispering, "Test, test," all of them pressed buttons that flashed rainbow colors, almost hypnotizing Sara. She closed her eyes to the glittering multicolored lights and tried to recall her relationship with her husband. Could she make them understand? A stillness gathered around her heart when she thought of how much in love she'd been after she'd first met Carl. Not too long after, on a drive up the coast, he described a small image that he carried of her in the upper corner of his mind; ready to retrieve and look at whenever he felt lonely, sad, or angry. She told him about her father—how he criticized her, how he drank too much, and how he washed down pills with a bottle of whiskey. *You have me now, Sara. No bad stuff will happen to you again,* he promised. And she believed him. He stopped the car and held her. They kissed and kissed. He'd pulled her onto his lap so she could straddle him. Who cared how uncomfortable they were? It was the best sex she'd ever had. But lots of bad stuff did happen. After they were married, he began to nag her about her appearance. He drank too much, not as much as her dad but sometimes too much and there were times when he was drinking that he got angry. She paled remembering when she had once overcooked their steaks and he raised his voice, berating her cooking. She answered back as loudly as he, *So fucking what? If you hate my cooking that much why don't you take over?* He'd struck her. On her mouth, and split her lip. She took a deep breath. She hadn't let that memory out since it had happened.

He'd gone to counseling with her and he never hit her again. But he hadn't stopped yelling at her. And from then on she was always slightly afraid of him. Yes, the sex was usually pretty good. If only she could have gotten pregnant!

She looked up to see their expectant faces staring at her. She'd better think of something to say soon. "Tell me what you think of this. Let's say the main character, Nickie, and her friend—her name is Joyce—run into a man, Peter, who's involved with Nickie. Peter is instantly attracted to Joyce. He wants to see Joyce again, so he asks Joyce for her communicator code pretending he has a friend he would like to introduce to her—"

"Hey, if they're contracted, that's against the Code," Natalie objected as she fluffed her red-gold, close-cropped curls.

"Yes, but the rules are more lax in this world. Anyway, he contacts Joyce and asks her..." Sara hesitated. Did they date here? It was better to not introduce too much alien material. "To meet him at a Pleasure Palace," Sara continued. "He just can't get her out of his mind. She's reluctant—after all, Nickie is a friend of hers—but she's been so lonely..."

"Lonely?" several of them asked.

Uh-oh, she thought, I bet that's a feeling very few of these people experience. "You know, when you have no one of the opposite sex in your life."

Natalie cut in. "*Lonely?* How bizarre. Why not just say she's sex-deprived?"

"That's not exactly it. Sure, she wants sex, but she also wants some man to care for her, to help her and recreate with her." This was getting harder and harder.

The quiet, tall, thin man on the end said, "I think I understand. You're talking about mixing two kinds of formal bonds, aren't you—the pair-knot and the heart-bond?"

Unsure of what he meant, she prayed Stan would come to her rescue. Instead, Tom saved her. "Yeah, Walter, but I don't get it. How could sex get mixed in with friendship? We all know pair-knotting is just a contract for exclusive sex. Think about it. How many of you ever wanted to heart-bond with someone you're pair-knotted with? And, for that matter, how many of you have ever heart-bonded with someone of the opposite sex?"

Natalie spoke up. "I wager quite a few, Tom, I think I can understand how this feels. I might have some experience...Never mind." She looked away.

Sara studied Natalie and wondered who the man was. Surely not Stan? She hoped not.

Stan said, "Mall Fathers warned us about the dangers of those kinds of attachments. Too much possible hurt involved, and if anyone felt like he or she wanted that kind of weird closeness, he could eliminate the desire with a dose of Ezydozit."

"It doesn't matter, Stan," Natalie interjected. "She's talking about something outside of most of our experiences. Just because this kind of relationship seldom happens in real life doesn't mean that it wouldn't fascinate consumers. Remember that kidnapping story that Real Tears did? And remember how we thought no one would find the idea believable, much less entertaining, that parents would take their bio-children out of Care and hide them in their living quarters? But, after six months, people are still renting that holovideo. Pure fantasy, but entertaining stuff. Go on about your idea. I think it has merit."

Sara warmed to Natalie, someone who seemed to understand where she was coming from. She hesitated and scanned the faces staring at her, interest glittering in their eyes, some of which were outlandish colors like purple, emerald green, and even gold. What should she say next?

"Sara?" Stan prompted.

"Sorry. Anyway, they meet, and the attraction between them is powerful. He breaks it off with Nickie, and they begin an intense romantic…"

Walter, the thin man with silver eyes, smoothed the sleeve of his gray silk shirt. "I'm sorry to interrupt, but what is this word, *romantic*? We need everything to be clear so when members of the audience reserve for interactive time—and we hope every single one does because that's where we make our profit—they will understand not only the plot but the reasons why the characters act as they do."

"You mean the characters' motivation?" Sara asked.

"Yes, I guess I do, although that's not a term we use."

"I need clarification. What do you mean *interactive time*?"

139

Stan answered, "Audience members reserve some time the day after a performance to take part in the action."

"I still don't understand."

Stan continued, "Let's say an audience member would like to be sitting near Peter and Joyce when they first meet. He or she may want to interact with them."

"Then what? The actors have to improvise?"

"Exactly, and the more time the audience member requests, the more profit we make."

Shirley looked up from her screen, "We still need to know what *romantic* means."

"The mixture of friendship and sex, I guess. A word I just sort of made up. We don't have to use it in the actual drama. Should I go on?" In a way Sara was enjoying herself. It was fun to stretch her imagination.

"Sure." Walter's smile was slow and easy. "Please continue."

"So they continue to meet and have sex, of course. One day, he takes her in his arms and tells her that she is his and that he loves her."

At the other end of the table, the Asian woman, busy whispering something into her headset, looked up and pushed back the black curtain of her hair, revealing an exquisite face with alabaster skin. Diamonds glittered throughout her hair, on her nose, in her ears, and on her fingernails. Her black eyes shone with intelligence and interest. So lost in admiration, Sara almost missed her question. "I need clarification. Will they pair-knot? If so, of course she will be his. No one can have sex with anyone besides his or her partner. Your Pod would shun you."

Natalie snorted. "Oh yes, they do. They're just very secretive about it."

Sara closed her eyes, trying to find the right answer. "If you remember, I was thinking of a world where enforcing rules was kind of lax. But maybe lax isn't the right idea. What about something more extreme, like a world where pair-knots and heart-bonds don't exist?"

The team members began asking questions all at once. Sara pleaded, "Wait a minute, please. I can't understand what each of you are saying." Stan activated the gong, silencing the clamor as suddenly as it had begun.

"Sorry, Sara," Stan apologized, "this sometimes happens when Rules of Brainstorming are in effect." Looking around the table, Stan admonished them. "Let's remember to ask questions one at a time."

"Sure," Walter said. He gazed at Sara. "I'm trying to picture a world without pair-knots, something I can hardly imagine. Wouldn't people suffer extreme jealousy? What little I've experienced was quite unpleasant, but nothing an ampoule of Smuthnezy wouldn't eliminate. Compared to what you're talking about, I realize how minor these incidents were, like a flirtatious smile or a pat on the derriere, but this is a world where a person might go to extremes to keep someone for himself or herself, am I right? In other words, without the safeguard of pair-knots, wouldn't people, well, amok? You know the trouble just one Amoker causes? Think of hundreds of them. We couldn't function."

"But we're not talking about that here," the Asian woman interrupted. "Would it work in a storyline?"

"No!" Natalie exclaimed. "Sorry, Delta, I didn't mean to be so abrupt. I think it would be far too complicated—more important, too credit-inefficient—to portray all that deranged confusion."

"Excuse me, please," Delta countered, smoothing the impatience from her porcelain- like face. "I wasn't suggesting that we do it; in fact, I am not in favor of this strange creation. I'm just trying to keep an open mind."

Sara looked at Stan with mute appeal. What should she do? She had to convince them or she might be out of a job, and then what? And a tiny but growing part of her liked this, the process of creating on the fly.

This time, Stan rescued her. "Let's hear more before we decide."

Improvising, Sara offered, "Couldn't we just show the relationship and what happens with a few supporting characters? Then the story would only be about two people who are in a sexual-love relationship that ends up hurting both people."

Shirley looked up. "Hurting? How could that be? Wouldn't they just get a practitioner to prescribe some pharm?"

"No," Sara declared. "Let's say this world doesn't have pharms as sophisticated as here. No one has the power to get rid of pain for more than a short period of time and usually with nasty side effects."

Looking fascinated, Shirley stared at Sara for a moment as the other team members whispered some of these ideas into the tiny microphones extending from their headsets. "So we're talking about a world filled with pain?" Shirley asked. "Maybe we're on to something. I suggest we hear the whole story; what do the rest of you think?"

Hearing the murmurs of assent, Sara knew she had to continue, but how exactly to tell it and make it acceptable? Should she tell how, when looking at the full moon in a black-coffee sky, Carl had turned to her with tears in his eyes and told her he loved her? And asked her to marry him? No, she would not talk about Carl and her marriage after all. They would not understand. Not in the least. They had no way of comprehending a long-term commitment especially if pain was involved. She closed her eyes, remembering the time he'd called her Janelle. He swore she was someone he'd been involved with long ago. *Stop the fucking jealousy*, he demanded when she cried. So thick was her suspicion, she could barely swallow it. But swallow it she did. Maybe these people had it right. Avoid love. Never commit. Anger and sadness began to leak through her defenses. About to ask Stan to ask for a recess, Sara opened her eyes and the lights blinked off, then on and off again.

"Those fucking Junkers!" a voice cried.

"Tom, you naughty boy!" Sara recognized the shouting voice as Natalie's. "Good thing a Courtesy Enforcer isn't here or we would be shunning you for hours on end."

"Yeah, well it's enough to drive any Mallite to swear. We can't work in the dark!"

"True," Natalie giggled, "but maybe we can play a little?"

"Not in the mood." Tom replied in a cranky voice. "How can we be..." he stopped when a high-pitched whistle pierced the air. Everyone moaned or cried out while covering their ears.

"Make it stop!" someone shouted.

Sara rose from her chair ready to flee only to crash into someone else running blindly.

"Where's the door? Help me find the door!" Shirley cried out. Sara drew back and knocked over her chair. Just as suddenly as the blackout and noise started, it ended. Shirley was on the floor on her hands and knees, her pajama-like bottoms rucked up. The Asian woman stood against the wall, part of her long black hair covering her face. Sara picked up her chair and sat down heavily. For several moments no one said anything. Walter was the first to speak, "So far, these disruptions—black-outs, coffee shortage, lack of hot or cold water, who knows what else—have caused us inconvenience, but this sound hurt, really hurt. This is not good."

"You're right, Walter. I had to do without coffee three mornings in a row," Stan said. "It's gotten so you never know when we'll be plunged into darkness. And this sound! My ears still hurt. Even worse, I heard they pumped in too much carbon dioxide into a neon artist's quarters. His number was almost up!"

Tom said, "Things *are* getting bad. I ate at the café of the Silver Moon in the Apparel Designers' Pod and a horrible smell drove everyone out. I felt—what's the word?—ill. Have any of you ever felt a discomfort in your stomach? It was horrible, like my insides would come out of my mouth. Thank God of Reincarnation I recovered once I was out of there."

"What is happening to our secure and pleasurable life?" Shirley whimpered.

Stan looked at Sara whose face scrunched with discomfort. "Are you okay?" He asked.

"Not really. Can we take a break?"

"Just a minute." Tom insisted. "I thought we needed to …" Stan's warning look stopped him. "Sorry. Didn't mean to be rude."

Stan nodded. "I know, Tom. I think all of us are forgetting that this is only Sara's first day and one where we went through a really bad experience. Don't forget that she's still recovering from the toxic effects of illegal pharms. I suggest we take the afternoon off and return this evening. I'm sure we can finish this in a few hours and maybe have a brief rehearsal."

Sara heard a few of them grumble. Overwhelmed, she suppressed a moan and walked toward the door.

Hurrying to catch up with Sara, Stan called, "Sara, wait." At her side, he whispered, "You look—how to say this—very disturbed. I know the darkness and that penetrating sound were far from amusing, but it's more than that, am I right?"

"I'm okay. The memories took me off guard. And yes, that damn blackout, and that terrible sound! Every time something like that happens I get scared. It makes me want to go home!"

Voice husky, words almost tripping on each other, Stan asked, "You're not thinking of quitting, are you?"

Sara rubbed her forehead. "I just need some time to gather my thoughts." She slowed her pace and turned her face toward Stan.

"What I need is someone to talk with who would really listen. Can you do that?" She moved closer. Was listening what she really wanted? Or did she want him to hold her, to whisper *you'll be okay*?

"Listen?" Stan asked, as he started to touch her arm. Quickly, he stepped back. "Wasn't I doing that?"

"Not the kind of listening I mean. You were listening with dollar signs flashing in front of your eyes."

"Dollar signs?"

"Never mind," she snapped, turning to walk away from him.

Matching his pace with hers, he said, "I wish I knew what to do. I haven't the slightest idea what kind of listening you mean or how it could possibly help. No rudeness intended, but why don't you just admin something to eliminate this, uh, distress."

Sara stopped and faced him. "Maybe I will. I don't know. I have such divided feelings about pharms. You know, maybe I should talk to Nona; after all she's my Mental Health Practitioner."

"Oh, I get it. You want the kind of listening MHPs do. I've never been to one or I would probably have a better idea of what you want." Stan followed her, close on her heels as she made her way through the throngs of people. "I have an idea. If it is okay with you, I'll contact Nona and, if she's not with a client, I'll arrange a meeting with both of us. Maybe I could pick up some pointers about the kind of listening you want. I don't want to lose you." He held her gaze. For a moment Sara swore she could see his eyes shine with what? Tenderness? Attraction? Averting his eyes, he asked, "How about we meet at the Maple Tree Arboretum on level seventy-three. I'll be there as soon as I dictate the meeting summary."

"I don't know." She stepped closer to him, stopping just short of taking his hand. "Will I be able to find it?"

"Sure, all the arboretums are close to the elevator exit."

This time she did take his hand. For a moment, he returned the pressure. Then slowly he withdrew it.

Sara looked at the hand he had released. "Oh, sorry—I guess I shouldn't do that. It's just that I am a little scared. What if someone thinks I don't seem Mallite enough?" She wished he would do more than hold her hand for a short minute. She wanted him to hold her. There it was again, that attraction and ramping up. Could she work with him and keep her longings in check? And what was happening to her? She hadn't thought about escape for several hours.

Sara sat alone on a small wrought-iron bench, grateful for the abundance of lace leaf maples and miniature oak trees. Her tension began to melt away until she felt almost languid. If only she could take these few minutes and stretch them, like taffy, into hours. She was tired. Tired of all the tension, the worry, the difficulty of fitting into this world. In a way she felt almost like giving up or should she say, *giving in*. There was a lot to like about this place. How could she not enjoy that heady feeling when so many people paid attention to her, something that she so seldom experienced?

She started when someone from behind called her name, a very familiar voice. "Paul?" she called out and he appeared. She had almost forgotten how tall he was. "What are you doing here?" She watched his face as he sat next to her. "Are you following me?"

"I have some business on this level, and I spotted you when the elevator door opened."

"How? I had my back to you."

"Your hair." He reached out and touched her bangs.

Before she could stop herself, she caressed his hand smoothing her hair. "I wondered when I would see you again."

Once again she heard the elevator swoosh open. She turned around to see Natalie sail out. "There you are, Paul and…Sara, hi. What a surprise." Paul stood up and went to her side. "Didn't we have an appointment," she asked as she stood on tiptoes to search his face. "Or were you slated to see Sara?"

"Of course, we have a meeting, Nat. Sara just happened to be here, so I stopped to say hi."

Jealousy trickled through Sara's body. So this was the man Natalie had mentioned in the meeting, and they were still together. Compared to tiny, adorable Natalie, Sara felt like a lummox. Tears stung her eyes. *Oh shit, here I go again,* she scolded herself, *always on the short end of the comparison stick. I'm making a fool out of myself.* She rose and stumbled toward the elevator only to bump in to Stan.

"You're not leaving, are you?" He caught her arm. "Wait, what's wrong?"

Sara leaned against him. "I just want to go…I almost said home, as if I could just turn around, get in that elevator and punch in the floor to exit to the parking lot in Lincoln Mall." She glanced behind her. Natalie and Paul were gone. When she turned back Nona stood next to Stan.

"What's happened, Sara? You look sad," she asked.

"I'm okay." She smiled at Nona, surprised by the flood of gratitude and relief to see her.

"I don't understand. Stan communicated with me that you needed to talk to me. He said it was urgent." Nona urged Sara to a bench and they sat down.

"I was a little upset during the meeting. I'm over it." She glanced around again in the hopes of seeing Paul and Natalie. "Stan, did you see Natalie with a tall man dressed in a cape?"

"Are you talking about Paul?" Nona asked sharply.

"Yes. He and Natalie were here just a minute ago," Sara answered.

Stan said, "Nope, didn't see anyone. Wait, do you mean the SP you were talking to the other night at the Pleasure Palace? You just saw Natalie with him?"

"That's the one and, yes, she was with him."

147

Stan shook his head. "I know she's been meeting someone often. Too often. And she's not pair-knotted to this man. More importantly, I think her carrying-on with this person is affecting her work."

"I have to go," Sara burst out. She rose so abruptly she lost her balance and fell against Stan who caught and held her for a moment, then dropped his arms. *Get out of here,* she urged herself, *before you embarrass yourself and cry in front of him.* It would have been better if she could have talked to Nona alone.

"Sara, wait," Nona reached out to her.

Sara hurried off to the exit. Stan call out, "Don't forget the evening work shift."

What she wanted to forget was the conflict jerking her this way, then that. She slowed her pace to keep from losing her footing. She almost wished she could slice herself in two. One half could go home and the other half could—what? Stay here, make lots of money—or credit, it was called credit here—and pair-knot with Stan or Paul? How could one person be so divided? When would she know with certainty what she really wanted?

CHAPTER SEVENTEEN

Nona walked back and forth in her office. She pulled out her communicator to listen to the list of upcoming appointments. None until later in the day. When she heard it announce the upcoming contest, she jumped. What contest? Then she remembered agreeing to Fabriana's suggestion to enter Barona's competition. Usually she looked forward to contests, but today the thought did nothing to ease the sensation of something gnawing on the edge of her stomach. Why was she allowing herself to feel this way? A dose of Ezydozit was just a step away. Yet she hesitated, her hand hovering on the drawer handle. Thoughts tumbled one after another. *Why was Sara disturbed after her team meeting? What about Paul? Was he really in charge of the Junkers? Was Sara involved with them?*

Nona needed to find out more. An idea occurred to her. *Visit Natalie.* Although not polite to drop by unannounced at someone's work place, she would go to her Entertainment Team studio. Courtesy rules would make it impossible for Natalie to refuse.

In the long, brightly lit hallway, Nona could see ten well-spaced and ornately decorated doorways. Whenever she passed an entrance, a melodious voice announced the team member's name and flashed his or her image. When Nona approached a copper door dotted with sparkling green stars and purple moons, Natalie's image flashed in the center at the same time her name rang out. Nona knocked and waited for several minutes until the petite redhead answered the door, panting slightly. "Please forgive the unannounced visit. May I enter?"

"Nona! Yes, of course, although seeing you here surprises me. Pardon me for asking, but I thought MPs were not allowed social visits? Please don't misunderstand me, I do want you to come in," she babbled as she stood aside to let Nona pass. "Actually, I'm flattered you dropped by."

Nona looked around the small room, all surfaces covered in green velvet shot through with copper threads. In the center stood a small circular platform, which Nona assumed was for practicing her parts in the dramas her team created. Her eyes moved to the easy chair where she spotted Paul, black cape lying on the floor, hair mussed. Nona sniffed and sure enough she could smell recent sex. "Again, please pardon the unexpectedness of this visit, and you're right, MHPs are discouraged from social visits with clients, although my reason for coming is not social." She pivoted to face Paul. "Hello, Paul. We met at the Pleasure Palace, I hope you remember."

"I remember. You were with Sara. Might I ask why you are visiting Natalie in her studio? It is rather surprising, if you don't mind my saying." He squinted with suspicion.

"No offense taken, and I hope you don't take exception if I ask what *you* are doing here? I thought SPs had their own places for meeting with clients, unless, of course, that was not the purpose of this meeting."

Paul rose. "No, I don't have an office for meeting purposes. I find that most clients are more comfortable choosing their own meeting places."

Nona stepped closer to Paul. "Forgive me if I point out that it's obvious that the two of you just had sex in her work place, something that, although the Code does not expressly forbid, is strongly discouraged." This man worried her. What was he up too?

Paul said nothing for a moment while staring at Nona. "Let's cut out the politeness. What Natalie does in the privacy of her studio is her business. What's it to you anyway and why are you even here? My business with Natalie is private." He picked up his cape.

"I do wonder what your connection is with my client, Sara, and why after seeing you, she was so agitated."

"How should I know? Ask her." Walking toward Natalie, he brushed against Nona without an apology. "Hey Nat," he said in soft voice as he scooped up his cape, "I have another appointment." He touched her arm. "We'll communicate later, okay?" He left.

Natalie perched on a small stool. "Please sit down, Nona," she said, indicating the easy chair where Paul had sat. "I'm curious why you wanted to see me."

Sinking into the chair's softness, Nona thought about her answer. To find out if she knew whether Paul and Sara were having sex? To find out why Sara met with Paul on the sly? Or to discover if he were not only a Junker but also their leader? Out loud she said, "I beg your pardon for my bluntness. Is Paul a Junker?" She removed her cropped white linen jacket. Why was Natalie's studio so warm?

Natalie's pink cheeks paled. "Junker? No, no! He's ..." She stopped to flick sweat off her forehead. "It's so hot in here; what's happening?"

Nona sprang out of the chair. "Something's wrong." She fanned herself with her hand. "I can hardly stand it." Silent for a moment, she said, "I think this is another Junker disturbance." Had Paul done this? Nona wondered. Fear flashed through her. Would this heat harm their bodies? *No,* she thought. *Paul wouldn't leave Natalie here to suffer harm.*

"Oh shit!" Natalie exclaimed as she tore off her green satin slip, soaked with sweat, the only garment she wore. "Oops, I just swore; you won't report me to the Courtesy Enforcers, will you?" Naked, she headed for the bathroom. "I'll run a cold bath."

"Please don't worry; I won't disclose anything you say, she reassured Natalie as she shucked her chemise and followed her. "Tell me, Natalie, don't you find it strangely coincidental that Paul left just before the temperature went up?" She leaned against the wall, feeling lightheaded.

Natalie snorted as she turned on the cold tap full force. "Of course not! He had an appointment."

"I hope you know that in coming here I grant you the client/MHP confidentiality. Please tell me about Paul. Everything." The need to know pushed against her chest. She slid into the tub, welcoming the icy water rushing around her calves. She and Natalie sat facing each other, gasping for breath. As the cold water rose Nona's temperature dropped, the uncomfortable heat in her limbs dissipating, though it still shimmered in the air around them.

"I don't know anything. Really." Natalie splashed water on her face.

"I think you do. Be assured I will not divulge anything you say. Maybe you could start telling me about your relationship. It looks like you are in a secret pair-knot."

The heat seemed to thicken in the silence until finally Natalie said, "I don't understand why you want to know."

"Because he seems to be involved with my client, perhaps in a sexual way. Doesn't that make you jealous?"

"No," she shook her head. "We are not pair-knotted, secret or otherwise. You won't understand what we are to each other."

Nona's interest quickened. Did they have some kind of forbidden strong attachment? "I might surprise you," she said in her gentlest tone. "You've already told me he's a Junker and I've kept your secret per the Code."

Natalie dunked her head and came up sputtering. She brushed the water out of her eyes, then squinted at Nona. "That was different. And you better keep that to yourself. Paul just told me about the MM meeting. I confided in you before that so it should be covered by the Code. But because of that MM meeting, I can't be sure of you, Nona, so I can't discuss this further."

"Please think of this as just another session with your MHP. The Code specifies confidentiality and I promise I will honor that." Nona swallowed. Technically, not if the discussion involved Junkers; not that she would tell anything Natalie said. What if she revealed that she, too, cared about Royce in a way discouraged, even banned by the Code? Or, maybe, if Natalie knew about her feelings about Sara, she would be more comfortable disclosing everything about Paul. "I do understand how you feel. I have a client who is in a relationship somewhat like yours," she improvised, "maybe with a Junker."

"You? And you didn't report her?"

"No. I still consider myself bound by my oath of confidentiality." She paused when a tremor of fear ran through her. Natalie could report Nona. "I'm very interested in this relationship phenomenon. It would be so helpful if you told me about you and Paul." She shivered in the water. Goosebumps rose on her arms. She stood in the bath. "I think it's cooling down." The air felt milder. She grabbed a towel and handed Natalie one. They dried and dressed.

Natalie dropped her towel and shook her head, wet coppery curls bouncing. "I can't tell you any more about him. I don't want him to get in trouble."

Nona took in a deep breath. Maybe if she admitted she cared for someone without naming Sara or Royce, Natalie would feel more comfortable talking about Paul. "Perhaps it would help if you knew that I also feel more strongly about a friend than is advisable. There is no need to worry that I won't understand or reveal anything you say. Please believe me."

Natalie paced for a few moments. Finally, she said, "He listens to me."

"You mean you need spiritual advice because your number is up?"

"No, no. He is like a heart-friend, only much more. No expiration. It's forever." Natalie sat on her stool.

"Heart-friends don't have sex; I don't understand." Or did she? She felt a sliver of recognition thinking about Royce and her relationship with him.

"Right—if you will pardon my abruptness, *you* might not. Sometimes we have sex, but that is not why I seek him out." She walked to where Nona sat and stood in front of her. "If you tell, I will deny it. I will tell that one of your clients revealed she was in some kind of relationship with a Junker and should have been reported."

"I told you, I won't reveal anything you say," Nona insisted. "I also just confessed to allowing myself to experience stronger attachments than is allowed. I did not admin the recommended pharms to deal with these feelings. So you see, Natalie, I am as vulnerable to shuns and official credit-debits as you. Who knows? With all the disturbances, all the turmoil caused by the Junkers, the sanctions could be much worse and involve Judgment. You and I are both taking big risks."

Natalie grabbed her arm. "Maybe you're saying all this stuff just to make me feel okay about telling you everything. Yes, it would feel good, but I'm just not sure I can trust you. And I can't be responsible for doing anything that'll hurt Paul. Or me for that matter. You would have to prove you're telling the truth. Now if you excuse me, I need to rest before I go back to the team for a night session."

Natalie gently pressed Nona's arm leading her out of the room, closing the door behind her. One thought after another piled up. How could she discover more about Paul and Sara? Were they planning to escape? But how? *Do the Junkers know how to get out? No, that can't be! There's no way out.* A new thought shocked her. *If there were, would I want to go with them to Outside?*

154

CHAPTER EIGHTEEN

Her mother lay on a white bed in a white room, her white cheeks grazed with pink. When Sara spoke her name, her eyes popped open and she moaned. *Where have you been?*

"Nowhere, Mom, I'm right here."

No, you've been gone for years. Now I'm dead.

Sara hurried to the side of the bed and leaned in to kiss her. Her cold cheeks smelled like cinnamon. She started to cry, "Mom, please don't leave me; you're all I have. Why are you dead?"

Her mother answered without moving her white lips. *We killed your dad.*   "No, Mom, he took pills."

We didn't love him enough.

"Not true! He didn't love *us* enough. He loved whiskey, not us. Don't you remember you decided to get a divorce?"

I killed him! A second pair of arms floated out of the ones motionless and glided to Sara. She backed away. *Why did you leave me?* The ghost arms pinioned her.

"I only left for a little while. I had to get away! I was eating too much, sleeping with too many men. I thought you understood!"

I had no one. Her mother wept. Tears rolled from her staring eyes.

Someone was tapping at the door—her father? No, no, he was the one dead. She woke with a start. The room was pitch black. She had laid down for a nap before returning to the ET. Had the dream awakened her? No, the soft knocking was real. Should she get up and answer it? Weren't visits to sleeping quarters forbidden? She opened her eyes wide, then wider; not one single drop of light floated in this vast lake of darkness.

Shit, she thought, *another one of those damn blackouts. What good were they doing?* And it was hot, really hot. She threw off her cover. When the tapping sounded again, Sara rose and groped her way to the door. Before she could try to enter the right sequence in the dark, the door opened. Someone gently pushed her aside. She gasped.

"Don't be scared—it's just me, Paul."

"What if we're caught? It's forbidden!"

"Don't worry—they're too stupid to even suspect someone would break one of their asinine rules."

"Why are you here?" She backed away a few steps.

"To let you know we're scheduling another meeting."

"I don't know, I don't know. I'm scared. What if we're caught? What would happen to me? Sometimes...I feel like I don't want to leave. My employment is more fun than I thought. In fact, I'm looking forward to going back this evening." Quiet for a minute, she said in a halting voice, "I like not being responsible for anyone but myself." A wave of guilt washed over her, but not quite as intense as before. Pushing her hair off her forehead, she asked, "Why is it so hot in here?"

"Sit down." He took her by the arms and pressed her into a chair. "Yeah, I know it's hot; that's something we arranged. Don't worry; you'll be okay, just uncomfortable. Are you having second thoughts? I hope not, because it wouldn't be good for you."

Sara froze for a moment. "Are you threatening me?"

"Let's say I'm giving you some advice, or you could consider this a friendly warning."

She used her tunic to wipe off the sweat from her face. "What are you saying? Something will happen to me if I decide not to be involved?"

"You won't want to make that decision. We have one MHP in our group who would be happy to put you through a Mem-wipe. He doesn't believe you're from Outside."

Sudden anger spilled through Sara's body. "Shit! To think I trusted you!"

"Listen, Sara, you *can* trust me. I'll try my best not to let anything bad happen to you, but if you decide not to be part of this group, it won't go well for you. You know too much, and I'm not sure I'll be able to do anything to stop the group from going against you."

"I'll go to the damn meeting. When is it?"

"Two nights from now. I'll be in touch."

Sara opened her mouth to ask where, when the muted sleep-light blinked back on, and the air began to cool. Before she could ask, he rose, wrapped the black cape around his body, and touched her cheek as he passed her. He pressed the door sequence and left.

Confusion swirled through her whole body. Shouldn't she be absolutely committed to getting out of here? Yet the pleasure of her new job, her satisfaction with her appearance, the drugs, too—yes, she had to admit that she'd loved the effects the two times Nona had given her pharms.

When had she ever been so deeply immersed in a job? When she taught? Maybe at first but not for years. What had happened to her vow to get back home? What about her mother? She needed Sara; didn't the dream prove that? Maybe, but her mother would be so proud of her—a job creating a new play. And her appearance! Finally, she looked as good as her mother had when she was young. Sara had never been as pretty as her mother and nowhere near as smart. Her mother had a Master's Degree, and she'd taught English at a community college until Sara was born. Why hadn't she gone back to work? Oh, Sara knew all right. Her father. His alcoholism. Her mother had tried to get him to stop drinking, until one day she said to him in an almost inaudible voice, *I'll file for divorce. And get a restraining order*!

157

He laughed at her. *What will you do without me? Do you think you'll be able to get a job? You haven't worked in years. And do you think a little piece of paper will stop me from coming into my own home, which I bought and paid for?*

After his suicide, her mother had never been the same, and, if Sara was truthful with herself, she would open her eyes to her mother's fragility—not just emotional, but physical and mental. Her mother had forgotten her doctor's appointment one day and the next she forgot how to get to his office. How long had it been since Sara had shopped for her? Did she have anything in her refrigerator? Sara squeezed her eyes shut. Her mom couldn't take care of herself anymore. She had to get home.

No, she couldn't, she thought. She was empty. She had no core. What had she ever done to help her mother except visit her once every week, buy groceries for her, and take her to the doctor? She'd never granted her mother's wish to live with her after her father's suicide, when she'd been so lonely, so troubled. But Dr. B had supported her decision not to ask her mother to move in. *You have to take care of yourself; you are as deeply affected as she is.*

Stop! she ordered herself as she turned on her side and curled up in a fetal position. Almost drowning in the memory, she forced herself back into the present where, if she chose to stay, she'd live in an airy, light-filled place. Maybe, she could learn to live in the present where the only responsibility was to be happy.

Sara took the same seat as she had during the initial ET meeting. As before, all turned toward her, blinking artificial hues: gold, silver, green, purple, and Shirley's, an unnerving pink. Stan rang the gong to announce the beginning of the meeting. "Remember, team, Rules of Brainstorming are in effect." Eyes on Nona, he continued, "You were describing a relationship between a man and a woman without rules that would safeguard them from pain. Let's go on from there."

Sara had been thinking about that. She remembered to turn on her Inset and push record before she began to speak. Taking in a deep breath, she realized what she had to say next would be a risk. Stan might fire her. If not, she could give them a story that would shock, and, she firmly believed, engage the public. "Well, Walter mentioned jealousy. What if Peter sees Joyce hugging another man—something people do in this world just to show they like them—and he assumes it's a sexual gesture? He is overwhelmed with jealousy and pushes Joyce to the ground and hits the man. Joyce gets up crying and breaks it off with Peter. Then Peter starts to cry and ..."

Shirley cut in, "What? Hit? Cry? This is too weird. Too extreme. How can an audience understand such outlandish actions?"

Once again, Natalie intervened in Sara's favor. "Isn't that just the point? To give them something radically different?"

"Yes, I agree with Natalie. We need a hit. Yeah, I know we're taking a risk, but if I'm right, this could be the drama of the season. Go on, Sara." Stan added, smiling broadly at her. "I think we can finish this tonight and start rehearsal tomorrow morning. We're just a day or two away from production."

Sara continued to outline the plot. Occasionally, one of the members would ask for a time break as they spoke to their in-sets, creating the scenes, and trying out dialogue. Once Tom interjected, "Wow, really original, Sara!" As they worked on, she understood clearly that never had she felt this way in her world—filled with the warmth of acceptance and acknowledgement. For a moment she felt the familiar sting of conflict. Did she want to return to her world or not?

CHAPTER NINETEEN

It was Nona's turn to stand on the small circular stage in the middle of a darkened room crowded with spectators. A brilliant spotlight amplified her signature white, this time a form-fitting jumpsuit with diamonds around her waist and scattered through her hair and her eyebrows. After the MC announced her name, loud clicks and red light from applause devices flashed in the darkness, almost blinding Nona. The next contestant, dressed in green satin shorts and top, wiggled her whole body, making her breasts and rear jiggle; even her red curls bounced. Nona immediately recognized Natalie. Judging from the sound of the clicks and the red shimmer, the audience loved her, maybe almost as much as they loved Nona.

After six other contestants stood for the audience's appraisal, the MC announced the top three: Nona, Natalie, and Roberta. Each one stood on the stage again, this time after each round of clicks and flashes, the judges' scores lit up just above each contestant's head. Nona scored the highest with 115. Natalie was close behind at 110.

After the lights came on, people in the audience crowded around Nona and Natalie, congratulating both of them. Natalie drew her aside from the crowd's swell. "Congratulations, Nona! You are truly the most beautiful." She moved closer to whisper in Nona's ear. "I do hope you can forgive me for my rudeness when you visited my studio. I just don't want anything to happen to Paul because of me." After she checked the room, she continued, "I thought about you and what you said. Maybe I can trust you. I have this sense that you may understand what Paul and I feel for each other. Am I right?" She looked into Nona's eyes.

Nona paused before replying. "You *can* trust me; you are a client. And if I decided to divulge anything you said, I would have done it by now. I thought about our conversation too—"

Natalie interrupted. "Do you think the Junkers might be protesting because we are limited to certain kinds of feelings? If so, I want to..."

Too late, Nona put a restraining hand on Natalie's shoulder. Fabriana, overdressed in a pink ruffled dress covered with tiny rubies, stood close by staring at Natalie, her lime-green eyes cold. With studied casualness, she turned and sauntered over to a guard leaning against the wall. She whispered to him and pointed at Natalie. Nona said in a low voice, "I think you are about to be—" In three strides, the guard reached Natalie and grasped her arm.

"Better come with me, ma'am." Natalie snatched her arm away, pivoting to run, but the guard clamped down and safe-braceleted her. Nona started toward the guard to protest but checked her progress. Not a good idea, she thought, unless she wanted to be apprehended too. She whirled around and glared at Fabriana. If it were the last thing she did, she would cancel their heart-friend contract. Just as quickly as the anger gushed inside of her, she felt fear displace it. *Oh God of Reincarnation, what if Natalie reveals what I told her about Royce and Sara?* Could Nona escape the consequences? Maybe if she told them she was trying to trick Natalie into confessing her involvement with Paul. She had to think of something!

"This is a mistake! Let me go!" Natalie cried out, struggling with the guard. By this time, the room was silent while all eyes tracked her every move. Finally, the guard picked her up and carried her to the exit. Loud voices broke out and some audience members stared at Nona.

Worried that Natalie would confess and cause trouble for Nona, even ruin her life, her body tensed to run, until a tall man with a dancer's body and grace approached. "Perhaps you would want to escape all this unpleasantness?" he asked as he took her arm and began to guide her across the room. "My name is Giorgio. May I say that you are just as beautiful close up, maybe even more. I confess I wanted to be near enough to smell and touch you, if that is agreeable with you. I was bold enough to reserve an Erotic Pleasures room."

Familiar warmth cascaded through her body. She had not had sex for at least a week, a long time to go without. What better way to forget the trouble she could be in for a while and get away from the melee? Looking over her shoulder, she was sure one of Finance Police was watching her. A very good reason to leave. She followed Giorgio down some hallways and into a small room, walls glittering white, a white velvet rug, and in the middle, a bed covered in black brocade. Throwing off his silk robe, the only piece of clothing he wore, he stood in front of her as if to be admired, and admirable he was, with his supple body and tawny polished skin. Drawing close, he pulled her in and kissed her on her mouth, neck and shoulders with sculpted lips, silky and pliant. He slowly unzipped her jumpsuit and helped her out of it. "Would you care for some Instantlift?" he offered. She licked the pharm off his upturned hand.

The powder and his deft hands and tongue worked better than she expected. After, lying next to her, he traced circles on her belly. "Ah, Nona, you are exquisite. Maybe you would like to stay for a while? I also have some Vibrata to enhance our pleasure when we repeat."

Nona considered staying—further diversion from her anger at Fabriana and from her worry about Sara, Paul, Royce and especially Natalie, all crowding her thoughts. Was she responsible for what happened to Natalie? Could she have stopped it? But how, without being apprehended too? Yes, she was strongly tempted to stay but she had to get her eight hours and she couldn't oversleep and miss her first appointment. Another thought's unwelcome bite: what if the people who'd noticed Natalie and her conversing reported her? She must not do anything to bring attention to herself. "No thank you, Giorgio. Maybe another time."

The pleasure and relief from her sexual encounter with Giorgio wore off quickly, and the bath she was soaking in did little to diminish the tumult surging through her. Nona's hand fluttered down and touched her stomach, rubbing small circles to ease the gnawing pain located in the center. How could she be feeling disordered thoughts in her stomach? The names of disorders she'd once learned while studying the History of Ancient Mental Maladies rusted and stuck in her throat. Using all her mental effort, she forced the words out and whispered those old terms: *worry, anxiety, depression, guilt, delusions.*

She stopped, frightened by the last word. At first, she'd been convinced Sara was disordered. No longer. Now she was convinced that Sara was from another world. Unless, Sara was experiencing *delusions.* No, that didn't fit. She seemed too reasonable. No, reasonable wasn't the right word either. Many of the events she described weren't what any Mallite would call everyday occurrences. And the way that Sara's description of painful experiences hurt Nona wasn't reasonable either. How could another's pain echo inside of her? Nona ground her teeth in an effort to understand. Was it because she cared about her in a way unheard of in Mall, from a deep, untouched place, different from the place Royce occupied and a part she didn't even know existed? And strange that when Sara revealed how her husband had hurt her, Nona felt pulled close, almost like she was falling into her. Also strange, how these feelings caused intense discomfort but also joy, a high more profound than any pharm she knew of, but also a plummeting, especially when Sara seemed not to return her…what would Sara call this feeling? Some sort of intense connection?

Ah, she thought, *this should be what a true heart-bond feels like;* however, the Mall Fathers forbade intense feelings. Instead they touted easy pleasures and developed pharms that made the user feel euphoric or peaceful or lustful or excited, all designed to enhance sex, eating, virtual reality experiences, anything to eliminate the desire or need for close connection. Abruptly, she stood up, almost slipping in her hurry to get out of the tub. Perhaps these thoughts, circling in her head over and over, were the first sign of a new kind of disorder.

She needed to see Royce! He was the only one she could talk to—the way she should be able to talk to a heart-friend. But not in Mall. And never Fabriana. So what if she'd revealed her secret pair-knot to Royce—that was so long ago. Since then, Royce and she had tried to follow the Code and only seen each other once in a while, although each had occasionally given in to that strong desire not just to have sex but to be together. Fabriana did not know about those times. If she did, Fabriana would not keep quiet. She loved being in the know. Besides being an exemplary Mallite, she was one of the worst gossips Nona had ever known. She would report Nona for sure.

So strong was the desire to talk about Sara, about Royce, about her confusion, and about her growing need for something more, she'd been close to telling Natalie everything at their last meeting. Now that Natalie was in a holding cell, what would happen next? Would it help if Nona went to the Finance Police to insist on Natalie's innocence? How much had Natalie disclosed? Would they believe her or would Nona also be arrested? Nona twisted her hands and moaned. So far the FPs had not checked in on her progress with Sara. Would her appearance at the MHP's Finance Police office jog their memories?

She held her head as all of these possibilities assaulted her. She didn't know what to do. Could this havoc of thought and feelings harm her brain? Maybe the Mall Fathers were right to simplify their lives. But she had no desire to go back to that one-dimensional existence. She could admin Nepenthe, Ennuend, or even

Freedomfrum; employ a masseur; go to a movement class; have sex. If she did admin, the deep interest, the unusual affection would be eliminated too. Even the most potent stim could not equal what she felt for Sara, Natalie, Royce, or even Paul. Each one of them made Nona feel stunningly alive. Perhaps the Mall Fathers were not so wise, after all. They'd eliminated possibilities for deep attachments so Mallites would feel little pain. Was experiencing pain worth it? If Sara left, Nona knew she would suffer. If Royce disappeared— just thinking about not seeing him again stung. Many pharms could purge her of these feelings, yet she resisted adminning.

Toweled off, she sat on the bed, sleeping prep in hand, when darkness engulfed her quarters. Not again, she thought, although she wasn't really troubled. Who cared when it was sleep time? Lying there, eyes squeezed shut in an effort to sleep, she heard a soft tapping at the door. She stumbled over, fingers touching blank buttons from memory, wondering who would take this kind of risk. When the door slid open, she heard a familiar voice say, "It's Royce."

She stood aside so he could enter. "Pardon me for my rudeness, but what are you doing here? You know the consequences for visiting someone in her quarters during sleep-time."

"I never would have chanced it if we weren't in this blackout."

"I don't want anything to happen to you or to me," she added. She guided him to her bed where they sat side by side. He put one arm around her while reaching around to cup her breast.

"Oh, Royce, I don't think we should." She gently removed his hand. "Damn," she added, "they're turning up the heat again." She used the sheet to blot the perspiration from under her breasts.

He pulled away and sat up. "Yeah, it's become almost standard procedure. I'm almost getting used to it. Anyway, I thought you would want to have sex; I know I do. It's been weeks since we've even touched, although I confess sex isn't why I chanced visiting you in your quarters."

Nona caressed his arm. "I do want sex, but I'm afraid if we start up again, someone will find out. We'll be sanctioned." She stopped for a moment. "But you know what? I hardly seem to care. Everything that used to matter doesn't seem to anymore."

"Strange you say that, because I feel the same way. I need to talk to you. You're the only person I can trust." He paused and took in a deep breath. "I'm thinking of doing something risky."

Nona gripped his hand. What if he confessed to being a Junker? It would be her duty to report him, but she wouldn't. She didn't seem to care anymore about doing her so-called duty. "You can trust me. Please tell me."

"It's a lot more than trust that I feel for you, Nona." He stroked her hair.

"I know. Are you concerned that would bother me?"

"No, not exactly." He drew in a deep breath. "I want to pair-knot indefinitely."

Nona's heart picked up speed. "We can't—you know that. No one will issue us a contract. And if Mall Guards notice we're seeing each other on the—you know all of this." Was this the kind of feeling Sara described when she talked about her mother and had felt once for the man Sara called her husband? That strong, deep-inside feeling. Did she feel this for Royce? And for Sara? "Do you mean love?" she asked.

"I beg your pardon. How could that be? Love is what people feel for children, like we would have if …" Nona felt him lie down and heard him moan. "What am I going to do? I guess *love* sounds right. Nona, it's so strong for me. For both of us." He sat back up. "Now I'm going reveal something else that is forbidden. I attended a Junker meeting and I'm going to another."

Nona was stunned into silence. Oh God of Reincarnation, what was she going to do? This was exactly what she feared. Either she reported him or she was complicit. Yet she knew she too was skirting the regulations with Sara. And with Natalie. And she felt something for Royce that seemed to be widening, deepening, and even stronger than before. Much more than sexual feelings. She felt a cord inside her attached to him, pulling him closer and closer.

"I'm afraid for you. If you get apprehended, you know what will happen. Are you willing to take that kind of chance?"

"Yes. And please go with me. Maybe the Junkers will be able to change the rules. Like being able to sleep in the same bed with you. Like being able to change employment."

Nona fumbled for his hand and then held it. "But how can these rules be changed? They have been in effect for hundreds of years."

"That doesn't mean they are right or beneficial. And the Junkers don't agree with them either. Why do you think they're causing so much trouble?"

"I don't think I could attend a Junker meeting. I—"

Just then a warning voice announced, "Please do not be alarmed. Finance Police will be entering your quarters in three minutes." Without a word, she and Royce rushed to the door. Nona pushed the code sequence, and Royce ran out.

Oh God of Reincarnation, she prayed, *I hope he makes it to his quarters without the FPs seeing him.* She waited for longer than three minutes. Had something happened? When the door slid open, she stood by the bed, naked, trembling. It was still unbearably hot and too dark to make out how FPs entered.

"Excuse the interruption, ma'am. We have been searching floor by floor for the presence of Junkers."

The sleep lights flickered on. In the dim light, Nona could make out two FPs pushing a safe-braceleted Royce in front of them. The

FPs were silent for a moment and then one said, "You may want to throw something on, ma'am. You know the rule."

Oh damn, she said to herself, *that stupid rule that Mallites can never appear completely naked in public.* "Please excuse me, but you are in my quarters, not a public space. It was too hot to put anything on." As she found and slid into her silk robe, she made eye contact with Royce. She couldn't tell if his glance revealed anything.

One of the FPs asked, "Do you know this man? He was outside your door. He may be the Junker we're looking for."

"Yes, he is a fellow MHP, one of our top profit-makers, certainly *not* a Junker."

"We'll see about that. Was he in your quarters about four minutes ago?"

Should she lie? What if Royce admitted being here? "Uh, no—how would that be possible? It is prohibited." *Please, please,* she thought, *let them believe me!*

Royce said, "I told you that I was merely walking in the corridor."

"Yes, you said that, but who goes for walk during sleep-time?"

"I did, because I could not sleep in that dark and hot room. I felt closed in."

"Sir," Nona tried to sound as respectful as possible, "this man is an honored, valued MHP; surely the last person to suspect in your search for a Junker."

They whispered among themselves and one said, "We'll release him, but if we find out that he was in your quarters, we will apprehend both of you." She caught Royce's eye and tilted her head in an effort to signal that they should talk later. Royce nodded slightly. The FPs ushered him out. When the door slid closed, she collapsed on the bed.

CHAPTER TWENTY

Sara stood before the mirror admiring the dress Antonio, the fashion consultant, had recommended for the opening of the play. Her pleasure dwindled when she went over her last conversation with Stan. Wasn't it too soon to present the play? she'd asked. They had rehearsed only once. Didn't he think the acting was sometimes a little wooden? Maybe, she suggested, she should revise the scene with violence? No, no, he had reassured her. This drama will be huge success!

Only Nona knew that this play sprang from her life, not just her imagination. If only Nona could be there and not at some beauty contest. Well, not exactly true—Paul knew, but she doubted he'd be there. Instead he was probably stirring up trouble with other Junkers. *Oh God, please don't let some big disturbance ruin this for me!*

Sometimes, she almost believed she had made up the play's entire narrative. Was it a sign that this Shangri La was working its magic on her? As she had worked with the team on the drama, they—especially Stan—had praised and encouraged her. When she had suggested that Peter threaten—she knew better than to use the word suicide—to end his life if Joyce left him, Stan had patted her back. How she had warmed to his touch and to his words, "Wow! Really original, Sara! I can't recall any ET using that in any of their dramas. I wager that we'll double our profits because of your efforts." She felt creative and appreciated. She felt special. She searched her memory for any time she'd ever felt that way before coming here and couldn't remember anything. *If only Mother were here. No,* she thought, *don't think about her now!* Instead, she daydreamed that Stan would whisk her away from the party to one of the dozens of special rooms for sexual liaisons. Just once, and then she would find her way home.

Was she kidding herself? Even her husband, who once seemed too attractive for his own good, would look average here, not that he worked at looking good. The thought of seeing him now, in this world, made her queasy. Besides, if she went home, her appearance might change back, a thought that caused bile-tasting panic to rise in her throat.

She concentrated on the celery-green silk dress with a plunging neckline, fitting tightly around her bust and then floating softly to the ground. Sara touched the taut springiness of her enhanced breasts, exposed almost to the nipples. Back home, so ashamed of her body, she would never have worn something like this. But here the dress felt exactly right.

Still too early to leave for the theater, she paced her room. If only Nona were here. She had begged Nona to cancel so she could attend the opening, but no, she'd said she had committed to the beauty contest. Finally, the soft bell on her communicator alerted her that it was time. *You're on your own, kid,* Sara thought as she exited the room.

Although the elevator was crowded, Sara squeezed through to the glass wall, where, through the arboretums on each floor, she watched rivers of people moving about. So many people—maybe too many, she thought while squeezed between two men who talked over her head about her play. "I heard it will be the talk of the first-raters—really different." Although she delighted in their excitement, she squirmed at their closeness. Was it her imagination or did the one on the right press even closer? When she turned to look at him, he grinned at her and touched the top of her exposed breast. Sara frowned and leaned as far away from him as possible. He shrugged his shoulders and looked out the glass wall.

Just before she exited at the Live Performance level, she closed her eyes and prayed, *If there is a God, please let this be a success.* She was the one who had created most of the play. Her team believed in her. She'd never had much success before; she needed this.

On the Throughway to the Theater Division, she went over the drama in its final form. *Will all the scenes work? How will the audience react?* She was so distracted that she stumbled in shock at the sight of the hologram of herself recounting the beginning of the story, followed by Walter, the narrator, recommending that people credit-transfer to *see the most unusual story interactive theater has ever offered.* She threaded her way through the throng of people crowding around the repeating hologram and slipped in the side door to take a seat in the back row of the circular theater. As she waited, she fidgeted, more and more nervous about the crowd's reaction. Would they respond to the concept? And how would they change it once they had seen all of it and were allowed to interact? Slowly the lights dimmed until they were in blackness except for the one light encircling Walter.

"People of Mall, you are about to experience an amazing story, and you will be entertained like never before. Before we begin, I would like to acknowledge Sara, the team member of Realized Fantasies largely responsible for today's narrative." The circle of light swung around to Sara, dazzling her eyes as she tried to smile nonchalantly. After the light swung back to Walter, he began the story. "Joyce had not pair-knotted for a long period. In fact, because of an intense attraction, she had been guilty of an illicit pair-knot several months prior to this time. Of course, she was discovered, but in this world, there are no real sanctions except for people shunning you in an informal manner. Still, it was unpleasant enough for her to break off this illicit relationship. After that, she had trouble finding a relationship as sexually exciting and, experiencing rather severe ennui, she sought the help of a Mental Health Practitioner who prescribed a potent pharm, followed by a visit to a Pleasure Palace and...Well, let's see what happens." The light on Walt dimmed while the circular stage lit up. About ten actors milled around the set of a typical Pleasure Palace. Two women sitting at a table began to talk.

Nickie: See that man over there? I recently pair-knotted with him. I don't know—Peter's good at sex, but he's kind of intense as a companion.

Joyce: Was it pleasurable enough to want to renew when the time is up?

Nickie: I'm not sure. I...Well, I'll confess to you. I'm also interested in Ted—you know, the one I introduced you to during the afternoon break two days ago? The trouble is the pair-knot with Peter lasts two more weeks. Oh, I guess I can wait until then."

Joyce: You mean, it's not worth breaking the knot?

Nickie: You of all people should know that. How did you—

Peter (walks over and interrupts them): Hi, Nickie, how are you? *(His eyes stay on Joyce as he speaks politely to Nickie.)* I'd like to greet your friend here, but I've never met her.

Joyce: My name's Joyce. *(Her eyes lock with his. The light narrows to a bright beam illuminating just the two of them.)*

Nickie (in the background, not visible): Would either of you mind if I left you for a moment? I just saw my employer, and I should greet him.

Peter: No, I don't mind. Do you, Joyce? *(Joyce shakes her head as Nickie leaves.)* Joyce, will you meet me here tomorrow at the same time? And come with me to the private room I use? *(He leans over and kisses her on the forehead gently.)*

Joyce: I... yes...

Sara froze. What was the audience doing? It sounded like tittering. Were they misinterpreting the characters' actions? *What's wrong? It must be the actors. They sound hollow and false, alternating between wooden and melodramatic.* They hadn't sounded like that in rehearsal, had they? Although the audience's faces were veiled in darkness, Sara looked around to see how they were reacting. She turned to Stan sitting next to her. Why was he smiling? She started to ask him when she heard someone chuckle. A few other laughed. They weren't getting it! This was too painful, she thought as she squinted her eyes to hold back tears. Not only were they misunderstanding, they were laughing at something deeply personal. Why had she drawn on these particular memories? She'd never really forgiven herself for getting involved with Carl. How could she have been so susceptible to him? Yes, he'd been charming until his jealousy became a problem, but hadn't she secretly been flattered, that someone had cared that much for her? And then after they were married for a while, he began to take her for granted. The tables turned, and she began to feel jealousy bite at her.

Turning her attention back to the play, she could hardly sit still as she watched the scene after Joyce and Peter pair-knot, when Joyce innocently hugged a male friend and Peter hit the man, then pushed Joyce to the floor. He screamed at her so loudly, some of the audience covered their ears. Joyce ran away, sobbing way too wildly. The actors, now madly overacting, reminded Sara of characters in old-time silent melodramas, with voices added. The audience guffawed, and she, too, had to fight an overwhelming impulse to laugh uncontrollably—or was it to cry? Embarrassed, she fought an urge to run. *It'll get better,* she thought. Twitching and squirming, she sat through the scene where Peter begged forgiveness. Finally, when he threatened to kill himself, his sobs loud and phony, she laughed with the rest of the audience, but her hilarity skirted on hysteria. Hand held against her mouth, she jumped up and stumbled out of the theater.

When the soft gong awoke Sara, the memory of the performance bubbled up, staining her usual early-morning happiness. A slight but insistent pain throbbed in her left temple.

How could she face the team? Burrowing into her pillow, she moaned. What was she going to do? Would she be fired? Maybe she could call in sick, but was that allowed?

Shut up! she whispered when the gong changed to a voice warning her to hurry. Slowly, she rose and dragged herself to her beloved bathroom, something she would have to give up because no doubt she would be fired today. So what, she thought, she was leaving this place. *Paul will get me out of here, if he can, and if they don't get caught.* She stuffed that thought in the back of her consciousness and threw on one of her new outfits.

When she arrived at work, she opened her mouth, ready to babble apologies for being late and mostly for the flop she had created. Before she could utter a sound, her eyes shut against the red lights flashing all around her. Loud popping sounds filled the air. She opened her eyes and spied black clickers in the team's hands. What was going on? Then she remembered these were devices audiences used instead of applauding. Stan hurried toward her and hugged her, announcing, "We have a huge hit, thanks to you!" Stunned for a moment, Sara stared at Stan and then looked around at the smiling faces. She grasped Stan's arm to pull him aside, "Stan, wait a minute. What are you talking about? The audience laughed at the story. I was so upset I had to leave the theater before the drama was over."

Stan's smile faded. "Hey, team, now we know why Sara left. She was embarrassed that the audience was laughing." He tilted her face up to look into her eyes. "Oh honey, don't you get it? Making people laugh is the hardest thing to do. But *you* did it. The actors took six flash calls! And, listen to this, we haven't received a count of how many also reserved interactive time, but I haven't any doubt that it will top our highest expectations."

Sara hovered between anger and confusion mixed with joy. "Are you trying to tell me that I created a comedy without knowing it?"

"Yeah, and isn't it strange that none of us saw how funny it was when we were creating it?"

Stifling the urge to cry, Sara said through clenched teeth, "I didn't mean it to be funny, and there is nothing the least bit humorous about the story."

Walter removed his headset and walked over. "Sara, I don't want to offend you, but may I offer some advice? Could the problem perhaps be a little hurt pride because it didn't have the effect you had planned? You've created a comic masterpiece, so why not take full credit? After all, creative inspiration sometimes works without our being fully aware, you know what I mean?"

Sara looked down. "I don't know. I want to believe what you're saying ..." Stopping herself before she made an inadvertent reference to her world, she said, "Never mind. Really, Walter, I appreciate your encouragement." Pulling on Stan's arm, she said to the team, "Excuse me, I don't mean to be rude, but there's something I need to talk about in private with Stan."

Stan nodded and announced to the group, "Listen, everybody, I think you'll agree we don't need to revise, so I am declaring today and tomorrow to be Success Holidays with two full days' credit transferred to your accounts. And don't forget the Celebration Festival tonight." Laughing and talking excitedly, they all surrounded Sara, touching, hugging, and patting her before leaving, except for Delta, who lingered nearby. After the others left, she said, "I wasn't quite sure what would happen with the crying scene, but it was a masterstroke. Actually, I don't know which the audience thought was funnier, the crying or the hitting. I want you to know"— she touched Sara's arm "—although I had some reservations about working with you at first, and I hope my honesty does not offend,

175

now I think you're the best-ever addition to the team. I hope you and Stan renew after the six-month probation period is up." Eyes now on Stan, she added, "You'll need her when I'm gone."

Stan caught her arm as Delta was preparing to leave. "What do you mean, *gone*? Are you crossing over to another team?"

Sara noticed that underneath the pearl-like perfection of Delta's skin, there was an ashy tone. Something must be wrong with her, but what? She couldn't be sick. Hadn't Stan or Nona told her that there was no more illness? Sara watched her whisper something to Stan, who sobered. With a perfunctory "beg your pardon" to Sara, Delta moved to the door. What strange behavior; maybe something she would ask Stan about later. Even though they were alone, she said in a low voice, "Shouldn't we revise it, so the audience can understand what I had in mind?"

Stan shook his head. "Are you disordered? Oh, pardon my overreaction. Why fix something when it works great? You're a success, and that's all that matters."

Sara looked him in the eyes. "I'm a success through a mistake. I don't know how I did it or if I could do it again. Besides, it hurt that people laughed at something that I wanted to show was so painful and important."

"Excuse me, Sara, but what's so bad about that? If you don't mind my saying this, it would be good for you to lighten up. Maybe if you laughed at this thing you created, oops, beg your pardon, that *happened* to you, you wouldn't get all disordered over it. Go to the next performance, and I'll wager you'll laugh too."

She rubbed her temples, trying to ease the headache that had been growing since she awoke. "Right now, I would have trouble laughing at anything. My head hurts. I could admin, I guess, but I am still a little uncertain about pharms. Do you have any suggestions for a way to relax that isn't through a pharmaceutical?"

"Baby, baby, how are you getting through the days without any pharms? No wonder you're acting, excuse me for saying so, disordered." He thought for a moment. "All I can think of is something Numbers-up do, you know, when pharms don't work; they go to Spiritual Practitioners."

"You think one might be able to somehow help?"

"Yeah, that might be the reason Natalie was meeting with that SP, Paul." His cheerful expression turned grim. "Did you notice that Nat didn't show up this morning? She was apprehended last night for something. No one knows. It must be a mistake. I thought they would have released her by now. She's a renowned actress who has never done anything against the Code." He ran his hand through his shiny blond hair. "I wager she's with Paul. If so, she needs to stop meeting with him. Missing a Team Meeting is unheard of."

"Does Paul have some sort of hold over her?" Jealousy burned in her stomach for a moment. Maybe she was the one he had a hold over...

Stan shook his head. "Like what? That woman can have sex with anyone she wants, and believe me, she does. I had to remind her more than once that sex with me was against the Code."

Sara's chest constricted. "What a stupid rule. What's the worst thing that could happen?" The urge to pull him close was so strong, she had to clasp her hands tightly behind her.

"Distraction from our primary goal—profit. Excuse me for pointing this out, but you should know by now."

She sighed. "I suppose. Anyway, you were saying that an SP might help me?"

"Right. I've heard SPs practice something called meditation. I'm not exactly sure what that is. Numbers-up supposedly get some benefit from it. It might do the same for you."

"I know what meditation is."

177

"I don't know how it works, but why not try it? I must admit, I'm worried you'll burn out, and we need you too much for that to happen. If this meditation thing doesn't work, you better self-admin."

"Okay, I guess I could. Are these Spiritual Practitioners located on the same level as the MHPs?"

"No, they're on the fiftieth level in the Spiritual Peace Sector."

Standing, she looked up and, for a second, his eyes gleamed with what looked like desire but quickly changed to a bland kindness. "Thanks for listening and for the advice, Stan."

"You bet, sweetie; I'd do anything to help. You saved our profit behinds." He wrapped his long arms around her and hugged her tight. Sara let her body lean into his, stung by the quickness of her arousal. She searched his eyes for matching feelings but found only the blank cheerfulness of an empty blue sky. He wasn't kidding when he said no sex with someone he worked with. Yet he didn't need to hug her so close.

"I hope, for your sake, that this success wasn't a fluke."

"If *fluke* means you think you aren't responsible for this success," he said as he released her, "think again."

Sara left the workroom and saw Delta crumpled on one of the chairs in the waiting area. Sara stepped over and touched her black silk hair. "Delta, what is it? Are you ill?"

Delta's head jerked up. "Is that more of your odd humor?"

"No, uh, I'm sorry, but you seem…" She stopped, wondering how to say it without sounding too strange, "I mean, you look like you're suffering."

"No, that can't be," Delta snapped then she softened. "Please excuse my discourtesy. I allowed too much time to pass between admins, that's all. I am surprised at how often I need Freedomfrum since I learned …" She looked down for a moment. "I might as well tell you. My number is up."

No use trying to suppress the meaning of these ominous words. She knew that was how Mallites referred to dying. It chilled instead of reassured her. She didn't know what to say next. Just how did these people die? She had nursed a secret hope that somehow they had discovered immortality or, at least, the secret of incredibly long lives. But here was Delta, clearly fading away, though she seemed so young, surely younger than Sara. Her youthful appearance could very well be due to cosmetic altering. She felt unsure of what to say to Delta who acted depressed in this world of little or no sadness. "What are you going to do next?'

"I don't have enough credit for more Freedomfrum." She frowned. "At least not at the strength I need. I plan to go to the Spiritual Practitioners section."

Was Delta really dying? Because of some disease? Could Sara catch it and die too? That couldn't be; Nona said Mall Fathers had eliminated all communicable illnesses. Still, she could not stop the fear spilling through her. She backed up to leave, then stopped when she saw Delta's pleading eyes.

"I know this is a lot to ask, but will you go with me?"

"What? Now?"

"Yes. We have the day off. Of course if you have something else ..." She bowed her head.

It was true; they had a day off. And what a lucky coincidence that Delta wanted to do exactly what Stan had suggested she do. Maybe the experience would be interesting, even uplifting. She might run into Paul. She wanted to see him. She could ask for his help with meditating or information about the next Junker meeting. Or maybe she wanted to find out about his relationship with Natalie. To fuck him? She almost moaned aloud. One minute she wanted sex with Stan, the next minute she fantasized about Paul. What was happening to her? This obsession with men and sex—hadn't she grown past that? Out loud, she said, "Sure, I'll go with you."

179

Like a tourist, Sara gawked at the church-like facades lining each side of the lane. Delta walked at a faster pace, searching for something specific. "This is the place—come look! Oh, I beg your pardon, I meant to say, please," Delta called back to Sara as she stopped to read a red neon sign. "Chapel of Unparalleled Renewal." On the stairs two holographic men, bare-chested and golden-muscled, sat in lotus position with eyes closed, breathing in unison. From somewhere a bassoon-like voice urged the audience to enter and engage in *this superior practice for the ultimate in peace and relaxation.* "I think this is just what I need. Would you also like to enter this place?" Delta asked.

For a second, Sara considered saying yes just to keep an eye on Delta. "No, I want to find the SP, Paul. Do you know him?"

"Only by sight. He's Nat's SP, although I have no idea why she needs one. Her number isn't up." She moved up the stairs. "Thanks for coming with me, Sara; I'll be okay now."

Sara continued to walk down the Boulevard of Renewal bordered by ornate chapels, their rectangular edifices plain except for brilliantly colored doors, and even a few church-like facades with tall spires. When she slowed in front of a gold and white high-arched door, hundreds of tiny angels emerged, darting and swooping around her face and singing in high, childish voices,

Sweet one, stop here a while!
Within you'll find a place
of pleasure so very rare.
Peace and beauty beyond compare.
Renewal anxiety will fade away,
preparing you for that fateful day.

Although delighted by their miniature perfection, Sara drifted toward a small crowd. Floating above the knot of people, a green neon outline of a woman cried silver tears. Sara couldn't see over those gathered, but she could hear a woman whispering, "I have so little time left." After a moment of silence, she continued, in a louder but husky voice, "Please, please tell me how to get through this!"

"Many find thinking about reincarnation, the opportunity to live a whole new life, reassuring at a time like this," a deep voice answered, a familiar voice, both dreaded and desired. Paul. She'd never quite believed that he was a practicing SP.

The woman cried out, "I want the life I have now. I don't want to start all over again." She stifled a sob and the crowd edged away. All Sara could hear now was the voice's indistinct whispering to the woman; she gazed into the air as if the SP stood there, but no one was there.

The woman snapped, "Don't give me any of those old myths about some sort of spirit life after death." She started to cry again. "I wish I *could* believe!" The crowd's murmured responses swelled as they wheeled around to scurry away. The neon sign disappeared. Left was a bone-thin woman, hair tinted cherry-red, clenching the back of one of two green and purple cushioned chairs.

Sara asked, "Pardon me, were you talking to Paul?"

She turned to stare at Sara. As she gasped, she sank into one of the chairs. "Yes," she managed to say. Then she glared at Sara. "I can't believe what I did." She turned, almost toppling the chair.

Lost, Sara asked, "What, talk to an SP?"

"No," the woman answered. "Cry." She peered at Sara. "Why aren't you repulsed, like all the others? I'm so ashamed." She rose, and then sat down again. Sara sat down opposite her, studying her made-up face, stretched a little too tight.

"It's okay; you're just upset."

The woman searched Sara's face. "How can you be this kind? Oh, you must be an SP. Where do you practice?"

Sara shook her head. "No, I'm not. Do you know where Paul practices?"

"Oh, you want a spiritual consult? Your number must be up, too. I don't know where he goes when he leaves. No one does. And he doesn't appear on a regular schedule. She paused, pressing her eyelids then said, "He did set up a private appointment with me tomorrow, thank the God of Reincarnation. Not here, and I can't tell you where we will be meeting; he made me promise."

"I understand. I hope your meeting with him helps."

"He has to help. Nothing else has." A sob erupted. As if she might be sick, she flew out of the chair with her hand on her mouth. Sara watched her disappear into the crowd of seekers. Behind her she heard a rustle. Turning around, she saw Paul. Did he appear out of thin air?

"What are you doing here?" he demanded.

"I was looking for you."

His mouth compressed. "Why? I told you that I will contact you when the time comes."

"I know, I know. I came because—well partly—I hoped you could teach me how to meditate. I'm stressed over the play, over escaping, over the changes I seem to be going through. I thought it would help."

"I don't think I am the best person to ask. If I were alone with you, I might get carried away, and now I'm not sure a sexual encounter would be a good idea. We need to be focused. I can give you a few names, if you'd like."

Almost the same argument Stan used, and she fought the same urge to reach out to him. She wanted to say *So what? Let's fuck ourselves silly.* "What about Natalie? You have sex with her even though you're her SP."

"We have a unique relationship. I'm not sure you or anyone could understand because..."

"Yes I could. Where I come from, we have all kinds of relationships not possible here. I wondered if she might be with you."

"Me? Wasn't she at the ET team meeting?"

"No, didn't you hear about what happened?"

"What do you mean? I went to the beauty contest for just enough time to see her take second. Your MHP won. Then I left. The crowd around them was so thick I couldn't get near her."

She shifted her weight from one foot to the other. "She was apprehended."

He stared at her a moment. "And she's still in custody?"

"I don't know. She wasn't at the team meeting. Stan was really worried."

"That makes two of us. I'll find out what's happened and I *will* find a way to get her out."

Butterflies danced in Sara's stomach. She had expected a small gathering for the Celebration Festival, not this huge crowd pulsing with color and ringing with melodious voices. She recognized Shirley from the ET team touching some of the tiny purple jewels scattered throughout her lavender-tinted hair as she studied her reflection in one of the hundreds of gilded mirrors lining the walls. She even emanated a lavender fragrance. Looking behind her image, she recognized Sara's reflected eyes. "I wore these amethysts in celebration of our success—actually, *your* success, Sara. Because of you, we will earn scads of credit in the future, and besides, you are so amusing to work with. I wish I could come up with such..." Shirley stopped midsentence to reattach one of the jewels.

At the mention of the play, Sara lowered her eyes, mumbling, "The success is as much the team's as mine. And I love how those jewels look in your hair." Sara looked around the room. "Do you know Nona, the MHP?"

Shirley's silken forehead creased. "I don't know her personally, but of course I know who she is, everybody does. Why would you think otherwise? Oh excuse me, if I seemed rude."

Sara squirmed inwardly at her error. "Oh, right, of course. She is so well known. Is she here yet?"

Shirley's sidelong glance caught her own reflection once more. "I don't think so." She slid her eyes away from the mirror to search the room. "When she comes in, believe me, everyone notices."

"I heard she won the contest last night." Sara also allowed her eyes to seek out gratification in the mirror.

"Yes, you can credit last night's info of the contest. Our little Natalie came in second. Oh, it's so worrying that she was apprehended. Really, what could that darling little woman do to cause her arrest? But I wager they'll let her go very soon. Anyway, the holo was quite diverting, you should have seen it. Everyone was talking about it; in fact, when I viewed it, I had to share a booth with two other people. At first, I was a tiny bit irritated, but one of them was this gorgeous man; you should have seen the bulge in his shorts. We left before the holo-cast was over. No point waiting, don't you agree? And after viewing the contest finale, I'm sure there wasn't much to see." Shirley's dancing eyes searched out Sara's in the mirror. "I just realized, if you missed last night's info-holo, you missed the critique of our play."

"You're right, I did. I was too upset. Darn," she added, hoping that was a mild enough expletive to pass the courtesy rule.

"Just rent day-old info. It's less credit that way. Anyway, not one negative review!"

"Oh, good! And I will rent the holo."

"Yes, you should and..." Shirley's words trailed off, her searching eyes hungry. "Ah, do you see those two men by the flower arrangement? They are delectable. How to choose?"

Sara laughed. "If you like sex so much, why don't you pair-knot for convenience?"

"Oh no, never. No man could hold my interest for a month. Hmm, that's not exactly true; there was this unusual man—actually, an SP. So unbelievably sexual. I had one encounter with him, but then he discovered Natalie and almost immediately they pair-knotted." She craned her neck to follow the two men's progress to the refreshment table.

"What about this SP?" Sara prompted.

Eyes still on the men, Shirley replied, "I just had one time with him." She leaned close to Sara to whisper, "Who cares about spiritual advice? Not me, but I'd pretend to need it, if I could have sex with him again. I'd gladly pair-knot with him so I could fuck him silly."

Sara stared, surprised at Shirley's use of the word *fuck*. No one else seemed to notice; no Courtesy Enforcers seemed to be around. She opened her mouth to comment when she saw Tom and Walter waving to them. Shirley waved back. "I want to admin with them, how about you?"

Sara shook her head. "No, I'll pass."

"Then, please excuse me. I'm sure you understand."

Alone, Sara wandered, openly staring. Above, a huge rotating chandelier of colored crystals poured rainbow light on the swirling crowd. Following a woman dressed in a sequined body suit flashing its own rainbow sparks, Sara stopped next to the refreshment table loaded with food and the drink, Rush, in a variety of brilliant colors. After choosing a few things, including her favorite, the crumbly little purple fruit tart, she chose the red beverage and maneuvered through the crowd to a vacant chair. Sipping slowly, she savored the flavor of a berry she couldn't identify, something like all her favorites combined. She sat and watched the guests move from one group to the next, stopping only long enough to admire themselves in the mirrors, to grab a chilled Rush or a pharm-soaked patch from the tray of a passing server.

After drinking half of her Rush, Sara's body began to echo the crowd's manic activity. No one sat or even moved at a normal pace, she thought. These drinks must contain some kind of stim. Too wired for eating, she bolted from her chair to pace through the crowd, eyes searching for a familiar face until she he caught sight of Shirley and Delta talking to a short, well-built, completely hairless man. Sara stared at the only garment he wore, a black jewel-encrusted silk loincloth designed to emphasize a very large penis. Delta, too, was almost naked, except for a spray of diamonds on the transparent filmy garment covering her pubic area and her areolas. She stopped talking long enough to embrace and congratulate Sara.

"Did you ever formally meet Xavier, our lighting technician, when we were rehearsing?" Delta asked.

The little man, almost clownish in his odd perfection, kissed her hand. "May I congratulate you on a work of remarkable originality?"

"Oh, thanks. You did a wonderful job on the lighting too."

The little man beamed his thanks and emptied a packet of a stardust-like powder in his hand. In a flash, he had licked and sucked up the entire contents. "Oh, I'm sorry—I consumed the whole packet of Instantlift without asking if either of you wanted any. My apologies."

"You better share next time, you cute, greedy thing!" Delta flirted, her voice almost strident.

Sara moved closer to Delta and whispered, "Are you okay?"

"Oh yes, I had an uplifting session with Armand. I highly recommend him. And tonight? I intend to be amused like never before. My last fete, you know." She pulled away from Sara and cried out, "Oh, there's Stan," pointing to the center of large group. "Stan!" she called out, waving frantically. Walking next to him was

Nona, cool and elegant in an ivory, form-fitting, floor-length silk sheath, with a high mandarin collar. A pearl barrette held her hair in a complicated twist. On her other side walked a tall, dark man dressed in black, with his shirt unbuttoned, a physical opposite that highlighted her pale beauty. Smitten, the dark man couldn't stop touching her. Sara pushed her way through the crowd, congratulating Nona for winning the beauty contest as soon as she reached her.

"Oh yes, that was pleasant; but you, so much more than I, deserve to be congratulated," she said as she leaned against the man accompanying her. Turning to look into his smoky-gray eyes, she asked, "Don't you think Giorgio is appealing?" Nona's loud laugh startled Sara. When she looked closely, Sara could see Nona's enlarged pupils and her flushed cheeks. Nona laughed again and said to Giorgio, "Maybe we should leave so—oh, dear, I don't want to appear rude." She wrapped both arms around him and closed her eyes. Sara thought Nona's mouth twisted down, but perhaps she imagined it, so fleeting the moment. Giorgio whispered something in her ear to which she nodded, eyes wide open again. "Sara, dear, we are rushing off to more pleasurable pursuits. Perhaps we can communicate later and schedule an appointment?"

"Maybe. I'll communicate with you in the morning."

Nona, already walking away, looked over her shoulder and nodded.

Sara jumped when Stan touched her shoulder. "I don't want to offend you, but are you aware that you are staring at Nona?"

"I guess I was," she murmured as she watched them leave. "I've never seen Nona like this. Was she loaded? High? You know, did she admin a lot?"

Stan, wearing only a pair of rainbow patterned shorts, stood so close she could smell his citrus cologne and see the sheen on his polished skin. "Of course, hasn't everyone?"

"I guess. So where were they going that was so much more fun?"

"Honey, I bet you can guess. They were pretty obvious."

"You mean Nona left so she could have sex with that guy?"

"What? You're surprised?"

"Sort of. I thought she was maybe above that. I don't know why. At least I thought she had more class and would be more discreet."

"Above sex? Are you joking? We all just about live for sex. We're talking about one of the most pleasurable activities there is, right?"

An ancient longing, like a strong undertow, pulled her closer to him. Her eyes caught his. "What about you?"

Indifference shuttered his eyes. "To tell you the truth, sometimes I don't want to take the time. It interferes with work. A one-timer here and there is enough for me." He shrugged his shoulders and smiled sheepishly. "Hey, this stuff is way too serious to be talking about at a fete. This is a night for amusement. What would be most pleasurable? You name it, and we'll do it." He scanned the room. "I hoped Natalie would show up but she's not here. I would be able to see those red curls bouncing up and down."

"Shirley thinks her arrest is a mistake and that she'll be released soon."

"Sure, that's what'll happen. No way would she be guilty of anything." He sighed and looked at Sara closely. "We need to do something special for you! You earned us so much credit. So what's your pleasure for tonight?"

Sara silenced her body's real wish. "How about music and dancing?"

Stan stared at her, his mouth open. "Excuse me, but what did you say? Dancing? Music?"

"Yes. Why are you looking at me that way?"

"Don't you know what you're asking?"

188

"Of course I do. You're acting like I asked you to rob someone of their credit."

"Sometimes, I really do believe you are from a different place. Everyone knows what music does to you! You won't hear it anywhere in Mall. Well, that's not exactly true; there is one place, but, trust me, you wouldn't want to go there."

Sara thought for a moment. It was true; she never heard music here. Why hadn't she noticed that? In her world she'd always sought out music—turning radio dials, pushing CD player buttons until just the right piece played. Was this more proof that she'd been changed by this world? "Why would anyone avoid music or dancing? Don't tell me. Is it against the Code?"

Stan glanced at the people streaming past them. He took Sara's arm and pulled her closer. Lowering his voice, he said, "Not a law, but the Code strongly discourages it. Almost no one from the upper rates would be caught *dancing*. Don't you know what happens when people hear music and when they do this dance thing?"

Incredulous, Sara exclaimed, "Music and dancing make people happy!"

"Are you joking? Music and dancing arouse people beyond what is normal. It's almost like amoking."

"What are you talking about?" She grimaced in frustration. "Dancing to music is the most natural thing in the world. Humans have been doing it since the dawn of time."

Stan frowned and looked away. "Well, if that's so, thank God of Reincarnation we're past that. Listen to me, baby. You would not want to go to the place where it's allowed. Only third- and fourth-raters go, like Mall Sweepers."

Sara waited for him to look back at her. "You mean, no first- and second-raters go?"

Stan looked again to see if anyone was listening. "Once in a while someone might go secretly. I guess it can help when someone is having a sexual problem. I don't get why, because there are plenty of things to do and admin when needed."

"Did you ever go?"

"I went once, when I was a kid. We all did, but once was enough."

Sara insisted, "I'm not afraid of a little music and dancing. I've danced hundreds of times. I had fun. A lot of fun. Just tell me where it is, and I'll go by myself."

"No!" Stan grabbed her arm. "You just don't get it, do you? Pardon the outburst. I have to make you understand. It's not safe!"

Sara yanked her arm away. "You can't stop me."

"You really mean it? You'll go by yourself?"

"You're damn right, I will. Just tell me where to go." She refused to look at him.

Stan shook his head and sighed. "Sara, it's so risky, I don't that I could be trusted if I were there with you."

Hope surged through her that he meant he would make love to her, that he wouldn't be able to help himself, that he would toss aside that stupid rule—no sex with employees—that he would pull her close and kiss her for hours, that…

"Why are your eyes closed?" Stan whispered.

She blinked. "I was remembering what it was like to dance."

Stan grimaced. "How could anyone stand to think about it? I can't believe you really want to do this."

That's not all I want to do, she thought, frustrated by not getting what she wanted. "Like I said," she insisted, "if you don't want to go with me, I'll go by myself."

"Nope, no way. If I can't stop you, I'll have to go with you."

On the crowded Throughway, Sara and Stan passed one elegant Pleasure Palace after another until they reached the Sex for Profit Division. Here the facades were garish, brilliantly lighted to feature explicit holographs of men and women disrobing and engaging in various sex acts. Sara averted her eyes. When she looked again, they had moved to a more dimly lit division featuring neon depictions of every kind of sex act one could imagine, including two naked men outlined in incandescent orange, kissing and fondling.

At the last stop they stepped off and walked in such feeble light Sara could barely make out the painted sign that Stan pointed to. "That's it, the Dancing Dungeon, and you're not going to like it," he warned as they walked toward it. No holograms, no neon pictures, nothing but the sign depicting a couple with their arms around each other on a dark shadow that must be a building. Instead, this establishment seemed to be promoting its form of entertainment with sound—at first a faint thump, growing louder as they approached until she both felt and heard the throbbing, an insistent drumbeat that made her body vibrate with the desire to move. Close up, all she could see was a massive black door blocked by a huge, thick-necked man, tattooed muscles bulging like a pro wrestler's, waving a handheld at them.

"Fingers and cards before gettin' in," he bellowed. After she finished showing him her ID, Sara moved toward the door, only to be barred by a large arm. "You also gotta finger-agreement to the disclaimer that this here establishment ain't gonna take no responsibility if you get hurt in any way."

"Okay," Sara said, ignoring Stan's worried look. After they both touched the cold finger indentations, the massive black door slid open to the full force of the drumbeat, so loud and insistent, the sound seemed to originate inside of her. If she focused her whole attention, she could, in the distance, hear a faint guitar twang a desultory tune.

On the dance floor, hundreds of people undulated, contorted, twisted, stamped, or jumped. Sara had to blink twice before her mind believed what she saw. Some of the couples pawed at each other, others rubbed against each other as if they were having sex while clothed. Looking to her left, she spotted two couples ripping off each other's clothes, staggering toward small cubicles lining the back of the room, each with just enough space for a cot and a straight backed chair. When the couple reached one of the tiny rooms, they didn't even bother to close the curtains. For a few minutes she stared, mesmerized, as they pulled off their remaining clothes, starting the act before even lying down, uninterested in any kind of foreplay. Looking away quickly, Sara concentrated on the Mall Guards, almost as numerous as the participants. Systematically, they closed open curtains and guided overly aroused dancing couples to empty cubicles.

"Oh, beg your pardon," one guard said as he brushed against her, thrusting out his arm to separate two men arguing over a dark, squat woman whose overflowing breasts had escaped her scanty dress. He passed close enough for Sara to see he wore earplugs—to protect his hearing, or was it to protect him from the music's effect? She put her mouth to Stan's ear to ask him what he thought, but the words stuck in her throat when she caught sight of familiar dark eyes drilling into her—hooded eyes, too close together, unaltered by any cosmetic procedure. It was Paul, his face arresting in its irregularities—large crooked nose, full mouth and shoulder-length unstyled hair. As always, he wore a black cape that touched the ground, obscuring his body while calling attention to his height. When he held out his hand to her and asked her to dance, she flowed into his arms, ignoring Stan snarling,

"Can't you see she's with me?"

Paul pulled her closer enunciating clearly into her ear. "Tomorrow night is the meeting." He drew her even closer, and, although she warned herself to stop, she wrapped both arms around him.

192

"Mmm," she murmured burrowing closer. "Okay, but can we talk about it in a few minutes?" Sara couldn't make out his reply when the music stopped and voices suddenly swelled. People pushed against them, and Sara would have tumbled if Paul hadn't been there to catch her. A man fell to his knees with a bloodied nose. Shouting, crying, and pleas for help thundered through the arena as the crowd drove the two of them toward the rear. Paul jerked her into one of the little rooms and yanked the curtain shut. "What's happening?" Sara shouted.

"A small riot we started," he shouted back.

"What? You Junkers are causing this?" Sara reached for the curtain, thinking of Stan, but before she could call out to him to see if he was all right, an ear-splitting whistle rang out. Silence followed by moans and soft crying. Paul stopped Sara from opening the curtain.

"Yes, and now quite a few guards are occupied with the rioters. We'll wait for the room to empty, and believe me it will, and fast." He looked down into her face. "Don't worry; nothing is going to happen to you." Again he pulled her close and began to stroke her hair. "You do know Natalie's been apprehended."

"I do, but not why. Do you?"

"No. Those fuckers are pulling in people right and left. Most have nothing to do with us."

After a few more minutes, the room was silent. Paul whipped back the curtain and Sara grabbed his arm. "Wait, are you going to do anything about Natalie?"

"I'm going to free her," he said and gently pushed her out.

Outside the building, the area was almost empty except for two guards who were picking up a man who couldn't move. Sara shuddered, remembering when she had been techno-netted. A silver-suited Finance Policeman watched the guard hoist him over his shoulders and walk toward the elevator. The FP spotted Paul and

Sara. "Where did you two come from?" he asked while sauntering over to them.

Paul grinned, "We were occupied in one of the little back rooms."

"Really? It must have been quite diverting not to be caught up in the riot. Damned Junkers," he snarled.

"Just my thought," Paul said, then asked, "Are we free to go?"

"Yeah. But don't come here again. This is *not* a place for first-raters, you should know that." He tapped his hand with his techno-net wand. "Now get out of here."

When Sara and Paul reached the Throughway, they saw Stan sitting on the ground, holding his head in his hands.

She rushed over and knelt next to him. "Are you okay?"

He took her hand and she helped him stand. "Yeah, I guess so. But, God of Reincarnation, did you hear the screams? Did you see the blood? Now do you see why I was against going?"

He started to walk but tripped. Paul caught his arm. "Are you okay to walk?" He turned to Sara. "Can you handle this? I have to go." He gestured toward the Throughway.

"Yes, I think so." Paul waved and left. To Stan she said, "You look pale. Can you walk?"

He took a few steps, still a little shaky on his feet. "I do feel a little strange." His eyes opened wide, he stared into the distance. He gripped his head. "I've never seen anything like that, not in real life. Those people were angry, so angry they actually hurt each other's bodies." He looked into Sara's face. "I think I'm okay now. Are you all right?" He studied her for a moment. "You look fine. Why aren't you more—what's that word—upset? Didn't this affect you at all?"

"Yes, of course. Well, maybe not to the degree it did you. Anyway, I hid." The excitement of the music and the brawl still pulsed through her and she found herself stroking his arm. Without thinking, she put her other arm around him, pressed against him and raised her head to kiss him. When she began to rub against him, he returned her kiss, rough and hard. But just as suddenly as he kissed her, he jerked away.

"I beg your pardon," he said as he turned his body away from her. "We need to get back to the Pod. I want to get my eight in."

"Stan, what's wrong?" she asked, sliding her arm around his waist. He jerked his body away and strode toward the Throughway. She hurried after him. "Stan, please talk to me. Tell me what's wrong. Is it the riot, or does it have something to do with kissing me?"

Polite but distant, Stan replied, "I was way out of line, but I did warn you that the music and all that rough sex might affect me." Turning his back to her, he added, "I don't care to talk about it anymore."

Why was she near tears? she thought angrily. She hardly knew this man and here she was feeling that sharp rejection she used to feel when someone she wanted didn't want her; like the time when Carl told her *sure I love you,* but he wanted to move out; he wanted to see other women. Almost crazed by the rejection, she had hurled books, grabbed the bedspread and dragged it to the car, and sped off wearing only her nightgown to park in a supermarket lot to sleep for the night. Yet she had taken him back and married him. What was the matter with her? *Damn it, stop!* she thought. The memories hurt.

Gripping the railing on the Throughway, she looked out at the sights, her unshed tears blurring the lights into long streaks of color. Twisting and squirming, she tried to think about something else. What did she have planned for the next day? Nona wanted to meet her, she remembered that. Maybe they could meet for coffee, if there was coffee anywhere. Nona was the only person she could talk to about what just happened and, for that matter, about her other life with Carl and her mother and her job as a teacher—memories now faded as an old tinted photograph, more and more out of focus and dream-like, the characters outlandish in the way only dream characters were. She was lost, wasn't she? She was ready to have sex with Stan and with Paul. This couldn't be a relapse back to the Sara before her therapy. No! The old Sara was a wimp. She had no belief in herself. Now she was different; she was more confident, stronger. Wasn't she?

She snatched a look at Stan. Was he softening? Reaching out to touch his arm, she was stung when he flinched. "I'm sorry. I just wanted to ask you if I could come in late tomorrow." She moved so far from him she had to talk above their usual low tones. He shook his head and put a fingertip to his mouth. They rode the rest of way in silence.

After the moving sidewalk stopped to let them off, Stan finally answered, in his usual cheerful mode. "About coming in late tomorrow, don't you remember? I gave everyone a work-break to celebrate your success. Wait until we see the ratings. I wager—"

Who cares about work success? Sara thought as she sped up to out-distance him.

"Sara?"

She kept moving. He called, "I guess you're annoyed with me for kissing you. I'm sorry. I know I've been rude to you. I promise, I'll make it up to you."

Sara stopped. At least he wasn't mad at her. Things would go back to normal, and she *would* find some way to get him into bed with her. Finding her casual voice, she turned and answered, "I guess what happened affected both of us." She waited for him to catch up and they walked toward their Pod.

"Sure, that's it." He patted her shoulder. "I've got a great idea. Let me choose another way to celebrate, something really amusing."

"What do you have in mind?"

"How about the Bon Chance Pavilion?" he asked.

"The what?"

"The best gaming center in Mall. How about two nights from now?"

Sara caught a whiff of his citrus fragrance, and she wanted to reach out to pull him close so she could inhale him, lick him, even swallow him whole. Instead, she said weakly, "Sure, I'll go with you," and turned away to stumble to her sleeping quarters.

Inside, Sara sat on the bed, reliving the night's events. Why had Stan rejected her? Was it just because of this stupid rule, no sex with employees? Why, when it meant curtailing pleasure? Maybe he just didn't find her attractive. Well, she would find a way to make him want her. For some time now he'd floated through her mind, sometime on the outskirts, other times center stage. She didn't want fantasy, she wanted reality.

Once again she cautioned herself. *What about my husband?* Better to completely forget about him. For sure, she did *not* want to go back to him. And he didn't want her. It had been weeks since they'd made love. No, not *love* and not for a long, long time. But her mother? How could she abandon her?

What good did it do to torture herself with regret and guilt? They both seemed to be a part of another place, another time, that may no longer even exist, erased by her passage into this world. Maybe it was better, no matter what, to live in the moment. And in this moment, she wanted Stan and Paul. The only problem would be how to choose which one to pair-knot with. Not that it mattered. She could probably find a way to have one and after the pair-knot was over, have the other. Her casual contemplation of sex startled her. Before she'd almost always coupled sex with the possibility of love ever after. Not here, because there was no such thing. If she stayed here, would she ever care about love again?

CHAPTER TWENTY-ONE

Nona had adminned two doses of Pumpup just to get through her three scheduled clients. Each one complained about the loss of pleasure, especially sexual. Yes, they sounded maddeningly the same, but it was more than that. Their stories, their experiences, came across as flat, insignificant, and silly—things a talking doll would say. Except for Freedomfrum, even the most credit-inefficient pharms were not as helpful as she wanted. She decided against adminning again. Nona wanted to be pharm-free when she met with Sara. The Pumpup would have worn off by then.

She sighed, trying to recall who was next. A mandated client was due in five minutes. She pushed the play button on her headset and listened to the tape spiel out one sound-bite after another. "Subject is male. Name is Jerry. Third-rater employed as a communicator and Inset tech. Apprehended in the company of a known Junker whom he failed to report. The Junker escaped. No evidence proving that he had converted to the group. Mem-wipe will be administered two days from now. Consultation with Mental Health Practitioner as per the Code requirement before treatment."

Anticipation ramped up the stim's effects, and she began to pace the room. This, she thought, is more like it. Someone who has had contact with a Junker, and I don't have to report it because they already have the background info. Maybe she would learn what they believed, or the identity of some of them, or even where they hid out. When a soft gong sounded, she scrambled to activate the entry code.

A young man sauntered into her room and flung himself into one of the client chairs. His appearance was surprisingly ordinary: sandy hair that could be transformed to gold; grayish-blue eyes she imagined could be altered to an interesting slate gray or at least sapphire blue, and an average build that could easily be buffed to well-defined muscles or dieted to a graceful slimness; puzzling because she knew third-raters had enough credit for some cosmetic alteration. With a start, Nona realized that she had been ignoring his questioning gaze. Sitting in her customary chair, she smiled, closed-lipped. "Would you like to tell me what happened to you?"

The young man shifted upright. "I got caught having contact with a Junker. It wasn't like I was gonna become one. I was just curious to see what he was like."

"Of course you know we're required to report anyone suspected to be a Junker. They're rebelling against all the Code's tenets and recommendations."

"Yeah, and I guess I would've, but the guy was real interesting, and he listened to this problem I got."

"Excuse me for pointing this out; that's what MPHs are for."

"Sure, but I don't have enough credit saved up to get a good one, you know? I could never afford one like you." He grinned sheepishly. "I like to gamble."

"Hmm. I see. Is that the problem? Gambling?"

"No, and I tried telling the Finance Police, my Confessor, and the Advocate—" he counted off on his fingers "—about this thing on my mind, but all they did was laugh like I was an idiot. Who cares?" He pursed his lips and snorted. "You're not gonna believe me, either." He regarded her closely. "Even if you did, so what? I have to get the Mem-wipe." He leaned in even closer. "But the other world will still be real."

Excitement fluttered, then pulsed. Nona said with calm intensity, "I might surprise you, Jerry."

Quiet for a moment, he sank deeper in the chair. "I guess it's okay to tell you. At least you'll pretend to believe me." He frowned and clenched his fist. "I never would've told anyone except the Junker guy, but the assholes have their ways. They adminned a who le bunch of Restzy and—get this, I talked in my sleep. Well, not exactly sleep. A sort of trance. Oh! Will I get sanctioned for swearing?"

"No, not during a MHP session."

"Good, I don't need any more trouble. Anyway, at Judgment, the People's Advocate thought I was so disordered, he sentenced me to the Mem-wipe thing. You'll probably think so too, but what do I have to lose? So I'll go ahead and tell you." He gave Nona a conspiratorial glance. "See, it's like this; I can remember another life, and it was nothing like Mall." He paused and raised his eyebrows. "You're not shocked. Why should anyone be, anyway? We're reincarnated." He shifted in his chair. "It's stupid to think that Mall is the only place that ever did or ever will exist." His eyes unfocused. "This last life, man, it was beautiful. My Confessor thought I was disordered to think anything could be greater than Mall. Just look around, he said. But what the hell does he know?" He leaned closer, his eyes shining. "If he could have seen what this other place was like. We lived in these high, and I mean high, structures—much, much taller than Mall. And there were thousands of these places all interconnected by covered bridges on the hundredth floor." His mouth twisted. "I can see the he-must-be-deranged look on your face. But I was there. And you know? These places floated."

"Floated?" Nona cut in. "Pardon the interruption."

"That's what I said—floated in a sea of pink-orange air. My— I guess it would be called a Pod—was very high-ranked. We all had our own rooms with floor-to-ceiling windows on all sides. You could even go out one of the windows and stand on these things called balconies."

She gasped. "Out? There is no out. And balconies? What do you mean?"

"You'd never understand. Here we're trapped; we're boxed in. You ever think of that? I could go out on a balcony any time I wanted, into this coral light. And get this. There were red-orange clouds in the sky. You know what clouds are?"

"Yes, I think so. In a nature virtual reality that—"

"Yeah? Well, in VR, all that stupid white puffed-up virtual reality air can't come close to this. Sometimes, when we were on the balcony, one of these clouds would come right through us, and it was like swimming in orange nothingness." He stared at the wall, eyes still unfocused. "And you know what else? If a lot of these clouds built up, it'd rain lavender drops. You remember learning about rain in baby-school, and how we were supposed to be so glad that we no longer had to put up with something so bad? It's not like that at all. Even the storms were great. We couldn't watch them outside, too rough. Man, were they ever something. The air turned red, and orange lightning splashed across the sky. We had to cover our ears; the thunder could be that loud. Sort of like the drums at the Dancing Dungeon. You ever go?"

"No, of course not." She dug her nails into her palm. Maybe she should go just once…

"I didn't think so. If you ever do, you'll know what the thunder was like."

As Nona listened to him, the pulsing of excitement turned to pounding. Reincarnation in another world! Reborn into Mall, even if she were different, everything else would be the same. She was tired of it. How she wanted the existence of other worlds or other realities to be true!

When the closure bell chimed, in her most nurturing manner, she reminded him that he could book one more session. "What for?" He asked. "Don't get me wrong, you're okay. Maybe how you listen is just an act, but it feels good. No one else even pretends. Oh yeah, except for that Junker."

Nona's interest was stretched to a breaking point. "This other person, this Junker, does he also remember other lives?"

"Not really. Look, I can't tell you much about this guy. He warned me to keep my mouth shut. When we were picked up, I didn't see what happened to him. I think he got away."

"Can you tell me what he looked like?"

"Yeah, like no first-rater I ever saw. Real tall, big nose, longish hair—black, I think and he wore this long cape. You know him?"

It was Paul, just as she thought. "Who or what I know isn't important here; you are, Jerry."

"Listen, I gotta be sure you aren't going get him in trouble."

"Please don't worry, Jerry, as an MHP, I cannot divulge what you tell me." Not true. She should. The consequences for not revealing any information about a Junker could be severe.

He held her eyes. "Okay, I guess if I don't tell his name, it'd be okay. A couple of times, I went to that Spiritual Peace Sector, thinking maybe I could find a guy who could understand and not think I was disordered, and one day I ran into this guy. He works outside one of those huge places decorated with gold and other stuff. No way would I ever have enough credit to get into one. Anyway, I started talking to him. And get this, he didn't laugh at me. He just listened."

Nona leaned forward. "Excuse me for being too inquisitive, but did he have beliefs like yours?"

"Sort of, but different, too." He looked around as if someone else might be listening. "Get this. He believes that another place exists right now—*outside of Mall*. He said all he had to do was find the exit, and he was outta here. Can you believe it? He even thought that place was better than Mall!"

"But didn't you say where you previously lived was preferable to Mall?" Nona asked.

"Yeah, but that was in a past life or a different reality, not here. I mean how could you get outta here? And, man, I don't know, I don't think I would even try it, even to escape the Mem-wipe. There's nothing out there, right? What I think is one place per lifetime. But he was pretty persuasive. Sometimes he kinda made sense, about Mall having some things wrong with it."

"We all know that there's a vast nothingness outside of Mall. To believe otherwise is disordered." Or is it? she asked herself, and not for the first time.

A smile lit up his uninteresting face. "That's what I thought." A soft gong repeated the closure reminder.

"Shall we make another appointment for tomorrow? I have a ten o'clock available. May I enter your name?"

"Nah, I don't think so. Talking about this has kinda made me feel heavy inside. Besides, I've got the Mem-wipe tomorrow evening." He stretched and rose to leave.

"Don't do it! You won't …" Her hand flew to her mouth. "Forgive me, I don't know what came over me. It would be beneficial to me if you don't mention what I just said to anyone."

He shook his head. "Don't worry. But I can't figure out why you'd be against getting the Mem-wipe."

Nona sighed. Looking down, she said in a low voice, "I am reluctant to see that beautiful world you described disappear into the fog of pharm-induced amnesia."

With a smile more like a grimace, he said, "Yeah, I know what you mean. I don't like it much either. But I gotta do it."

She activated the door and he left. Sitting back down she thought there was no doubt Paul was a Junker and a very dangerous one. But she was not going to report him either. Instead, she wanted to find a way to talk with him. If only Natalie were free, she could arrange a meeting. If it weren't for her, Natalie wouldn't have been apprehended. Maybe if she asked to appear before the FP in charge, she could convince him of Natalie's innocence. Were the Junkers demanding more freedom, especially when it came to relationships? If so, maybe she *would* join them. She wondered if Royce had met with them yet? She should have agreed to go with him. What would happen if she were caught at a meeting or someone found out that she'd failed to report Paul and Royce? Most probably a Mem-wipe or some kind of imprisonment. There would go her life as the MHP top profit-maker, something she didn't seem to mind, very much. It wasn't enough and hadn't been for a long time, yet it was a part of her and something she could count on. But then maybe she wouldn't mind losing her position as number one as much as she thought. Not since meeting Sara and the others—Natalie, Royce and even Paul—who circled her mind in an almost constant orbit.

What if there really were a way out to a new world where things could be better, where she would be able to have friends that were real heart-friends? Or what if there was something worse? Inside her chest a push-pull tugged hard, a feeling she could easily eliminate with a small dose of Ezydozit. She fetched a patch and stared at it in her hand, then discarded it. No point in adminning something to ease this soaring/plummeting feeling, a more potent experience than any pharm she'd experienced. Besides, pharms sometimes blurred the edges of her thoughts, and she wanted to think with knife-like precision. She had to decide what to do next.

CHAPTER TWENTY-TWO

Throughout Bon Chance, the male croupiers' sequined cummerbunds and the women's jet chokers shot black sparks as they moved. Sara walked from table to table until she settled on a game similar to Blackjack. After watching for a few minutes, she began to play, concentrating so completely that Stan and the rest of the room faded away. Over and over, she pushed buttons and watched the blinking. When she had won the equivalent of two weeks of credit, she signaled the croupier to quit her, and walked over to Stan sitting at a nearby table with two other men. "How are you doing?" she asked him.

"I'm down a month's worth," he admitted.

"Are you going to keep on?"

"Nah, that's about my limit. How'd you do?"

"I'm up two weeks' credit."

"What'd I tell you?" Stan asked as he swung around and pushed away from the table. "Doesn't this beat the other night?"

"Considering that there was a riot, yes." Sara peered through the hazy golden light, punctuated by white lights circling above each gambling table. She pointed to a door at the end of the glass bar stretching across the length of the room. "What's in there?" she asked. When Stan didn't answer, Sara looked up at his serious face.

"Not there, honey; it's not for you," he finally said.

Sara's eyes widened with interest. "How do you know that? What's in there?"

"A game called Take a Chance. Trust me, babe, it's not the right time in your life to play it, especially if you don't remember it. There's stuff that you don't—"

"Oh, I get it," she cut in. "The stakes are really high. Can't we just go in and look around?"

Stan sighed and rolled his eyes. "Okay, but don't say I didn't warn you."

Although the room was decorated in the same motif of gold, black, and clear glass, an ominous ambiance sucked up all lightness and sense of fun. Over of the heads of a small crowd, Sara watched huge, rapidly changing numbers flashing like diamonds against the black background of an Inset the size of the wall. A small group of people huddled together, silent and unsmiling. A few slumped in the corner, including a woman with her head in her hands, silky black hair falling over her face. Was that Delta? Suddenly, bells rang and five numbers glittered red on the black screen. "We have a winner!" announced the dealer, and a shout of joy erupted from a woman in the front.

"Oh God of Reincarnation! I can't believe it. I won one hundred. Did you see that? I won!" She hugged everyone around her, laughing almost hysterically. Sara stared at her for a moment, then turned to woman she thought was Delta. She had disappeared.

At that moment, a tall man, thin to the point of looking skeletal, broke away from the clump of people and stumbled blindly until he bounced against the wall and slumped to the floor. He moaned. A server knelt beside him to offer a choice from a tray of pharms, only to have the suffering man flail and overturn the tray. Ampoules and patches flew and the man sprawled on the floor to reach the scattered pharms. He snatched one, and with trembling hands, he tried to admin. "Help me, someone! I can't..." The waiter crab-walked to his side and pushed the dart into his neck. "What am I going to do?" he cried as he yanked the waiter's lapels, pulling him to the ground. At that moment, the door crashed open, and everyone, including the sobbing man, fell silent, their eyes flying to the guard sweeping through the crowd. He jerked the man to his feet.

"Let's go, buddy; you're makin' a scene, and we don't want that, do we?" With his brawny arm around the man's waist, the Mall Guard dragged the man out the door.

Stan, lounging against the gilded wall with his hands in his pocket, frowned and looked away. Sara, who had been sitting in the front, hurried over to him. "What kind of place is this? That poor man! And look at everybody. No one is having a good time except the woman who won one hundred—what? A hundred months of credit? Just how much is the limit? Are people betting their whole savings or what?"

"Savings? Most of us know that we can't save any of it. We don't have that much control."

"Something's really wrong here, something worse than losing some credit. That man taken away was out of control; and what's the matter with the man in the corner with his head in his hands?" Sara shook her head. "I am not enjoying this at all. Can we just leave?"

"Honey, honey, I told you we should not come here. A lot of people end up playing this game when their number is up; I probably will ..."

"Wait, why?"

"Because I could win and more time would be added to my life or I could lose and my death..."

"Are you kidding?" Shoving aside his reference to death, Sara cried, "No! I couldn't stand to see you in pain like that man."

He glanced sidelong at her. "So does that mean you'll work even harder since you care about what happens to me?"

Sara turned away. "Please don't tease. You must know by now how I feel. I wish we could pair-knot."

He turned her face toward him and sighed. "I feel the attraction too," he said gently. "I would agree to a pair-knot in a flash, but it's impossible while you are employed on my team."

An idea occurred to Sara. "So if I found employment with someone else, we could pair-knot, right?"

"That's the last thing I'd want you to do. You're too important as an employee. Please don't, Sara."

She would wait until she was sure she could create more hits and then, yes, she *would* look for other employment. She flinched inwardly. More and more of these kinds of thoughts were disrupting her goal to return home. She wouldn't even call it a goal anymore. She held her head in her hands. Stan gave her a questioning look. "Are you okay?"

"Yes," she lied, tired of being battered by confusion. When would she know what she really wanted?

CHAPTER TWENTY-THREE

Nona watched with pleasure as Sara examined the mass of flowers encircling the bench they sat on. This, she recognized, was how one should feel when she meets with her heart-friend. Sara looked up and asked, "The flowers here, are they artificial?"

"No, pardon me, why would you ask something like that?"

"They seem too perfect, too bright, like little crayon-colored puff balls."

Nona shook her head. "Nonetheless, they are real. It's a rule."

"A rule? Who for?"

"The MDs who—"

"What? Doctors have something do with arboretums?"

Confused, Nona paused for a moment. "*Doctors?* I don't understand. As I said, MDs or maybe I should say, Mall Decorators, are the ones who create and maintain the arboretums."

"So what would happen if they broke the rule and sneaked in some really good artificial imitations? Forced labor?" Sara asked as she picked one of the purple zinnia-like flowers. Almost instantly an identical bloom replaced it.

Nona's lips tightened. "Of course not. Oh, I see you're joking again. It's difficult, sometimes, for me to follow your humor. I have a difficult time finding anything about Forced Labor funny, not even those who sort through discarded items like old shoes or used underwear to find items to be recycled. And yes, the decorator would be sanctioned."

Sara shook her head, eyes scanning the whole garden. "I wonder if this world will ever stop surprising me." She looked back at Nona. "That reminds me. You know what really surprises me? That sex with someone you work with is forbidden. I don't get it. How would a little sex interfere with that prime objective, *make profit and consume?*"

"Ah, you want to have sex with Stan. He *is* attractive, but think about it. To get the best products, to give the best service, expertise has to be carefully fostered. Think what would happen if you and Stan had sex. You might put it before accomplishing a work-goal. You might even want to pair-knot, and then your priorities would be confused. You would be distracted while working. Best to keep these things separate, don't you agree?"

"Oh, I don't know." Sara pushed her hair behind her ears. "I get mixed up. I guess you're right, but why should people's personal lives be managed like this?"

Nona gave the stock reply. "If we didn't, financial setbacks could cause suffering." Did she even believe this? she asked herself, avoiding Sara's eyes.

"I don't think a few love affairs in the workplace ever toppled an economic empire," Sara retorted. "I thought this was a place where people could have what they wanted. I'm not exactly suffering." She paused. "Nona, there's something else I wanted to ask. Stan and I went to the Bon Chance Pavilion, and I *did* see people suffering. Really hurting. They were playing that game, Take a Chance. The losers reacted as if they had lost their savings—I mean, all their accrued credit, their pair-knots, and their employment. I only saw one person win, and she nearly freaked out with joy. What exactly was going on?"

"People only play when their number is up. That would explain why they were so disordered."

"Why do you people always refer to dying that way? It sounds so cold and heartless."

"Excuse me, but isn't it obvious? It describes the way we die." Nona watched Sara's face crinkle with concern. "Why are you concerned? Your number isn't up." Nona puzzled over why Sara didn't understand how people died. Wasn't it obvious?

"But how would I know? You told me there's no disease here, right?"

"Of course not. There's been no disease since Before Mall."

"So people here could live, well, indefinitely." She shuddered. "I hate it that we have to die. We never have enough time to make our lives the way we want them." Head bowed, Sara took a breath and continued in a soft voice. "Dying seems to be some horrible trick thought up by some monstrous god."

Nona struggled to understand. "If our numbers weren't called, we might expire from boredom. We all return as newborn babies, so we get to have new bodies, new talents, and so on. Mall Management monitors how many can be born or reborn to keep the population constant because we live in a closed space." The idea of rebirth made Nona squirm. Not enough for me, she thought. *Not anymore.*

"Oh, you mean reincarnation. But I would need proof to believe it."

"Proof? The babies born are proof." Nona breathed in sharply. *What about the baby I didn't have? Did that mean someone didn't get reincarnated?*

Sara gazed at Nona. "Are you okay?"

Nona stopped before she said yes. "I was thinking of the baby I was assigned to have."

"Oh, it made you sad? I understand. I almost always cry when I think about not being able to have a baby."

"Yes, I guess I am when I think about it." And so much more, she thought, after she'd stopped Nepenthe. "What if my inability to conceive meant someone could not be reincarnated?"

Sara shook her head. "That's silly. Oh, sorry. Tell me, please, how do babies prove reincarnation?"

Nona pressed the center of her chest, where Sara's assertion tore at the fabric of Nona's beliefs. "But where else would the life force come from? Void is just Void; there is nothing out there to create this..."

"Consciousness? I don't know where it comes from. Your belief is just one of many theories; that's all."

"No!" Nona felt the hot denial erupt without warning. "Everyone knows reincarnation is a fact." It had to be true or how could people stand dying?

Sara sighed. "I don't want to argue about this. You say that there's no more disease. If people don't die from being sick, how do they die? Not from old age, I bet. I haven't seen one old person yet."

"You mean someone who has lived a long time? Yes, you have, all the time."

"Do you mean no one would look old? Just how long could a person live?"

"With good luck about two, occasionally three, hundred years."

Sara's eyes caught fire. "That long? But how? Wouldn't the body's organs give out? And there's really no disease, ever?"

Sara's inability to believe in Mall's defeat of disease and bodily suffering bewildered Nona. "There has been no disease in Mall for hundreds of years. And we have pharms that maintain the integrity of the organs. If an organ failed, we have synthetic ones to replace it."

"What about murder? Does anyone ever die that way?"

"*Murder?*"

"You know, when someone kills—takes the life—of another."

Shocked into silence, Nona felt her stomach jump. What kind of place did Sara come from? A world where people took the lives of others? Was Sara capable of violence? She shuddered inwardly at that word, one so ugly, so seldom used. Maybe she was dangerous. Yet Nona cared about her. How was it possible to feel this way about someone who could not be trusted? "As far as I know, no one has ever taken the life of another. It's unthinkable!"

"Okay—no illness, no old age, and no murder. I don't get it. How do people die?"

"Everyone dies through the lottery."

Sara's face stretched in shock. "Lottery? Oh my God. Do you mean...?" She stopped her words with her hand over her mouth.

"Yes. How else could it be determined when someone's life is to be terminated? I'm sorry, Sara—everyone knows about the lottery from the moment they can understand the concept."

"How does it work?" Sara croaked.

"The last four numbers of the ID code are lottery numbers. We have drawings every Sunday, and those whose numbers are chosen pass over at the Passing Ceremony the following Sunday."

Silent, Sara stared at the ground. When she looked up, her face was drawn and pale. "What about me? Do I have those kinds of numbers in my code?"

"Yes, everyone does." Nona thought of how, so apathetic and fatigued on occasion, she had sometimes wished her number to be up. But not since she had opened herself and Royce and Sara had flowed in to fill empty places.

"What if they pick my number?"

"If your number is chosen, one week later you must report to the Chamber of the Final Resting where you'll be prepared for the process of leaving your body. That part of the ceremony is secret. I understand it is a joyful and peaceful event, especially if you're a first- or second-rater. You have the most skilled SP guiding you. Don't you see? You don't need to be afraid. You're a first-rater now, so you'll get the best, including the most effective pharms."

Bolting from the bench, Sara cried out, "I don't want to live here! I don't want my ID numbers in the fucking lottery. Can't you explain and have my numbers taken out?"

"You *do* live here. You *have* to be in the lottery." Nona fought back the fear zigzagging through her. Would this discovery renew Sara's commitment to find a way home so she'd leave her? When she reached out to touch Sara's arm, she jerked away and scanned the flower-filled arboretum as if she could find her way back to her world if she only searched hard enough. Finally, she turned back to Nona. "What are the odds? Tell me my odds!"

"No one knows exact odds."

"Even children can be chosen?"

"Not until they reach sixteen."

Anger glittered in Sara's eyes. "They're still children at that age! My God, how can you people do something so horrible?"

Anger also scalded Nona. "Do you think your world is so much better? You describe a place where there is disease and bodies wear out, and haven't you admitted the existence of violence? And it isn't uncommon?"

Sara spit back. "And didn't you just admit that only people with a lot of money—oh, excuse me, credit—can have a humane death? Is that so very advanced?"

"Pardon me, but I did not say that. It's a matter of degree. And if you would think about it in a calm manner, you would see how much sense it makes. Everyone should have a clear reward for his or her hard work for sustaining the economic standard that is the backbone of our way of life, and …" Nona hesitated, the way of life she extolled did *not* and had not satisfied her for a long time, not at all. Why was she saying a lot of things she didn't really believe in anymore? *I want to convince Sara to stay, to give up the idea of somehow escaping Mall because if she did manage to leave, I might very well join the Junkers to leave too.* She swallowed hard, feeling lightheaded, and closed her eyes.

"I can't listen to this. I don't care what you say; you're talking about sanctioned murder."

Trembling, Nona opened her eyes. "You make it sound like the murder you describe in that alternate reality. Why don't you try to understand? Why can't you see there is no other way? Think how stale it would be to live for hundreds and hundreds of years in the same body. We need to have the opportunity to have new bodies, be attractive in different ways, have different employment, maybe even change sex." A thought occurred to Nona, unbidden and frightening. If she believed what she said, could she find a way to end her life before her number was up and return as a new person freed from this push/pull inside of her?

Sara shook her head. "You can bet that I am not going to go like a lamb to be slaughtered."

Nona clutched Sara's arm. "I don't know that phrase, but I get the gist. Listen to me, please, Sara; you do not have a choice. If your number is chosen, you have to undergo Passing. It's the law."

"Fuck the law. It's not my law." Sara tried to break away, but Nona held her arm tighter.

"Yes, it is. That you come from a different world doesn't matter because you are here, and you can't go back. You must face this."

Sara stared at Nona. "What if my number comes up soon?"

Nona's heart leaped. "What are the last four numbers in your code?"

"I can't remember." Sara clawed at the tiny drawstring bag tied to her belt. Her hands shaking, she fumbled with the card before she finally pressed the indent. "Two, eight, five and one. Oh, please, tell me those are lucky numbers."

"No one knows for sure. I'm trying to remember the numbers rumored this year least likely to be chosen. Let me think." Nona tapped her forehead. "I think ones and eights are rumored to be lucky numbers for the next couple of weeks." Nona could not stop herself from wringing her hands. "Please, please stop thinking about returning to your world. You can't go back. Even if you could, I would try to stop you. I won't let you go." She jumped up from the bench and walked a few steps away then whipped around and said, "Please excuse me … I don't know what the matter is." Her hands flew to touch her hot cheeks. She was embarrassed to reveal her feelings. Would Sara reject her?

Sara looked at her as if Nona were the one who was disordered. "I don't know what to say. It's almost like you're ill."

"I do feel strange, certainly not myself."

"I don't get it. Aren't you supposed to admin some sort of pharm that will erase bad feelings?"

Shocked to feel tears sting her eyes, she squeezed them shut, her body trembling with fear at this reaction. How could she be this close to crying? A Mallite never cried. "Yes! I should be adminning anything and everything. Not to do so is disordered. I don't because I care about you more than I should, and if I admin, the feeling will be eliminated while the pharm is in effect. I don't even know how to describe what I feel. It's like waking up from a stupor."

Sara stared at her openmouthed. "This sounds—disordered."

Fists clenched at her sides, Nona faced Sara. "All I know is that I feel something deep inside. Sometimes, I hurt. And even then, I don't admin. All the time, I worry—I'm afraid that somehow you will find a way out and leave me. I'm afraid of losing Royce too if …" Her hand flew to her mouth. She'd almost revealed Royce's plan to attend a Junker meeting and maybe even join them. "When you spend free time without me, I feel jealous."

Sara continued to gape at Nona. "I can't believe this. I see tears in your eyes. Are you trying to say you're in love with me?"

Nona scrubbed at her eyes, trying to think. "In love—is that your term for sexual attachment?"

"Sort of. I don't know how to explain it. Every time I try, I get confused. It's more than sex; it's love—you know, sort of like a really close friendship too."

"I don't have any desire to have sex with you, but I do want to know where you are all the time. I'm afraid that you'll lose interest in me." Nona stopped, rubbing the pinpoints of embarrassment stinging her face. "Am I making any sense at all?"

Sara shrugged her shoulders. "I've never had a woman talk to me this way. Really, Nona, it sounds like love, and I don't mean that heart-friend kind of feeling. Are you sure you're not talking about some kind of sexual feeling?"

"Yes, I told you."

"Okay..." Sara paused. "Ah, I think I do know what you're talking about. I felt that way about my best friend when I must have been around ten. Remember? When you loved your friend so much you just about wanted to possess her? And you were so afraid of losing her, like she was some kind of precious gift?"

Nona shook her head. "No, never."

"I remember I would have done just about anything to keep her." She looked closely at Nona. "Does this sound anything like what you're feeling for me?"

Nona shook her head. "I don't know."

"Because you never had a real friendship? Maybe this is sort of a stage, part of learning how to have friends."

"But why is friendship filled with so much discomfort?" Nona hesitated. "This makes no sense." She searched Sara's face. "If it used to be this way then this must be why we have a contract and rules for a heart-friendship. All you have to do is sign the contract, agree to meet a certain number of times, and share experiences."

"From what I gather, heart-friends have a watered-down relationship, nothing like those early friendships I'm talking about—" Sara's eyes grew far away "—long afternoons and late nights telling our deepest secrets, sort of like melting together." She looked closely at Nona. "I'm still friends with a few of them and we remain close, not as intense of course. Maybe I should use the past tense because who knows if I will ever get back to them."

Nona ignored Sara's reference to returning to her world. "You mean adults and children in your world have different kinds of feelings?" She drew in a deep breath. "Are you saying that there could be a variety of relationships based on strong feelings?" Seeing Sara nod, she exclaimed, "Oh, this is disordered." No, she suddenly realized, it was not disordered, not at all. Only recently had she realized just how much she cared about Royce. And she felt connected to Natalie too. She wanted these complicated relationships, really wanted them, even though they brought discomfort—worry about Royce, guilt over Natalie, and fear of losing Sara. She'd taken risks, big risks. She'd never adminned Sara the Mem-wipe; she'd failed to turn in Natalie and Royce for Junker associations, not to mention Paul, who she knew was a major figure with the Junkers. Suddenly, she was filled with the desire to escape. But where would she go? Sitting back down, she cried, "Sara, I don't know what do. I seem to want to have this and other relationships, in spite of the discomforts."

"I don't know, Nona. Maybe you should think twice. Believe me, I've been there, and a lot of hurt is involved." Sara shook her head. "It might be better if you adminned or went to one of your MHP friends for some help. I'm not sure that you would enjoy close relationships. Too many hurt feelings; too many expectations that are never met. I could go on and on." She pressed a hand to her mouth. "Oh God, will you listen to me?"

"I *am* listening," Nona insisted.

"Here *I* am trying to convince *you* to follow the ways of Mall."

For a moment, Nona was silenced by the irony of the role reversal.

Sara continued, "Listen to me, these kinds of relationships can hurt. I'm almost convinced that I don't want to care about anyone that much anymore."

Nona touched her throat, which ached with the tears she'd held back. She cared more for Sara than Sara did for her. *How did you make someone love you?* She took in a deep breath. If she were able to ease Sara's fears about passing, she might love Nona. Or—she struggled to identify feelings previously felt in a shallow, fleeting way—would Sara feel thankfulness? No, the better word was gratitude. Could gratitude turn into love? It was worth a try.

"Sara would you come to Passing with me? After you experience it, maybe you won't be afraid of death anymore."

Sara folded her arms across her breasts. "I guess. If I can be sure my number isn't called."

"Passing is tomorrow. You would have been notified by now."

"Is it possible that my number could come up, let's say, next week?"

"Yes. None of us knows until early in the week before the next Passing."

"Then I really do have to get out of here!" Sara's face fell, then suddenly brightened. "Nona, if you really want to have these kinds of relationships, maybe you would want to find the way out of Mall? We could ask a Junker to help us."

Nona's hand flew to her mouth. "Oh, the thought—what's a word that means more than just scared?"

"Terrified?"

"Yes, terrified! I … feel tempted but, what a risk. It would be so dangerous!" She got up and walked toward the row of red tulips. She whirled around. "Anyway, who would we ask?"

Sara avoided her eyes. "Paul thinks he may know a way out."

"He's under suspicion. Even my heart-friend knows about him."

Sara raised her eyebrows. "Who's your heart-friend?"

"Fabriana. I sometimes forget so I haven't mentioned her. If we contacted Paul or some other Junker, you and I could both could be apprehended."

"Don't you think I'm scared, too? I'm not even sure I could go through with it."

Nona stared at Sara. Confusion swirled through her. Would she be able to find the courage to do this? What about Royce? If he came with her, maybe she could. "If you agree to come to Passing with me, I might come with you, but I need Royce to join us."

"I don't know who he is. Why do you want him?"

"He is a former pair-knot, the one selected to be the father. We are still in contact."

"So you must have feelings for him?" Sara asked, surprise widening her eyes.

"Yes, although I find it difficult to put into words."

"Can he be trusted? I'm scared of being caught."

"Yes, absolutely." After Nona said those words, she understood clearly how much Royce meant to her. She knew she could rely on him completely.

"Okay, Nona, I'll go with you to Passing. I don't know what will happen next with Paul. And to be honest, I'm not sure what I really want to do."

Nona's chest filled with warmth. There was a chance Sara could love her. Maybe it would be worth leaving Mall to find out.

CHAPTER TWENTY-FOUR

"Is this a church? It looks more like an auditorium," Sara asked Nona, as she craned her neck to look at the people, most standing, many moving up and down the aisles, all dressed in a dizzying variety of colors and styles. Behind her two rows up, Sara recognized Delta wearing a purple satin band across her breasts and a matching sliver of panties, "Delta?" Sara called. With an obvious effort, Delta turned her head toward them, the light catching on the jewels in her hair, on her ears, and around her neck. Her amethyst-studded eyelids almost hid her drug-enlarged pupils.

Sara started to ask, "Can a Mallite refuse...?" The question dangled in midair as three burgundy-robed men climbed the stairs and walked to the middle of the stage. As they stood side by side, unmoving and silent, a melodious voice repeated, "Please, take your seats; the Ministers of Passing have entered." The light drained away. Someone moaned, and then a velvet curtain of silence fell over the crowd. After several more long moments, the voice intoned three sets of ID numbers. A moan vibrated through the auditorium.

"No. I won't ... I'm too young. Let me go," Delta cried. "I'm only seventy-five!" Sara could just make out her figure wobbling with the effort to stand. Louder this time, she shouted, "I won't go!"

Someone shouted, "Communicate with the Mall Guards." Light bled through the darkness until Sara could see Delta crawling over people who either lifted or pushed her off. A guard ran up the aisles, grabbed her leg, and pulled her to the ground. Sara fought off an impulse to help her. There was nothing she could do. "Use dart," another guard shouted. Moments later they dumped her unconscious body at the feet of the other Passers waiting on the stage, visible until the light blinked out once more.

MALL

Quiet beat against Sara's ears, and the darkness thickened, relieved only by the appearance of a tight circle of light around the Passers and the Ministers. Sara's muscles tensed as she watched the entrance in the stage floor slide open to swallow each member of the procession. After the last one was lowered down, the circle of light changed to yellow, orange, red, and purple and then disappeared.

A new voice, deep and sonorous, intoned, "Let us ask the God of Reincarnation to grant us the ability to accept our Passing with grace and good humor. Let there be silence until the Rite of Passage is complete." Sara fought an impulse to cough against the anxiety closing her throat. Finally, in the center of the stage, a tiny light flickered and then flamed to magenta brilliance. Three times a gong boomed, announcing a shower of opalescent sparks that shot up to the top of the arena. The glittering specks floated down, washing over the audience's bodies, leaving a thin film of iridescence on their skin.

"What is this stuff?" Sara tried to brush off the sticky substance. Nona caught Sara's hand.

"Sara, don't. Those are the Passers' Sacred Remains. They bring good fortune."

"Oh, ick."

"Please," Nona hissed, "don't talk anymore."

Sara shuddered, holding her arms away from the sides of her body. The purple-red light brightened, revealing two Ministers half-dragging a man to the center of the arena where they shoved him onto a stool. The light shrank until only he could be seen.

"Oh God of Reincarnation," Nona whispered, "that's Royce!"

A robed arm insinuated itself into the light and snapped a tiny microphone around his neck. "This man's name is Royce. Fellow Mallites, he broke the Code in a way that shames me to mention. He was rude. Not in a minor way that his Pod could have dealt with. He pushed aside two people waiting in line for a place on the elevator."

A murmur swelled and then quickly died. "That, of course, is bad enough, but there is more. In his unseemly—no, his immoral—hurry, he jumped ahead of two others waiting for the Throughway and squeezed in between two people so they were *uncomfortable*." Little disapproving sounds flitted through the air. "He must be taught the seriousness of his crime. From this moment, the audience will shun you for five minutes. Tomorrow, during morning work-break, all of your Pod will assemble in the commons and will ridicule you for five minutes." The Minister paused for effect. "You will be laid off for a half-day, and during that time, you will remain in your quarters. And, now, at the sound of the gong, the shunning will begin!"

Once again, the auditorium lit up. Sara watched as the whole audience turned their backs. Nona grabbed Sara's arm to spin her around. Sara could hear him moan.

Abruptly, a voice cracked the silence—not one of the ministers, but an angry loud voice, "Fellow Mallites, I wager that some of you cringed at Royce's punishment for such a trivial thing—a moment of rudeness!"

People began muttering and whispering objections: "What's going on? Who is that?" Someone shouted, "Apprehend him!"

"And you third-raters, why shouldn't you have the same process as the first-raters? Yes, I'm a Junker. Have you wondered why we are causing all this trouble? Because we want change! We want—" just then two guards aimed techno-net wands at the speaker. Before the guards could release the nets, five men in the front row shot forward and wrestled the guards down. Three guards stationed at the exits ran forward, brandishing techno-nets. The crowd shouted, some ran toward the exits, and others surged forward, knocking down those who stood frozen with indecision. Nona pulled Sara back into their seats where they crouched to avoid being trampled. Cries, moans, and screams punctured the air, followed by an even more piercing whistle. Dozens of Finance Police marched down the aisles wielding batons to make way through the clogged passageway. Some crumpled beneath the blows and others threw themselves into the rows of seats to escape. In almost no time, the crowd quieted, standing, sitting, or lying silent while watching the FPs techno-net the Junkers and those who seemed to be protecting them. One of the FPs proclaimed, "All of you, show's over. Please exit in an orderly manner. Those of you who have been harmed, we have communicated with the Body Healers. They will attend to you, please stay where you are."

Walking out, Sara squinted in the bright light. "Oh my God, here I am in Mall, this supposedly perfect place, and I've been in two riots! What the fuck is the matter with this world?"

Nona stumbled but caught herself. "I don't know. I need to sit down." Before they could search for a bench, they heard a voice calling Nona's name. Sara turned to see a small overdressed woman with pink hair rushing toward them.

"Oh Nona," she cried out, grabbing Nona's hand, "I was so scared, weren't you? David—one of the MHPs for the second-raters—was with me, and he—" She drew in a sharp breath. "He ran to help those damned dirty Junkers. He was apprehended. And I came this close to be stepped on when..." She stopped and eyed Sara. "Oh pardon me, have we met?"

"No, I don't think so. I'm Sara."

"Please excuse me, Fabriana, I too have been affected and neglected to introduce the two of you. Sara, this is Fabriana."

"Oh, yes," Sara said, "you're Nona's heart-friend. Nice to meet you."

For a minute Fabriana stared at Sara. "Yes I am, although in the last week, I have hardly seen her. She has been so busy with your treatment."

"Oh, I'm not being treated anymore. I have recovered much of my memory and am now employed." Sara reported, a little surprised how easily the partial lie rolled over her tongue.

"Really?" Fabriana said coolly. "How advantageous for you." Her eyes flew to Nona. "My dear, we will have a lot to catch up on, won't we? I'm so glad you could find time for me tomorrow, or perhaps it will slip your mind like it did two days ago?" Fabriana's mouth twisted.

This is not a happy woman, Sara thought. *And more angry with Nona than she is letting on.*

"Please forgive me for inconveniencing you. So much was happening," Nona said.

"Well, perhaps tomorrow our appointment won't be blotted out by these *happenings.* I hope you won't think me rude if I remind you that the heart-bond dictates that the heart-friends meet three to four times a week and not meeting the requirements is a reportable offense. Of course I would never—I'm too softhearted." She strode off.

"Pardon me," Sara said, remembering the politeness rule, "for pointing this out, but your heart-friend does not seem friendly. In fact, she seems—if you will excuse me for saying this—she seems pretty mean."

"I have been a little worried about her and our contract."

"I think you should be afraid. Could she do something to hurt you?"

"Yes, indeed. She could denounce me to the Pod; however, I will try to be very careful when I next see her. Let's get out of here."

CHAPTER TWENTY-FIVE

Nona sat staring at her reflection without seeing when her communicator beeped and Fabriana's paper-doll face filled the tiny screen. "Hello, darling Nona, I certainly don't mean to offend, but I wanted to make sure you remembered our breakfast date."

Nona blanked the irritation out of her face. Of course she remembered. Fabriana had come close to threatening her if she forgot. "Yes, I was just finishing my hair. I am almost ready, but I do admit to forgetting where we are meeting. In fact, I was just about to communicate with you to ask you."

A strained smile stretched across Fabriana's face. "Now, I find that odd since you were the one who suggested the place. Don't you remember? You wanted to go to Kelly's Kitchen. I'll see you in about fifteen minutes."

Fabriana, already seated, was drinking a large vanilla frappé when Nona walked in, breathless from walking as fast as politely possible. Fabriana smiled. "Hello, darling, you weren't hurrying just for me? Your beautiful hair is a little mussed. Oh well, you're here, and that's all that matters." Her eyes never left Nona as she sat. "I am simply famished. Let's order, shall we? So sad, but you have to forget about coffee. The Junkers have still cut the supply."

After ordering, they both sat in silence until Nona asked, "Are you displeased with me, Fabriana?"

The other woman pursed her lips. "Well, darling, wouldn't you be? I admit I was offended that you forgot to meet me, not once but twice! Not only that, when I tried to talk to you at the beauty contest, you ignored me and instead talked to that other contestant, who was not someone you should have been talking to." She shivered dramatically.

Erasing the anger from her voice, Nona said, "I'm sorry, Fabriana. I wasn't ignoring you; I was in the middle of a conversation with Natalie. Then the Guards apprehended her, as you know. You reported her, didn't you? Why, if I may ask?"

"Indeed I did. I overheard part of your conversation. Obviously she's a Junker. I left soon after. They suspected you also, although I insisted to the guard that you were completely innocent." She smiled smugly.

"Thank you for your concern," Nona lied, tightening her lips against the words ready to jump out of her mouth. *You horrid woman. You have perhaps ruined Natalie's life and probably wouldn't mind wrecking mine, too.* "I don't really think Natalie is a Junker. It's just a misunderstanding."

Fabriana took another sip of her frappé. "No I don't think so. Why are you defending her? Why do you seem to be more interested in other acquaintances than me? Pardon me if I am being too abrupt."

"No, not true, dearest Fabriana," Nona lied again, nervous over Fabriana's jealousy. "All of this was due to odd circumstances." Aware of Fabriana's intense interest in sex, she added. "Did you see the man I met after Natalie was taken?"

"No, why?"

"He was gorgeous beyond belief and oh, what technique!" Nona saw interest spark in Fabriana's eyes.

"Who, who?" she asked.

"Giorgio, do you know him?"

"Of course I do. Oh, you lucky woman. Was it sublime?"

"Yes!" She enthused, relieved to have successfully changed the subject. "He wants to see me again."

"Which of course you agreed to. Right?"

"Yes, I attended the Realized Fantasy Fete with him. Actually, we barely made an appearance, if you know what I mean."

"Twice in such a short amount of time! He must be quite taken with you!"

"I guess so. He even asked to pair-knot."

Fabriana's eyes widened. "Nona, you are one fortunate woman. I have never heard of Giorgio pair-knotting with anyone. Have you signed the papers?"

"No, I asked him for a waiting period of two weeks. It's just been too busy and, well, almost chaotic."

"Are you disordered? You didn't grab at the chance to pair-knot with one of the most desirable men in Mall? I can't understand what has happened to you!"

Surprised at Fabriana's rudeness, Nona stared at her for a moment. "Well, I've been dealing with Sara. You know that."

Fabriana's eyes slid away from Nona's. "You've never spent so much time with a client before. It's like she's your heart-friend, not me." She shook her head. "Please excuse my rudeness. Well, you know how it is without coffee. I wish I had adminned a stim before you came."

Nona took a few moments to eat some of her roasted grain cereal before replying. "I have been thoughtless; I hope you can forgive me."

"I guess." Fabriana looked around and then whispered, "Please don't be annoyed with me if I ask. Are you having sex with Sara?"

"Absolutely not. It's against the Code and you know that I am not a same-sexer. Why would you think that?"

"My intuition. Maybe your voice when you talk about her or the way I saw you look at her."

"I care about her welfare, that's all."

"Are you sure? Sometimes we MHPs can be powerfully attracted to a client and both of us know of a few who have crossed the line. Really Nona, I would understand. Didn't I understand about you and Royce? And wasn't that one of the reasons you agreed to be my heart-friend? I just want to help you."

Nona hesitated. Maybe she should tell her some of what had happened, a little about the feelings she had about Sara, just enough to appease her. "I don't have sexual feelings about Sara, really. I do admit to a stronger attachment than is usual."

"What do you mean?"

"I can't describe it. Sort of a deep caring."

"What? I mean I beg your pardon. Do you mean something like sexual feelings without sex?"

"I don't know, maybe something like that." Was she getting into risky territory? She shifted in her seat.

Fabriana's upper lip curled. "If so, you must be disordered with boredom. It sounds like you are experimenting with something very much against the Code or for some reason you are too embarrassed admitting you want to have sex with her." She grabbed Nona's arm. "Have you taken advantage of a client for your own pleasure?"

"No, I told you. No sex. Just a kind of closeness."

In a sickeningly sweet voice, Fabriana went on, "Remember, you are talking to another professional; one of the best. You're talking about sex without sex, and, let's face it, a kind of perversion. Obviously this Sara has replaced me in your affections, and this unnatural closeness has caused you to avoid healthy sex; probably why you didn't pair-knot with Giorgio. And the fact that you did not admin the Mem-wipe! I should report you. You need help, Nona; maybe you ought to be my client. It's not the first time an MHP has turned to me for help. If I let the Pod know what has happened I will be the one with the number-one ranking. I should have that ranking anyway. I wager most of your clients are men because of your sex appeal." Fabriana's eyes narrowed. "*Nothing* to do with your expertise. When you come to me for help, I could instruct you how to be a better MHP." She pressed her lips together and two red spots appeared on her already pink cheeks.

Shocking white-hot anger spurted through Nona. "You're the one who needs help, you and all the stupid Mallites who think empty pleasure is all there is to life." She couldn't stop the scalding flow of words. "You know nothing about friendship. No one does. She's my first and only real friend, and I don't give a damn about our heart-bond." She stood up. "Go ahead and turn me in, and while you're at it, dissolve our bond. How I ever agreed to bond with such a boring nonentity, I'll never know."

Fabriana also stood, eyes glittering. "You will be ever so sorry for this!" she spat and spun around to walk away. Halfway out of the room, she turned back. "And I *will* be attaching to your credit the cost of the pharms I have to use to get rid of these dreadful feelings you caused. You will pay it or else."

Trembling, Nona slumped back into her chair. She could not believe what she had done. How could she have been so stupid? Her need to confess had blinded her to the risk. Thank God of Reincarnation she hadn't mentioned Royce or Paul or told her all about Natalie. She should have known Fabriana wouldn't understand anything about Sara. She didn't really know Fabriana. No one in Mall knew anything about anyone. Everyone might as well be talking mannequins. Neither did they know anything about themselves. Before, she'd believed there was nothing to know. Now, she knew there was something under the beautifully designed surfaces. Even Fabriana exhibited a hidden self—a jealous, angry one—an inner self that Nona should never have yanked out of its dark recesses.

Possible consequences piled up until she had no more room except for one thought: *this is what happens when you allow anger.* Hands shaking, she spilled several drops of sweetened tea as she brought her cup to her mouth and managed to sip it slowly. After a moment, she looked around to see if anyone had been watching her. Someone familiar was sitting two tables away from her. Who was he? She continued to stare until she remembered. He was that young man who believed he had lived in that beautiful cloud world. No wonder she hadn't recognized him, he was so altered—hair tinted red and cut close to his head and a jumpsuit contributed to his androgynous look. "Jerry?" she called out tentatively.

"Pardon?" he said. "You must have me confused with someone else. "I'm Roget."

"Oh, I beg your pardon." Nona turned away, saddened at how Mem-wipe had changed him. Sorry, too, that he couldn't remember her. Perhaps he would have been sympathetic to her. Certainly no one else would be. What was going to happen to her? She would have to undergo a Mem-wipe. What would that mean? Most probably, her memories of the last week or so would be wiped clean. Would she lose her license to be an MHP and never be able to practice again? Or even do Forced Labor?

Almost panicky, she couldn't conceive of a way to avoid the consequences. All she could think of was escape. But how, where? She would have to find a Junker to help her. Maybe Paul. Could she wait for the Junker meeting Sara planned on going to? She didn't know when it was. She sprang up. Natalie would know how to find him. If Nona acted before Fabriana had a chance to denounce her, she might be able to talk the FP into releasing Natalie. Another thought stopped her cold. Natalie may have told her all that Sara revealed to her.

CHAPTER TWENTY-SIX

Paul and Sara emerged from the elevator on Level K heading for the Junker meeting. Without thinking, Sara linked her arm through his and drew him closer. Paul turned his head toward her without breaking his stride, "No time or place to fuck, much as I would like to. You got to admit we have more important things to do." Sara flinched at the word, 'fuck.' Why? It had never bothered her before. No doubt the ways of this world had scattered its seeds within her, seeds that were beginning to sprout, especially the sexual one now flowering, not just for him but also for Stan. And here there was no shame for desiring more than one partner unless you were pair-knotted, and then only if you acted on it. Did she really want to go home? Part of her cried out, yes, to avoid that damn lottery. It frightened her. And another part of her cried out just as loudly, no, this is the kind of life she was meant for.

"I'm trying to keep up with you so we can talk."

"Nothing to talk about. You *are* going to this meeting with me." He increased his pace.

"I'm scared! I sort of feel like going back."

He stopped and turned her body to face his. "If you refuse, like I said before, I'll have Royce, who is an MHP, give you a Mem-wipe, or I'll have someone report you to the Finance Police." Holding her shoulders, he added, "You have no choice and neither do I. I couldn't risk you giving us away."

She pulled away. "Okay, okay, but why do you want me at the meeting so much?"

"I already told you. Someone might ask questions about Outside. And you may be able to help me once we're in your world. You *are* going to help Natalie and me." Grasping her hand, he pulled her alongside of him. This time they quickened their pace.

"Only if we land in my world." She panted in her effort to keep up. "Who's to say there are no other worlds, places, or times we might venture into? Wait, did you say you want Natalie to go with you? Did they let her go?"

"No, and I won't go without her. After this meeting, I'm going to get her out."

"How?" She almost ran to keep pace.

"I'll figure it out, don't worry about that." Reaching the door, Paul raised his hand to knock. "When we get out, even if it's not your world or time, you have more experience getting around in an unfamiliar place."

"What about Mall Guards or Finance Police? I don't get it. They know the technicians are causing the problems. Why haven't they arrested them?"

"They can't arrest the whole bunch of them. No one knows how to do their work, and they have no idea who's guilty."

Paul knocked at the door and the same jump-suited Techno let them in.

"Her again?" he asked as he stood aside.

"Yeah, and mind your courtesy rules." Paul threaded his way through the crowd, many more people than last time. Sara stood aside as he sat in the chair saved for him. In the sea of jumpsuits, she recognized Royce who, dressed in a gray and yellow silk-lined velvet suit, stood out among all those in overalls. Before Paul reached the table, a navy-blue jump-suited Techno blocked his way and pulled him aside. Sara couldn't hear what he whispered to Paul, although she overheard Paul say, "Thank you, David, for this info about the portal. If we use it to escape, you could very well get apprehended. Are you sure you don't want to come with us?"

David smiled but shook his head no. "No, I don't think so. I'm too afraid of what's out there."

When Paul stood at the head of the table, all talking ceased. In a commanding voice, he said, "Thanks to all you Technos. We have sickened countless first- and second-raters with noxious odors, caused a riot in The Dancing Dungeon and at the Passing Ceremony, even caused the deaths of two first-raters. One of them was a Bureaucrat! Because of your efforts, you're ready for your next move. I made a list of our demands to present to the Mall Management."

"Wait," shouted a Techno at the end of the table, "won't they apprehend whoever delivers the demands?"

"I've thought of that. We will threaten to release carbon monoxide into the Bureaucrats' meeting place if they do not give us safe passage. It can't be me because I will be attempting an escape through a portal tomorrow—"

A loud bang stopped him mid-sentence. Three Mall Guards and one Finance Policeman stormed through the blown off door. "You're all under arrest," the FP in the lead shouted. In seconds, techno-nets shot out into the air, dropped over the gathered Junkers, knocking everyone to the ground. Sara struggled only to find the net tightening around her.

"All right, you Junker Techno freaks, all of you are going to get the Mem-wipe," one of the Mall Guards snarled.

In a quiet voice, Paul asked, "Isn't that a mistake? If you take all of them in, very few will be left to run the electrical systems, monitor the air quality, run the food processing— well, you get my point."

"Shut up," the same Mall Guard roared and tightened Paul's net. "That hurt? If you say one more word, I'll net you so tight, you won't be able to say anything!"

The tallest FP, who seemed to be in command, motioned to the guard. "Calm down, Hal," he ordered in a quiet but authoritarian voice. He pointed to Paul and said, "We know you're a Junker, but who exactly are you?" He pointed to Sara, lying next to Paul.

Oh God, what should I say? Sara pushed down on the fear threatening to morph into panic. "No one, really! I was just curious. You know, I was bored so I came along for an adventure."

"Yeah, that's right, and I'm Paul, just an ordinary SP, not a Junker. I thought these men might need some guidance."

"Oh, I doubt that. I suppose this other first-rater will say he's an SP too." The FP spoke in a silken tone.

The burly rough-voiced guard kicked Royce. "You too? Just a do-gooder trying to help?"

"Yes, I'm a Mental Health Practitioner here to help these men by listening to their problems."

"What do you take me for? This is a Junker meeting and every one of you is a Junker." The FP raised his satiny voice a notch.

One of the men in an off-white jump suit piped in, "We were meetin' to try to come up with ways to stop the black-outs and the other things causin' problems ..."

"Why should we believe you?" the FP cut in. "I'll tell you what I'm going to do, I'll choose a few of you to take to Judgment. They'll find out soon enough if you're telling the truth." He pointed in succession to six Technos. The Guards loosened the nets enough so that, with one guard in front and one in back, they could stand and shuffle out the door.

"All right, the rest of you get back to your stations." Then he pointed at Paul, Sara, and Royce. "You three come with me. We're going to visit Mall Management."

CHAPTER TWENTY-SEVEN

Nona stood in front of a plain gray door, the only identifying mark a holographic gold baton floating eye-level. A deep masculine voice announced, "Finance Police, Entertainment Sector."

Nona touched the keypad, and the door opened to an austere office—no holographs, plant material, wall hangings or sculptures. Behind a plain wooden desk empty of ornament sat a severe-looking woman, wearing a simple black suit with a cream-colored linen shirt, brown hair pulled back into a bun and a face devoid of make-up. "Do you have an appointment?" she demanded.

For a moment Nona stared, shocked at her appearance and her lack of courtesy. "Uh, no. I was hoping to talk to the FP in charge."

"I doubt he'll see anyone without an appointment."

"I beg your pardon, have I done something to offend you?" Nona asked.

"No, why would you ask that?" the receptionist asked as she retrieved her headphones lying on the desk.

"Please forgive me for pointing this out, but your manner is lacking politeness."

"Oh, that. We are not about pleasure, entertainment, sex or anything like that. Courtesy wastes time. Here we strive for efficiency and results. Sorry if you are offended," she added.

"Oh, I see. No offense taken." She stepped closer to the receptionist. In the corner of her eye something glinted. Casually and quickly she looked at the wall to her left and caught sight of techno-net batons stored in a rack, something she'd failed to see when she first entered. A random and shocking thought occurred to her. Could she grab one and net this woman and the FP? *No, no,* she thought. Talk to the FP like she planned. "It really is important that I see him. Would you be so kind as to check to see if he is free?"

"All right, but you're wasting your time and mine. Who should I say wants to see him?"

"Nona, MHP."

She looked up at Nona. "Oh yes, now that I know who you are, I'll see that you get in." She pulled on the headset, turned away and spoke too softly for Nona to make out what she said. After listening, the receptionist rose to key in the entry sequence. "You can go in now," she directed.

Nona walked into an office as austere as the reception area—same wood desk, bare walls, and gray-carpeted floor. "You wanted to see me?" the man asked as he rose from his chair behind the desk. At the sight of this FP, tall and powerfully built with an unaltered angular face, Nona took a small step back. Would she be able to address him without showing her discomfort?

"I am Nona, the MHP. Please pardon my unexpected intrusion, but I have an important matter I wish to discuss with you."

"State your problem in a timely manner. We are all occupied with the Junker upheaval."

"Yes, of course, and it is a Junker matter I wish to discuss—"

"You have info about a Junker?" he cut in.

"No, not exactly. Please excuse my abruptness. I want to point out that you have apprehended someone who is not a Junker. It was all a misunderstanding." She paused to see his reaction.

The FP harrumphed. "I doubt that very much. We always have good reasons for arrests."

"Please pardon me for disagreeing in this case. The person I have in mind is Natalie, a performer with Realized Fantasies—I'm sure you have heard of that Entertainment Team—she has no time or inclinations for anything but her art. All she did was use the word *Junker* and some woman reported her."

He squinted with suspicion. "Now I know who you are. You're the woman guards reported seeing with Natalie and you disappeared. We've been too busy coping with the increase of Junker activities or we would have apprehended you by now. And here you are making our function easier." Opening the desk drawer, he retrieved a set of safe-bracelets.

As he walked toward her, Nona backed up until she ran into the wall. "No, no, this is a mistake; I'm not a Junker!"

He caught hold of her wrists and locked on the bracelets. "Maybe, but I bet you know something, maybe even a lot about them, and when—" A soft clanging stopped him midsentence. After inserting his headphones, he listened for what seemed to Nona a long time. When he was done, he looked hard at her. "I just received two messages and one of them involved you, Nona. It seems your heart-friend, Fabriana, has filed a complaint about you."

Ice-cold fear poured into her bloodstream. "No! She's lying; she's jealous of me! She's angry that I spent so much time with Sara." Her hand flew to her mouth.

"We also are aware of Sara. The Finance Police Commander on the MHP level communicated yesterday that she had not been cleared of charges. You are quite tardy with your report. And we have a situation with Junkers on Floor K where they secretly meet. Things have taken a turn for the unpleasant, shall we say? Sara is in the thick of this Junker altercation."

Nona sagged against the wall, slowly lowering her body. She'd missed the meeting. She'd failed to free Natalie. Sara was in huge trouble.

"Get up," the FP ordered. When she didn't comply, he picked her up and threw her over his shoulder.

She didn't resist. *My life is over,* Nona thought.

CHAPTER TWENTY-EIGHT

A Mall Guard, navy blue jacket topped with shining red epaulettes, pushed the entry sequence, and the gold and silver inlaid doors slid open to admit the FP Commander and his three prisoners. When the guard shoved them into the room, Sara stumbled, catching herself on a gold damask cushioned couch. Holding on, she took in the room carpeted with overlapping Oriental rugs where two Mall Managers sat on red velvet chairs. Gold mirrors covered three walls, and a huge Inset made up the fourth. She fought against trembling while she tried to catch Paul's eye. He stared stonily at the MMs.

"Sirs, we've brought you the first-raters suspected of being Junkers," the FP commander announced as he motioned to the small group to sit in the chairs opposite the MMs. The purple-robed MMs gazed at each prisoner before speaking.

The one on the left said, "I am Richard. Please be seated. The lead FP communicated your names and professions." He studied each one of them. "I must admit to a feeling stronger than surprise. In fact, this whole Junker business has caused all eight of the MM's the distasteful feeling of worry. Each one of us has found it necessary to his health to admin large doses of Freedomfrum." He again looked closely at all three. Sara was sure he looked at her the longest. Again she sought Paul's glance while clutching her legs in an effort to stop their shaking.

"Excuse me if I discontinue Rules of Courtesy. Each of you has profitable employment.

Why were you at a Junker meeting?"

Before Sara could think of an answer Paul lied, "Royce is an MHP and I am a SP. We thought these men must be troubled, and, you know, we might have been able to help them."

Richard scoffed, "I beg your pardon, but that is nonsense, and I know Claude will agree. No one does anything just to help. Where would be the profit in that? No, you were there as Junkers."

Royce answered, "I tried to tell the FP commander that we thought we might learn something about their work then maybe we could help out when they were arrested..." his improvising ended.

The first MM snorted, "No one but the Technos can know their procedures. You know very well that they started their training as children specially chosen for abilities in those areas. That you could learn or even want to learn how they do what they do is preposterous. Everyone has his own skillset. None of us is able to learn someone's specified employment."

Paul chimed in, "How do you know that? And why should we be restricted to one kind of employment for all of our lives when our life spans could be up to two hundred years?"

"This is what the Mall Fathers decided. Who are we to question?"

"Why shouldn't we have the right to question?" Royce asserted. "I'm tired of being an accountant, the work I've done for seventy-five years. Maybe I could stand it if I could pair-knot with the woman I want."

Claude frowned. "I don't understand. What stops you from doing so?"

"We did, but the knot is up, and we cannot renew. We knotted for four months so..."

Claude shook his finger at Royce. "The Mall Fathers determined four months is long enough. All kinds of problems can occur if two bonded for longer; it's something we all know."

For a moment anger cut through Sara's fear. She opened her mouth but Paul hissed "No!" and shook his head.

The same MM looked at Sara and Paul. "I want to be clear, there is to be no contact among you three; do you understand?" After they

240

all nodded, he continued, "We know who you are. Sara, you are Nona's client who has amnesia along with erroneous memories. A fellow MHP informed us that you have not undergone the Mem-wipe. Please excuse my abruptness, but why should we even listen to anything you have to say because—"

Paul interrupted, "Have you also been informed that she is profitably employed with an Entertainment Team?"

"Yes, we do know that, and in fact, saw the interactive drama she created. What does that—"

Paul broke in again. "That success came about because of her supposedly disordered memories."

"Those memories are neither made-up nor disordered." Sara took in a deep breath surprised at her newfound courage, "I did come from Outside. What I remember are things that truly happened to me in that world." Sara quivered. Maybe she shouldn't tell them, but what else could she do? If they believed her, there was a chance they would let her go back to her world. Otherwise, she would have to undergo a Mem-wipe and what or who would she be then? The thought of a complete loss of self petrified her.

Shock sparked throughout the room. The FP cried, "She is deranged. We'll see to it that she gets a Mem-wipe immediately!"

"I am not deranged! Ask me a question, any question, about the world I come from. You'll see that I know stuff that I couldn't be making up!"

Claude signaled the FP to remove Sara. She struggled with his hold and cried out, "I don't come from a *mall*. I come from a world where thousands of malls exist. We don't live in them. We live in houses or apartments, and we go outside all the time where there are buildings and trees and gardens and mountains and oceans. People get around in cars—"

Claude turned toward Richard, interrupting Sara, "Does what she just said sound like the way it was before the Last Days? How would she know about that? Only MMs have that kind of detailed knowledge."

"I know because I was there!" Sara shouted. She gasped for breath. "Did you say that something like what I described once existed outside of Mall?"

"You all will have a Mem-wipe, so I'll answer your question. Although Mall Fathers allude to things like vast forests, mountains, and oceans, we have almost no visual records. Virtual reality designers have done their best to recreate these things by looking at a few children's picture books that were somehow saved. What we know about Before Mall comes from one image and a pad of notes written on paper that—"

Royce cut in, "Written? What do you mean?"

Sara's heart leaped at the idea that her world was recorded somewhere. "On paper?"

"Yes, paper. I know, almost nonexistent now. And it seems that long ago, all people wrote words on paper. The original notebook has been lost, but the Fathers made a sound tape. This much we know: some kind of cataclysm occurred. A war, and a device that destroyed almost everything but not this mall where many sheltered. The air outside was toxic so these survivors stayed, and their children stayed, and their children. Over the years, they created Mall as we know it, a place not only safe but free of the risks involved in living outside before the event."

Sara couldn't wrap her mind around the thought of humans surviving in a mall after what sounded like the end of the world. "How did they do it?"

"The Fathers left little or no record of their endeavors. Why would anyone want to know when there would be no way to improve on our home, full of pleasure, with a Code that eliminates feelings and actions that lead to violence. No rudeness, none of the dangers."

Paul said, "It must be safe to leave now. Hundreds of years have passed."

"Maybe, but we don't know. Mall Fathers sealed off Mall. Why would anyone want to chance it? Here we're safe and have everything we need. Here there is no reason to set off bombs that poison the air. We're safe; we have a comfortable life."

Now panic fluttered in Sara's stomach. What if there had been some kind of time warp and she'd entered Mall created years and years in the future? Or was this a parallel world? What should she do; what *could* she do? She went limp in the FP's grip and whimpered. Everyone stared at her. Finally, Claude said, "You are suffering. Don't you understand that you will be happier and at peace after you undergo the Mem-wipe?"

"No!" Paul cried out, "She is going Outside with me. Sara's world has open spaces, trees and freedom to make choices. Besides, if what the writings described did happen, that was so long ago; things might have changed for the better. I want to go Outside with her and you won't stop us."

"Because you—" Sudden darkness swallowed Claude's words followed by a loud voice warning, "Mall Managers are doomed. Junkers will be taking over! Surrender your control or we will end each of your miserable lives!"

One of MMs or FPs shouted, "Stay where you are until the lights come back on!" Paul gripped Sara's arm and pulled her back. She could hear him patting the wall to find his way out when someone wrenched him away. While they struggled, Sara stood stock-still. Someone cried out—*Royce?*—then a thud. An arm circled her waist. "It's me," Paul whispered. He held her still while people stumbled around and, occasionally, a guard or FP would shout for everyone to stay where they were. "Let's get out of here," he whispered again. If she fought him and escaped his hold, she would get the Mem-wipe for sure. Had she changed too much to be able to resume her former life? What if they crossed over to some other world, one she would have to adapt to all over again? Here in Mall she would be safe from that kind of event, and she would escape the sadness, pain and guilt of her life in her world.

Paul hissed at her, "Move, Sara, or I will drag you out!"

No choice, she decided, almost relieved. She let go of her resistance and allowed Paul to pull her toward the door.

Darkness persisted in the corridor outside of the MM's office. High pitched whistles rang out followed by a new voice shouting, "Warning, warning, Junkers surrender to Mall Guards or Finance Police!"

Sara dug in her heels and covered her ears. Again Paul jerked her to force her to move. Together they staggered and groped their way toward the elevator. When Sara tripped and almost fell, she snapped, "Don't you people have flashlights?"

"What? You mean some sort of traveling light? No, why would we? Lights have never gone out until Junkers made it happen. Keep walking and no more questions."

Sara ignored his order. "Where are we going?" she whispered, afraid to say anything out loud now that the voice had stopped repeating the warning.

"We have to free Natalie. Otherwise she gets a Mem-wipe and will be forced into some kind of meaningless employment. I can't let that happen to her."

"Do you love her?" Sara asked.

"I don't know the name of what I feel … something like a kind of tight connection."

"But you seem to want to have sex with me."

"What's that got to do with anything? She has sex with others too. This is something different. Would you please stop talking and concentrate on getting out of here?" They continued to lurch along until they reached the elevator.

Paul punched the red glow of the stop button and they got on. "Entertain sector, top speed," he ordered.

Sara clutched the railing, closing her eyes as they sped down. Things were happening too fast and she could do nothing about it. Nowhere to run.

CHAPTER TWENTY-NINE

Nona sat on the edge of the padded bench in a soundproofed gray room. Any Mallite would find the lack of color difficult to endure. Even the silence seemed gray. What would happen? They would take her to Judgment and then what? Fear buzzed throughout her body until she got to her feet and began to pace.

A noise? She stopped pacing to listen. The keypad outside beeped as someone punched in a code. The door opened on a stocky guard, his face as dark as his hair and close-set eyes. "Time to take you to your new home," he growled. Before he could safe-bracelet her, the door slid open again, and Paul stormed in with a baton. Sara followed and relief and joy swelled through Nona. The guard shoved Paul into Sara who crumpled to the ground, then seized Paul around the waist. Paul struggled against falling and dropped the baton. The guard hit Paul on the jaw with so much force, he fell back against the wall. Nona ordered herself to do something, anything, but she couldn't move her legs. On the ground, Sara's hand crept toward the baton. She clasped it and when the guard moved toward Paul, Sara aimed the baton at the guard and techo-netted him. Down he went with a satisfying thud.

Nona gasped. "Sara, you saved us!"

Paul stopped massaging his jaw and shook his head several times. "We have to get out of here now!" He pulled Sara up and grabbed Nona's arm and dragged them out of the FP's office. Once in the foyer, Nona glanced with satisfaction at the receptionist who lay crumpled on the floor, held fast by the invisible net.

"You will regret this. Count on that!" the woman croaked.

Paul kicked her. "Where's Natalie?"

"Who?" the reception asked in a guttural voice.

He kicked her again, harder this time. "You know who I mean, the redheaded actress."

"Too late, traitor!" She coughed. "They took her to Judgment."

Paul groaned. "Fuck! We're too late!" With a final kick to the receptionist, he snatched another baton. They ran through the door and down the corridor until they reached the elevator, seeing no one. Nona pulled against Paul's hold. "Where are you taking us?" Fear hoarsened her voice. Off and on, the warning whistle blasted through the air.

"Keep up, Nona, or you'll get us all apprehended. We're going to Mall Management Level," he answered. "One of the new Techno recruits who works on the maintenance level for Bureaucrats tubes spied a small portal deep in the tunnel that seems to have no use. He says there are code sequences that open almost all the portals in the tunnel. The portal he discovered may be the gate to Outside. We're going to give it a try."

Nona's body felt divided in two. One side wanted to bolt, the other wanted to give up. Paul made the decision for her as he held fast to her arm.

CHAPTER THIRTY

When the elevator reached the MM level, Sara spied a small pine forest arboretum and beyond it, lights flooded the area. Ahead rose at least ten tall gates cutting off access to areas beyond, each with a floating neon picture of the BCs' functions. Even before the doors opened, she could hear the call for "fingerprint and dictate" ring out whenever someone neared a gate. After alighting, instead of moving toward the bronze gates, Paul herded them through the thickly planted trees to a hidden gate, not as tall or ornate. When they were close enough, the same demand for fingerprint and access code sounded while the sign above pictured a Techno repairing a tunnel track. Nona balked. "Only Maintenance is allowed into those tunnels. We'll be apprehended!"

"Shh!" Paul hissed through clenched teeth. "Override," he said quietly, then pushed several luminescent buttons. The lock clicked and the gate opened enough to allow one person at a time to slip through. When it closed behind them, through the charcoal-gray light, Sara could see that in the center of the darkness, tracks were suspended as far as they could see. On either side of the tracks were walkways just wide enough for one person at a time. Paul motioned them to get behind him as he took the first steps onto the passageway. Nona and Sara followed as he crept as close to the wall as possible. When a slight vibration announced passing tube cars, Paul hurried to a small alcove ahead with just enough room for the three of them to scrunch in while the tube roared pass. Out on the ledge again, they inched forward. Dizzied by the almost-black emptiness when she looked down, Sara trained her eyes on Paul. He stopped at a terminal and studied small circular lights blinking on the wall. His fingers touched a sequence and a soft click broke the silence. With a flick of a wrist, he turned a huge handle, and the gate opened, with just enough room for each of them to squeeze through.

Inside, a booming hum made talking impossible. Paul beckoned them to follow down a narrow corridor flanked by huge, vibrating pipes. He stopped at another terminal. Again he pressed the lighted squares, and the circular gate opened to another dimly lit corridor. Nona and Sara ran to keep up with Paul, who raced toward a gate with a terminal so small it was almost hidden. Much more deliberate this time, he touched three tiny lights glittering red, blue, yellow, and green. The gate stayed closed. "God of Reincarnation!" he whispered, "We're in trouble!" A musical voice silenced him with the warning, "You have entered an erroneous code; please reenter." Each repetition grew louder until a red light flooded the tunnel, and the warning thundered, "Security breach, security breach."

"Fuck!" Paul cried. "Run!" They sped to another gate. Heaving at the handle, he strained to open it manually, stumbling back into Sara.

Nona screamed. "We're going to be apprehended!"

Sara scrabbled at the wall for a handhold when something slammed into her, hurling her to the ground, immobilizing her. A techno-net, she registered. The grip loosened. Mall Guards stood behind them, laughing. In the space it took to perceive this, the techno-net jerked her up and embraced her with steel arms until she could barely breathe. Now a living sculpture, she was helpless to do anything but watch the guards, each holding a control, striding toward them. "Still feel like running?" laughed the one with green hair and red-tinted glasses. "Go ahead and try. This should be fun, watching you get squeezed tighter and tighter."

The second one, so muscular he looked distorted, laughed too and said, "Oh, I don't know, Al, she's way too pretty to foul up, dontcha think?"

Al laughed, a harsh grating sound. "Nah, I've seen better—maybe if you like 'em plump. Didja see her nose? But we won't find out what you feel like anyway, baby, 'cause we'd be sanctioned big time if we hurt that fat body of yours." Al looked at Paul on the ground. "Hey, Jack, who's this guy anyway? He looks familiar."

"I think that's the Junker guy everyone's lookin' for," Jack answered.

"What the heck is he doin' here with these ladies?"

"Beats me. But if it's him, I bet we'll get a special reward for nabbin' him." The burly guard jabbed Paul with his control. "That right? You that guy?"

Paul spit out, "Yeah, yeah. But these ladies had no idea who I am. They came along for the fun. They just wanted something to tell all their friends."

Jack barked, "What d'ya take us for? They're Junkers just like you." He jerked Paul to his feet and loosened the net. "I'm gonna bracelet you and march you to Judgment. We'll be heroes and heroes get big-time rewards."

"We're not Junkers. If let you us go," Nona pleaded, "I'll prescribe sexual-enhancing pharms, credit-free."

"Tempting, honey, but jacked up sexual acts can't come close to the extra credit we'll earn when we turn you in." To the other guard he said, "Let's get these guys to the holding rooms."

"No!" shouted Sara. "It's all a mistake! I don't even live here." The net gripped her and she stopped struggling.

Jack's attention focused on Sara. "Shut up, little lady, or we'll squeeze you until you feel like your insides are oozin' out."

"But you don't understand, I'm from a different world..." Sara stopped midsentence; her words changing to grunts and whimpers as the iron net tightened around her.

"Please," Nona begged, "please, let her go. Stop hurting her!"

"Get this, Al. A same-sexer. They always did give me the creeps."

Before Jack could tighten the net even more, Paul broke free of his net and took off. Al sprinted after Paul who was almost through the portal. Sara felt a flicker of hope. If Paul escaped, maybe he could free her and Nona. To distract Jack she began to moan and gurgle in such a way that he turned to look at her and failed to see Al pursuing Paul. Too soon Jack noticed Al's absence. He drew something out of his pocked and approached her. After the sting, before the darkness spread through her body, Sara thought, he got away, as a familiar lassitude spread throughout her body. Her last thought before losing consciousness, Will we be sentenced to Forced Labor?

MALL

CHAPTER THIRTY-ONE

Sara opened her eyes to white on white—white light, white bedding, white floors, ceiling, and walls. A borderless continuity relieved only by an open door. When she tried to sit up, pain from techno-net bruises pushed her down. The memory of their capture filtered through her consciousness and adrenaline jolted her out of bed and to the doorway, through which she could see nothing but gray shadowiness. I'm unguarded, she thought. I could get away. But before bolting through the door, she remembered how efficient and technically proficient these people were. She'd been held in this place after she'd entered Mall. She could only bring up a drug-blurred memory of struggle, sleep, confusion, and panic. She reached out to touch the dimness in front of her. A shock stung her hand and a loud buzz sounded, changing to that impersonal voice repeating, "Warning, warning, touching the bar-net can result in injury." She rubbed her stinging hand. How stupid to think she could escape a holding cell. Even if she did get out, what would she do? Where would she go? How did Paul get around all this security? He'd hacked access codes, something she had no idea how to do. Maybe she could talk her way out, explain that she went along with Paul and Nona because it was something new and different.

She had to persuade them she was innocent. Then try to get out again? No, not after that escape attempt. She couldn't ignore that her whole self had begun to yield to the temptation to stay in this world where so little would be expected of her. True, that if she stayed, she might be chosen in the lottery, but wasn't life in her world filled with risk, too?

She would have no problem fitting in if only she wouldn't be forced to undergo a Mem-wipe. She needed her memories to turn into dramas. Then she would have years to sample the myriad of pleasures this world offered. If her number wasn't called. Was it worth the gamble? Mall life had tempted her almost since the beginning and the appeal had only sharpened over time. She loved it that two men desired her. She loved it that she could have sex with either or both and no one would think she was a slut. She loved being beautiful. She loved her new employment. She loved being free of—oh God, horrible to admit—her mother's misery and pain. Each time after she visited her, the weight of guilt consumed her.

She had little going for her in her former world. A husband who was tired of her and one—*let's be very honest,* she thought—she'd stopped loving a while back. She'd wanted to win his approval and adoration, which wasn't love. Back home she had a job as a mediocre teacher. She didn't want to be average. She couldn't see her value as a person in that. When she inventoried her inner self, she found a void with smatterings of love for her mother and a feeble commitment to the kids she taught.

Yes, her mother needed her. Sara had never been able to persuade her to see a therapist or to make an effort to meet people. If Sara didn't return, maybe her mother would be forced to reach out to others. And had she ever really eased her pain? If she were a loving daughter, Sara would have visited her more. She would have asked her mother to live with her and Carl. He cared about her mother, even visited her occasionally. They had an extra bedroom. Too selfish, she had never made the offer. If she ended up staying in Mall, who would miss her? Her mother, but certainly not Carl. Women loved him; he would have no trouble finding another wife. Why should she return? She had been unhappy almost all the time. But here? Nothing to feel down about. No heavy responsibilities.

What about her punishment? Would they force her to have the Mem-wipe? Could she keep her job? Her stomach writhed with anxiety.

CHAPTER THIRTY-TWO

Nona sat on the edge of the cot while she absently rubbed her arm where the techno-net had squeezed especially tight. There was no escape, and there was no way to avoid punishment. For several moments she contemplated hurling herself at the bar-net. Would the injuries end her life or just wound her? Unless her life ended, any Healer could treat a wound in a matter of minutes. If she couldn't escape Mall, she wanted her old life back; although flat and unfulfilling, still it was the life she knew. *Please, oh please, no Mem-wipe,* she begged any god, anyone or anything with the power to change the minds of those who controlled her fate.

The bar-net crackled as her Confessor swept in. Nona struggled to still the quivering that rippled through her body. No comfort was to be found in the Confessor's gold-tinted eyes or her frowning lips. After she activated a tiny recording device with bronzed fingernails, the Confessor recited, "It is my duty to listen to how you committed this crime and why. Sometimes I find there are extenuating circumstances allowing me to recommend an easier Judgment against you." She stopped to play back what she had dictated and then continued after reactivating the recording device. "I began with you because you have been an exemplary Mallite. You excel in your profession, and you have consumed heavily." She sighed and shook her head, swinging her long coppery hair. "To be frank, your recent actions astonish me. The only conclusion I can reach is that you are disordered, but that puzzles me. You of all people should have recognized the symptoms. Your heart-friend, Fabriana, certainly did. She also suspected that you might be aware of Junker activity without reporting it." She leaned forward, frowning slightly. "It would be best for you to confess the whole story."

For a moment, Nona longed for the clarity with which she used to see life. If she told the whole story, what would happen to Sara? To Paul? Would she ever see Royce again? And what about Natalie—had she revealed everything Nona told her? Maybe Natalie had already gone through Judgment because a confession had been forced out of her. The pressure built inside and tears filled her eyes. Nona squirmed and clenched her fists. Words piled up at the base of her constricted throat. Seconds trickled by.

The Confessor's face molded into cold disdain. "Time is up, Nona. Better tell me the whole story. Sara confessed to all."

Nona started. Could the Confessor be lying? She didn't know if they were capable.

The Confessor continued, "If you don't, we will proceed with the harsh alternative of electric shocks. And if we find your narrative does not agree with Sara's, your sentence at Judgment will be much harsher. Sara's sentence, also, will be more severe because, well, you can see how difficult it would be to know who is telling the truth."

After another few seconds passed, the part of Nona that wanted to protect Sara and herself curled up into a compact ball of dread, rolled to a corner of her brain, and watched a frightened Nona spill out the whole story to the Confessor, whose expression seemed so forbidding. Nona realized she was alone, totally without anyone to help her.

When Nona was through, the Confessor asked, "Forgive me, Nona, but I'm a little confused. Are you saying that you believed Sara?"

"Not at first, but later, yes, I did."

The Confessor absently stroked her hair. "What were you thinking of? Why in the name of God of Reincarnation didn't you treat her with appropriate pharms and admin a Mem-wipe?!"

"I already told you. She didn't want it."

"Yes, but you could have applied for an exemption to the Force-No-Pharms rule. You know it will be granted when the client's refusal greatly diminishes his or her ability to flourish in our society. And you never reported back to the Finance Police. If they hadn't been so busy tracking down Junkers and found out you had not treated her, they would have re-apprehended her and brought her to Judgment. At the very least, you should have referred her to someone else."

"No, I never would have done that."

The Confessor moved her chair closer to Nona. "That doesn't make sense. You are a renowned MHP. Not to have taken the recommended steps to treat Sara is incomprehensible. What were you thinking?"

Nona bowed her head and whispered, "I wasn't *thinking*; I was *feeling*. I … I love her."

Tension straightened the soft curves out of the Confessor's body. "What? I mean, I beg your pardon? Love? You thought of her as a young child and you as her mother?"

"Child? No. I know you won't understand. No one can unless she or he stops adminning and shares himself or herself with someone."

"Share yourself? You mean have sex without adminning a sex-stim pharm?"

"No. I mean where you have a relationship, an intense friendship, a closeness with someone with whom you share what's deep inside of you."

The Confessor leaped from her stool. "This is an obscenity." She pursed her lips in disapproval. "I've heard enough. You can be sure that I will not recommend leniency for you."

Nona watched her sweep out of the room, then threw herself on the bed. Why in the name of the God of Reincarnation had she told the Confessor she loved Sara? *I had to. Because Sara probably told her something like that.* No, it was more than that. She wanted to tell her and everyone so that all would know there was more to life in Mall, much more.

Was there any way she could escape consequences for all she had done against the Code? She doubted it.

CHAPTER THIRTY-THREE

Sara searched every corner of her mind for a reasonable story—something to say that might make them go easy on her, and if it meant that Nona or Paul would be in more trouble, well, she had to think of her own welfare.

I could say I was a patient who was only following her MHP's advice to go with her on this adventure, that it was part of Nona's treatment plan. If I'd known Nona planned on entering an unauthorized place, of course I'd have refused to go. Or should she tell the whole truth to this woman? Would she lose everything: her job, her status, her new friends? No! She would do anything—*please, please*, she would beg; *let me go, and I'll never do anything against the Code again.* But if she told the truth, wouldn't they decide she was disordered, maybe even deranged? Then they'd administer the Mem-wipe and Nona and Paul would be implicated but she couldn't help that. She had herself to think of now there was no going home. There was only life here, and she wanted it be a continuation of what had begun to unfold. If only she'd avoided Paul; if only she'd known that escaping was never an option.

The sudden deactivation of the bar-net, a crackling and sparking sound, startled her. She couldn't stop herself from cringing when the Confessor entered, a crimson padded stool in one hand, a small device of some sort in the other. Sara gathered the sheets around her and scrambled to the side of the bed.

"Don't be concerned," the Confessor said. "I'm here to help you. Really, all you need to do is to tell the truth and submit to the pharm-rehabilitation we recommend." She tilted her head, looking kindly at Sara, then placed the stool close to the bed and sat on it. "It would best for all if you continued creating works that motivate so much consuming. As soon as I test the recorder, we can begin."

The Confessor momentarily occupied, Sara studied her. She was so beautiful, with a kind of perfection Sara saw every day. Every inch of her was pleasing to look at, especially the coppery curtain of her hair. She'd almost forgotten what it must be like to look at ordinary people.

Fighting down the nauseating fear, she ground her teeth in frustration. Why in the hell had she ever agreed to go with Paul anyway? Because at first all she'd wanted to do was get home. *And,* she thought, *to be honest, because I was so attracted to him.* She couldn't have known what the consequences would be.

What about Nona? Had she confessed how much she cared for Sara? A spasm of guilt pinched her. She couldn't control Nona's feelings for her. Besides, Nona had always known the consequences. A spurt of anger shot through her. Why was she even worrying about Nona? She had to take care of herself!

Finally, the Confessor broke off Sara's endless stare and rose to her feet. "You do know that Nona told me all about you. Judgment will go more easily if you confess. And we do have some ways to persuade that you would not find pleasant. Please begin."

Sara recoiled. "Do you mean torture?"

The Confessor regarded her closely. "Ah, just as I thought. You would prefer not to undergo this method. So I suggest you admit to all you have done and seen against the Code."

Nothing else I can do. "I'll tell the truth—really, I will." Sara curled up, closed her eyes, and began. While she spoke, part of her mind split off trying to find a way to get out of this mess. Would she be sentenced to Forced Labor? Or would they order the dreaded Mem-wipe?

CHAPTER THIRTY-FOUR

Sara and Nona sat safe-braceleted next to each other on a hard metal bench in the burgundy velvet-carpeted Judgment Room. Fifty people chosen to witness this event filed in, talking loudly about the proceedings. The People's Advocate, tall with closely cut silver hair and dressed in a red and green cashmere robe, sat on a raised bench behind a gold lacquered table. After the audience was seated, he signaled the Confessor to proceed. The Confessor played Sara's confession, and, when she touched the off button, the audience bolted out of their seats, pushing and shoving toward the front to get a better look at her.

"The woman is disordered," one audience member cried out.

"Deranged," another shouted.

The People's Advocate's demands for silence were swallowed in the din. Twice he pushed the silver circle in the center of the table, activating an automated warning. "Order in the Judgment Room, or you will be stunned and netted." Grumbling and whining, the audience members worked their way back to their seats. When the noise faded to whispers, the People's Advocate signaled the Confessor to play Nona's tape.

Sara only half listened as she turned around, searching for Paul. *He must have gotten away,* she thought angrily. It was his fault she sat in this courtroom, but had he done anything to help her and Nona? Not one thing! Would his absence and his side of the story affect her sentence? Cold dread pinched her heart. Maybe the audience's reaction to her tape was a sign that her confession was so out of whack with their worldview that her sentence would be memory obliteration. She snapped back to attention when the tape tumbled out Nona's declaration of deep connection with Paul, Royce, Natalie and especially with Sara who was the impetus for this change in her. "I love her," Nona divulged. Shame burned Sara's face as the crowd stirred, whispering excited shock. She glared at Nona who mouthed, *I'm sorry.*

The People's Advocate warned, "I will not allow any more unruliness. All quiet in the Judgment Room, or the proceedings will be conducted in private." The murmuring died, and in a few more minutes the tape finished.

"The other prisoner, where is he?" The People's Advocate asked the Confessor, pointing to Paul's empty seat.

The Confessor looked down. "Advocate, I am loath to disclose what happened with Paul. Three of our most elite guards allowed him to escape while still in the tunnel."

Speaking to the whole room, the People's Advocate announced, "These guards will be demoted to Forced-Labor surveillance." He shook his head sadly and continued. "The threat of Forced Labor or Mem-wipes doesn't seem to be an effective deterrent against Junkers. The few we have apprehended so far have refused to name other Junkers. In fact, all but two denied even being a Junker. Unfortunately, we will be forced to use other means to extract their confessions.

"At our last meeting, the Mall Managers authorized a substantial incentive for information that leads to apprehending a Junker." He paused to take a deep breath. "A credit-free, three-week vacation designed by Fly Me to the Moon Vacations Unlimited." A loud cheer rose from the audience. He raised his hand to quiet the excited throng. "As for these two women," he continued, "I concur with the Confessor's recommendations." Turning toward them, he said, "Sara, please rise. There is no doubt that your crimes, your strange behavior, and your belief in some other world were brought about by administering illegal pharmaceuticals. You will be allowed to go free after you sign the notarized document wherein you abjure using illegal pharms. As soon as possible, you will undergo the

Mem-wipe treatment with a court-appointed Mental Health Practitioner. From then on, you will report monthly to your Confessor for a period of six months to assure the efficacy of treatment. Failure to follow any of these stipulations or refusal to agree to the Mem-wipe will result in an automatic Judgment of eight months Forced Labor. So, Sara," he asked, "do you agree to the recommended pharmacological treatment?"

Sara's stomach tightened. *Oh God,* she thought, *how do I choose? If I say yes, the memory of my life before Mall will be erased. Without doubt, there's no way to escape now.* Saying no meant she would lose her new life filled with pleasure. She wanted Stan; she wanted to create plays, but without her memories, she wouldn't be able to. The other choice—Forced Labor? No! Voice trembling, Sara said, "I accept Judgment. I agree to the Mem-wipe."

His voice more solemn now, he said, "Nona, please stand. Your misdeeds went beyond entering an unauthorized place and associating with a known Junker. Not treating someone as disordered as Sara is not only illegal but also morally reprehensible, especially since you made this decision in order to meet *your* needs. Your Judgment is complete Mem-wipe. Your new identity will be one of a third-rater, specifically a clerk in the Ready-Made Fashion Division. If you refuse treatment, you will be sentenced to Forced Labor, Division One which means you will sew Forced Laborers' clothes every day of the week except for Sunday mornings. After six months, you will be offered this option again. What is your decision?"

Sara averted her eyes from Nona's imploring look. Nona sighed before she said, "I refuse Mem-wipe." The buzzing of voices filled the room until the People's Advocate silenced the onlookers. He rose, declaring the conclusion of Judgment. As a white-robed man led Nona off, Sara turned away and saw a woman signaling her. Sara waited until the woman, pink hair, pretty in a kewpie-doll kind of way, reached her. Where had she seen her before? Oh yes, after the Passing Ceremony. She was Nona's heart-friend.

"In case you don't remember, I'm Fabriana, and I will be your court-appointed MHP. We'll start your treatment immediately." She paused after each word, almost clipping the endings off. Her overdone face was impassive except for glittering eyes that burned with coldness.

Sara asked, "Will you be the only one there?" Fabriana's face stiffened. Instantly, Sara wished she could suck those words back into her mouth. "Not that it matters." Sara smiled so broadly, her mouth ached. "Your expertise is renowned." The sight of Fabriana's face softening reassured Sara. Fabriana was susceptible to flattery.

"Yes, well, it's to your advantage to be cooperative."

"I so agree. And that will be easy because you're the one doing the treatment. I have so much confidence in you. I'm sure that life will be quite pleasant after you're done."

Fabriana squinted at her. "That remains to be seen. What you believe doesn't matter anyway. What's important is to treat you as soon as possible." She seemed to swell with self-importance. "I will make sure your memory of this perverse, disgusting affair is completely wiped out."

A moment of emptiness took Sara's breath away. How could these people believe that a close friendship was a perversion? Then, as quietly as possible, she wrestled in one breath and then another, willing herself to blot out any regret. "Oh, that's fine. Those memories don't matter to me." Sara looked sidelong at Fabriana, noting the satisfaction swell in her face.

"Really? I'd wager Nona's reaction to the idea of Mem-wiping you would have been, shall we say, a tiny bit different?"

Sara shrugged. "That's none of my business, is it?"

Fingers drumming on the floor and left foot wiggling, Sara sat on a huge multi-colored pillow and waited for Fabriana to leave her bathroom to start the session. What would this Mem-wipe be like? Would it hurt? Even more important, what would she do afterwards? Would she be able to create dramas with Stan's team? Maybe it would be possible for Fabriana to do the wipe in such a way that she could keep her memories but make them seem....what? Dreamlike? Anxiety tickled her stomach and prickled her legs. Her eyes flew around the room searching for something calming to look at. Nothing like Nona's tasteful, comfortable space, this room jangled her nerves. Too much riotous color and overabundance of furniture: purple overstuffed chairs, magenta and gold lacquered tables, yellow and blue pillows strewn on the multicolored velvet carpet. Too much oriental fragrance saturated the air, and too many mirrors—dozens of them in different shapes, all ornately framed in gold and studded with huge amethysts, rubies, and topazes— climbed the walls.

Squirming, she glanced up, only to see hundreds of painted figures engaging in explicit sex acts across the whole ceiling. Snatching her glance away, she wondered again what Fabriana was doing. After bringing Sara to her office twenty minutes ago, she had coolly instructed her to sit on one of the pillows and disappeared into the bathroom. Why was she doing this? Sara's eyes wandered again to the ceiling when Fabriana, in a purple turban and a gold and midnight blue sarong, sailed into the room. "I see my ceiling interests you. I am the one who created it." Her eyes gleamed. "If you weren't suffering from a severe disorder, you would remember that I won a large credit award for best nonholographic, nonvirtual reality, medicinal pornography for the sexually disinterested. I'll show you one of the reasons why."

She walked over to the largest table and touched a glittering purple circle. "Now, look up," she prompted, smiling proudly. Suddenly, the ceiling figures began to move. In one corner, a woman performed fellatio on her partner, while next to that couple, a woman astride a man began to undulate. Opposite them, a man and a woman watched both couples while masturbating. Embarrassed and angry, Sara jerked her head down.

"Why are showing me this? What does it have to do with my therapy?" Sara demanded.

"Therapy?" Fabriana asked, pulling down the corners of her mouth. "You're here for a Mem-wipe, in case you have forgotten. I suggest we get right down to business." She sat on a sapphire-blue cushion and crossed her arms. "Preliminary assessment is unnecessary. I am well aware of how disordered you are. And I want to warn you. I did not self-admin today." She paused, eyes widening with surprise. "You're not shocked at such an idea? Do you mean to tell me that you joined Nona in this reckless, non-adminning experiment?"

"No." Sara ran her hands through her hair. "Well, sometimes, but I can't seem to…"

"Stop. Obviously, you went along with Nona. Well, without pharms in my system, I will discover for myself what it is like to engage in this aberrant behavior. To allow yourself to feel everything, especially if unpleasant and—" Fabriana stopped, mouth open. "This is quite shocking, but I have to admit that allowing all this anger toward Nona is not pleasant, but it *is* exciting. I feel so much that I would have to admin all sort of pharms just to take the edge off."

Sara shrank back, frightened that this woman might hurt her in some way. What could she do to get Fabriana on her side? Should she try to escape? How? Where? Maybe there was some way to convince Fabriana to leave most of her memories intact.

Fabriana narrowed her eyes at Sara. "I am filled with—I can't think of a word to describe this feeling."

"Rage?" Sara fought to keep her voice steady.

"Rage? I never heard of the word, but it sounds right. Yes, I will use that word. I am filled with this rage, especially when I think that she was having sex with you while neglecting to even contact me. She broke all the rules stipulated in our heart-friend contract."

"No, really, Fabriana, we were not lovers. I mean, we never had sex. Never."

"Yes, you were; well, maybe you didn't fuck physically," she smirked at the obscenity, "but it was a kind of fucking. Shall we call it mind-sex? Too bad if you have pleasant memories of this disgusting act. We will begin treatment immediately." She rose from the cushion.

Struggling to be conciliatory and stalling for time, Sara asked, "Would you mind explaining the treatment to me? What should I expect and what should I do?"

Fabriana snorted. "What do you mean, *do*? Since when do clients do something in a Mem-wipe treatment? I'm the one doing; you just lie back while in a pleasant pharm-induced state."

"Of course, yes, I'll do whatever you say. I get confused, you know, because of my disorder. I'm just so glad you're the one doing whatever needs to be done. I've heard so much about your skill," she gushed. Stealing a quick glance at Fabriana's face, Sara noticed the slight warming in her eyes. "But before we start, I need to confide in you. I'm worried about my credit-building potential. I know you will understand. I would hate to go from first-rater to who knows how low? That would be such a terrible punishment for someone who didn't really know what she was doing because of being disordered. Don't you think so?"

"What are you trying to say?"

Sara cleared her throat. "You see, my supposed memories are the basis for my creating stories, like the interactive drama I recently created—you've attended, right? Anyway, I realize now these *memories* are merely products of a disorder caused by illegal pharms. Please listen, Fabriana, I need those memories, I mean, products of my disorderedness..."

Still standing, Fabriana glared. "You're not making any sense, and you're wasting my time. We must begin treatment."

Sara got to her feet. "Please, let me try to explain. I think Nona let me go on in this state because my memories—these ideas—were so entertaining. You may not know, but I have ..."

Fabriana's mouth curled into a sneer. "Oh, spare me! That she let you go on in this state is morally shocking. Besides she told me all about those so-called memories."

For a moment, Sara couldn't speak. Was Fabriana lying? Or had Nona told this horrible little woman about her other life, even about her father's suicide? How could she? Well, she'd show Nona. "The bitch. I hope you erase every bit of her memory."

Fabriana licked her lips and smiled slowly. "How delicious. *Bitch*? A very naughty word." She barked a short laugh.

"What I'm trying to ask is that whatever these things in my mind are, they remain in some form so I can still earn substantial profit. Do you see what I mean?"

Fabriana looked at her with blank eyes. "I suppose, but why should I do that? It would make the treatment much more difficult because I would have to change each one of those disordered memories into an image or story that you believe your imagination created. Besides, Judgment only allocated credit for the standard Mem-wipe."

Sara struggled to come up with something to make her change her mind. "Of course, you need to make the appropriate profit. You can understand how much I want to make profit too." She gazed at the multicolored carpet, noting absently how her feet sank into the depths of clashing colors. Her heart lurched. "Wait, I have an idea." Her eyes flew to Fabriana's. "I could form my own company—my own creative team, that is—and you could be a partner, a full partner. What do you think?"

"Partner? Of course, I can see why you would ask; you've seen the ceiling. My talents are going to waste. But Mall Management never makes exceptions to the Code about changing professions. So it's out of the question."

"What about being a silent partner? Who's to know if we have some sort of arrangement?"

Fabriana raised an eyebrow. "Me? Do something against the Code? My, my, this is getting more interesting." Quiet for a moment, she nodded. "Of course, it's done all the time. What you call silent partners is such a quaint term for invisible co–team leader. Anyway, I already make a lot of profit. Why should I want to risk doing something illegal?"

Appeal to her ego, Sara urged herself. "Your ceiling, that's what. It shows what a creative person you are. Think what you could do in the entertainment field."

Fabriana smiled with tight lips. "Yes, I *am* quite creative. But you already have profitable employment with Stan. Why would you need an invisible co–team leader?"

Sara gripped the sides of the chair. "But that's just it. I don't want to work with him. Not anymore."

"Why ever not? He's top in his profession."

Sara looked down. "Yes, but I want *him*."

"Ah, you want to have sex with your employer." Her eyes glinted. "You want to start your own team so you can pair-knot with him? I can see why; he's really quite delicious."

"Yes, that's it. And with you and my ideas and stories, we could give Stan a run for his money."

"I beg your pardon?"

"I meant, we could compete with him on his level."

Fabriana stared at Sara with dead, calculating eyes. While the seconds ticked by, Sara fidgeted. Was Fabriana going to turn her down?

Finally, the other woman spoke. "You're right—with my creative talents, especially in the sexual area, we could be very successful. I would get 60 percent of the profit, of course."

"Yes, of course. Then you'll do it?"

"Yes, I like to be challenged. Lucky that you were assigned to me. I am one of only two or three MHPs who *can* selectively eliminate parts of the client's self while implanting new memories. So, as you have asked, I will use a technique to make you believe those memories you think are real seem to be products of your imagination. And then I'll create new memories of a previous Mall life before you adminned forbidden pharms. I know: when you awake you will be the Entertainment Artist, similar to what you do now, and you got involved with a Junker by mistake. When you discovered what he was, he gave you red-market pharms, without your knowledge. He was correct in assuming that the pharms would adversely affect you."

Sara stared wide-eyed at Fabriana. "You can really do all of this? I won't remember myself as I think of me in this moment?"

"No, however, your new ID will feel comfortable and familiar." She looked sharply at Sara. "I see; you're afraid. Too bad, because you agreed to this Mem-wipe. No way to get out of it now."

Sara sat unmoving while a storm raged inside of her. She had agreed to a termination of herself, a kind of self-murder. She gripped the sides of the cushion to keep from crying out. Finally, her thoughts stopped spiraling. She had no choice, she repeated to herself. She had no choice. This will be like dying and being reincarnated and hadn't she wished for that to happen so many times?

"Time for you to stop stalling. Before we start, let me record our little agreement. You must agree to and follow every little detail because, my dear, if you don't, I will report that you have violated Judgment terms. We know what will happen then—a very unpleasant Forced Labor vacation."

"What will the process be like? Will I be aware of what you're doing?"

"No, you will be in a state of bliss. You will be able to answer my questions, and hear my directions, but you will not remember any of it. After, I will personally guide you to your quarters, where I will admin the sleeping prep. When you awake, you will be an exemplary Mallite."

Hadn't she always wanted an easier life, one where her beauty made people want to know her, maybe even love her? A life where people admired the work she did? One where self-doubt didn't gnaw at her every moment? One where she was free of guilt over her mother? Free from the anger and depression Carl caused because she wasn't enough for him? She took in a deep breath. Maybe it was worth it. Yes, it was.

Sara awoke to a hand clamped over her mouth. In the darkness she could just make out a tall figure leaning over her. "It's me, Paul. I'm going to take my hand away. It would be best for both of us if you do not scream." He removed his hand and activated the light sensor next to the bed.

Alarmed but not frightened, Sara sat up and yanked up the sheet to cover her naked body. "I think I remember you. We met at a Pleasure Palace. Oh yes, and I spoke to you at the Spiritual Peace Sector. That's right, you're an SP." She shook her head to clear out the fuzziness. "What are you doing here? How did you get in?" She reached for her communicator to call for help.

He snatched it away from her. "Don't do anything disordered like call for a guard because I will see to it that you get in as much trouble as me."

"No I won't. I'll tell the truth that you somehow entered my room without my permission." Sara tried to wrench her hand free, but he strengthened his hold.

"You could try that, but I will tell them that you were hiding me," he countered still gripping her hand.

"Why would I hide you?" Something nagged at her, what else should she recall about this man? "Now I remember! You're a Junker. You were apprehended and didn't you go through Judgment? No, that's right; you got away, and the FPs from every level are looking for you!" She fought to get free of his grip. No use—he held fast. "Please, please get out!"

"Not yet. I'm here to tell you that you have been a Mem-wipe victim. You and Nona came with me in an attempt to get Outside, remember?"

"No! I would never do that."

"Yes, you did. You wanted to go home to your world, which you hoped would be on the other side of the portal. Only I didn't have the right entry code, and we were all arrested."

His words scratched and knocked at a closed door in her mind, which vibrated with anxiety. "I did not and would not ever attempt such a thing. And the idea that I came from some place outside of Mall? You must be deranged. Nothing exists Outside."

"Fabriana wiped that part of your memory clean. You don't remember one thing about your former life in a different world?"

"No! I told you! Except for the stuff I make up for interactive dramas. I may be able to picture a different world in a lot of detail, but it's fantasy. Now please, leave!" She twisted and pulled to free herself to no avail.

"You don't even remember Nona, your MHP?"

271

A picture of the beautiful white-blonde woman formed in her consciousness. "Of course, she helped me through the illegal ..." She broke off when the word *drug* came to mind. *Where did that word come from? Does it mean anything?* She tried again to pull away. "I want you to leave now!"

Paul dropped her arm. "I just want to ask one more question. Do you recall we almost had sex? We both wanted it."

Sara felt an undertow of longing. Why did she suddenly want him? She hardly knew him. "No I ..." she stopped. What was that noise? Someone was accessing entry. Paul grabbed her arm and whispered, "Don't say a word or you will be sorry. I'll try to hide in the bathroom."

Two minutes later, an FP and a Guard entered. Sara, still sitting, pulled the sheet tighter against her body. "Please excuse the unannounced entry," the FP spoke softly but coldly, "we're searching for that Junker, Paul. I'm sure you are aware of his escape."

"Yes, I heard about it." If only she'd alerted them when Paul had first entered. Now they would think she was hiding him, and she would be apprehended. "I would've screamed if he came in my room, although I don't understand how that could happen. Only I know the code. Besides you," she added.

"You are naïve to think that. He can access almost anyone's quarters." He looked around the dimly lighted room. "Please pardon us if we offend," he added, "but we are duty bound to inspect your entire quarters." To the guard he said, "No place to hide here; let's go in the bathroom."

Somehow, she had to stop them. She got out of bed and followed them. Standing naked in the bathroom doorway, she murmured, "Can I help?"

Both turned to look at her. She was close enough to the FP to hear him swallow before he spoke. "Please cover yourself, ma'am; you know the rule, no complete nudity is allowed."

"Oh dear, I forgot I had nothing on," she lied. Anything, she thought, to distract them. Where was he? Had he managed to hide? Before following the SP's order, she looked in the bathroom to see towels strewn on the floor. He was nowhere. He must have managed to fold his length into the linen cupboard. "I hope you won't judge me too harshly for the mess in the bathroom. I overturned the stack of towels where I placed them after the laundry delivery. I meant to pick them up after my bath." Slowly, she turned away to get back in bed, aware that their eyes followed her every move.

At that moment the FP's communicator buzzed loudly. He listened for a moment, then spoke sharply to the guard. "All hell's broken loose. The Junkers have gassed the Mall Managers!"

The guard hissed, "All of them? Their numbers are up?"

"Yes," he roared, "now move!"

Sara lay in her bed, relief surging through her body. She was safe. When Paul emerged, she said, "Thank the God of Reincarnation, you weren't discovered. Now nothing will happen to me."

"Didn't you hear what he said? Life as you think you remember will *not* go on as usual. The MM's are dead. Junkers will be running things soon, or they will all be executed."

Just then, loud clanging rang through the room's speakers followed by a voice shouting, "Mallites, stay in your quarters! If you are in a Pleasure Palace or in Virtual Reality, find someplace to shelter." Sara heard muffled voices and a thud coming from the corridor

"Did you hear that? Probably chaos, even a riot. You should come with me. This is your last chance!"

"No! Why would I want to go with you? You heard the order to stay in your quarters. It's not safe out there." She flung herself onto the bed. "The Junkers *will* be apprehended. And things will go back to normal, back to the way it has been for hundreds of years. Who'd want to live any other way? Not me, that's for sure!" A memory tried to surface, a woman with sad eyes whose lined face drooped around the mouth, submerging as quickly as it had arisen. Who or what was that? No one looked that way in Mall. She tried without success to recall the image. *Oh well, it was nothing,* she said to herself, *nothing at all.* She would stay in her quarters until things quieted down. When the clanging started up again even louder, she held her ears. *This will pass,* she told herself. Then she could go on with her pleasurable life.

CHAPTER THIRTY-FIVE

Nona wriggled and squirmed in her small, hard bed. Accustomed to the softest fabrics, she quickly discovered that the shift she was required to wear irritated her skin, and the less effective sleep-prep was not working. She craved something, anything to ease the pain and boredom. In no time, she had mastered the process of attaching sleeves and collars on rough cotton shirts, all white, no color to ease the monotony. Now she understood why people amoked.

What could she do? Should she give in and undergo the Mem-wipe? She would have relief, but distaste at the thought of that flat, two-dimensional existence rose in her throat like the bitter reflux from the greasy food served here. They would never let her practice again; instead she would work in some Ready-Made Division, using all her energy to sell, sell, sell, and still she would make little profit. And she would remember nothing about Sara or Royce, who she would probably never see again anyway. Her thoughts circled back. The alternative was life as a Forced-Laborer. She considered throwing herself against the techno-net, hoping against hope to breach it.

A footstep. Not a Mall Guard. Techno-nets made their presence unnecessary. She listened. There—a faint creak. She strained to see through the dense blackness for anything that would give shape to the tiny, almost continuous rustling. Right in front of her, a blacker darkness coalesced. Suddenly, she felt something close around her wrist, and a hand slapped against her mouth, damming the scream boiling up in her throat.

"Nona," a familiar voice whispered and her heart surged with surprise, "don't scream, and I'll take my hand away. It's me, Paul."

Slowly, he withdrew his hand. "Listen to me very carefully. I'm going to get you out of here."

"What? No! We'll be caught again, and I'll get a worse detail than sewing shirts for other Forced Laborers."

"You won't want to stay here or anywhere else in the Mall. The Mall Managers have been killed. FPs and guards are running wild, netting everyone they see. What's going to happen next, I don't know. Probably a kind of … war? Something like what we found out went on Before Mall. Listen, Nona, people are going to get hurt, even killed."

Suddenly a shrill voice announced, "Emergency! Emergency! All Finance Police report to levels 101!" The clanging sound reverberated.

Nona's hand flew to cover her ears. "Oh God of Reincarnation! How can we get out? The techno-net will paralyze us. Wait, how did you get in here?"

"Junkers have shut down the electricity. It won't be off for long so let's get moving."

"We might be killed!" she whispered.

He pulled her out of the cot. "I have a techno-net baton and that should be … Shh," he whispered in her ear, his arm around her waist holding her still. "Someone's coming; don't say a word and don't move." Nona strained to hear the sound. Footsteps echoed in the corridor then stopped.

"Hey, you in there! Somethin' bad's goin' on. Junkers are everywhere, maybe even here, so we gotta come in. Don't worry about bein' naked 'cause the electricity isn't working," a voice ordered. Just as the Guard entered, lights in the hallway sputtered to life. He spotted Paul and lunged for him. Paul whipped off the techo-net baton attached at his waist and struck the FP in the face. As the FP stumbled back, Paul used the baton to strike his head and he dropped to the ground.

Nona backed away until she was up against the wall. "You've hurt him. Is his number up?"

"Maybe. I had to silence him. Now we have to get out of here!"

Without stopping to think, she let him pull her out into the dimly lit, narrow corridor. As they ran, she glimpsed other Forced-Laborers looking out of their quarters. One shouted, "Wait, wait, what's happening?"

Another cried, "Can you get the electricity to go off again?"

Ignoring them, they continued to run until they reached the first escape-proof exit. Paul held her arm. "Don't move," he ordered.

"What are we going to do?" Nona whispered, trying to pull away.

"Just wait a few more seconds." The twinkling access lights went dark, as did the hallway. "Electricity is off right on schedule. Good, because we can't be seen; not good because we're going to have to feel our way to the exit. We may have to take the stairs instead of the elevator."

Nona trembled. "I don't think I can move."

"I'm going get you through this. Get behind me and hold on to my belt." Hugging the wall, they began to walk as quickly as they could.

Nona heard someone yell, "I think they went that way!" followed by a crashing sound.

"Now's the time to go as fast as we can," urged Paul. This time they fast-walked facing the wall using both hands to guide them. "We're almost there. Now we need to find the elevator." When they bumped into a wall, he whispered, "This is it." Quickly he moved his hand until he found and pushed a button. Footsteps neared them. As the door opened, Nona heard something whoosh, a cry and then something heavy falling to the floor.

"Got him!" the guard cried in a low voice. Someone else who had managed to escape his or her quarters wasn't going to make it out. They heard a ping and a door sliding open.

"Hurry, we can't slow down or it's over for both of us!" Paul pushed her into the elevator.

"Floor M," the elevator voice announced once it stopped. Paul held Nona back while he took one step out to search the corridor. All quiet. Releasing her, he motioned her to follow him past several closed doors. They rounded a corner into a wider hallway, one side bordered by large roll-up doors and the other side with recessed doorways to smaller rooms. Behind them they heard voices and footsteps as Guards or FPs closed in. Paul jerked her into one of the alcoves, and with fingers moving faster than Nona thought possible, he coded entry into a small, barely-lit storage room. "Here!" he pointed to a small area behind a stack of boxes and they squeezed into the space. A moment later the door opened and guards entered. "Nah, there's no one here. I told you that guy Paul wouldn't come down here. I say he's hiding in some Junker's quarters."

"Do we gotta check all the Life-Support hangers, too? We're done with all the little rooms except for the two at the end. This place gives me the creeps. You think there's no one around, you know, but there's lot of places to hide."

"Yeah, I know what you mean. Let the FPs check the hangars. They always do a follow-up search anyway. They never trust us, the bastards."

Nona heard them stomp out and activate the closing sequence. "Now what?" She couldn't stop shaking.

"We'll give them time to finish their search and then we go into the utility hangar."

"Is that where the portal to Outside is?"

"Right, and we will have to hurry. That guard was right; the FPs will follow-up."

Nona fought an urge to bolt. *Stupid,* she thought, where and how could she get out of this room? To distract herself, she asked, "Why did you do this—come for me?"

"No one else to ask. Natalie," his voice faltered, "and Sara both had the Mem-wipe. I admit I don't want to go alone. I tried to convince about a dozen Junkers, but it was no use – too afraid." He sighed. "Then I thought of you, trapped, without anything or anyone, you know, to live for. Man, refusing the Mem-wipe, an easier way out—that took a lot of courage. Sara jumped at the deal."

Nona looked away. "I've wondered how much they erased."

He grimaced. "I paid her a visit."

Nona ran her fingers through her tangled silvery-white hair. "Did she remember what we did?"

"You mean what we got arrested for? Nope."

"Does ... does she remember me?"

"Yeah, as the MHP who helped her with illegal pharm use. Nothing about the world she came from. She seemed more than satisfied with her memory-created life."

Nona's body wilted with sadness. Now Sara was just an ordinary Mallite. "What about Royce; did you ask him?"

"Didn't really get a chance. He didn't make it out when Sara and I escaped from the Mall Manager's workplace."

Nona moaned. "That means Judgment and Mem-wipe?"

"Yes."

She stifled the urge to cry. The three people she cared about—all no longer who they were. "Paul, what will happen if we're apprehended?"

"It won't happen if the Junkers come out on top, but if the Bureaucrats and Finance Police regain control, our lives would be ended before our numbers were up. I hope my guys take over, but I still want to leave."

There was no doubt in Nona's mind that the BCs and FPs would come out on top. No reason to go back to Mall then, none at all, even though crossing through the portal might mean death. So what? Whatever she chose would be the end of her life. Would she suffer when she stepped through? Would they be able to blend in? Would she be able to make new friends? That felt very important.

"We need to go," he ordered.

"I can't move!" she moaned. He lifted her and carried her to the exit pad where he punched in the correct code. He set her down and they crept out into the quiet, dim hallway. She took in the walls lined with three massive bay doors. "What are these?" Nona whispered.

"This is Life Support. See that third door, with the picture of an electrical plug?" he asked, pointing down the hallway. "That, according to the latest tip, is where the portal is. Hurry, FPs may appear any minute." Nona ran to keep up with him. Once there, his fingers stabbed in the code. Slowly the door rolled up revealing a room littered with machines flashing with lights.

A Techno in navy blue overalls stood in front of a solid piece of black glass, bordered with bronze panels, lights twinkling in a line down the center. "You have to hurry or our numbers will be up!" he called to them.

Paul grabbed his shoulder. "Where are the other two guys?"

"They ran for their quarters when they heard about the commotion."

"Not commotion. Riot," Paul said as he looked around the room. "Where's the portal?"

The Techno pointed to an area on the opposite wall without machines and panels, just a blank wall except for three tiny blinking lights. Paul and Nona hurried over. "Didn't you guys wonder what these lights were for?" Paul asked.

The Techno stood behind him. "We only discovered the lights a while back when we moved the portable Inset. Daniel figured out what it was, and he was fairly certain this access code did not follow the pattern of others." Looking over his shoulder he urged them, "You have to hurry! Daniel said to punch the red light three times, the yellow twice and the blue once."

"Thanks, Jeff. Come with us or you'll end up dead or Mem-erased," Paul said as he moved closer to the wall.

"No, I don't think so. Who's left that can run the electrical department?"

"Shh," Nona cautioned, "I think I hear someone outside the door. Someone is entering the code!"

Paul pulled out his techno-net baton and netted Jeff, knocking him to the floor. "Tell them I overpowered you, then ran away."

"Good luck!"

"Come on!" he shouted to Nona, who stood immobile. He rushed to her and pulled her to his side. Behind them they heard the bay door roll open. Through what seemed like honey-thick air, Nona grasped Paul's hand, and he pulled her toward the portal. He keyed in the code and a round door appeared and slid open. She sensed rather than heard the FPs and guards entering the room. Paul shouted, "Let's go!"

THE END

MALL

Made in the USA
San Bernardino, CA
05 December 2019